An Infantryman in Stalingrad

From 24 September 1942 to 2 February 1943

Adelbert Holl

Translated by Jason D. Mark and Neil Page

An Infantryman in Stalingrad
Adelbert Holl

Translated by: Jason D. Mark and Neil Page

Published by: Leaping Horseman Books
                   Sydney, Australia
                   info@leapinghorseman.com
                   http://www.leapinghorseman.com

Colophon

This book was created with QuarkXPress 4.11 on an
Apple G3, illustrations and maps were created in Photoshop
6, while word processing was completed using Microsoft
Word. Fonts used are Gill Sans for headings and Bembo
for the main text.

Notice of Rights

We are interested in hearing from authors with manuscripts
or book ideas on related topics.

First published: 2005

National Library of Australia
Hardcover: ISBN 0-9751076-1-5
Paperback: ISBN 0-9751076-2-3

Printed and bound in Australia by Southwood Press Pty Ltd

**This book stands not as a memorial
to war, but to the fallen soldiers.**

\- - -

Dedicated
to
Adelbert Holl
(15 February 1919 – 6 June 1982)

Many German memoirs are coloured by the author's attempts to justify his wartime actions and quite often plagued by gross factual inaccuracies. Both can be understood given the lack of reliable sources at the time and the climate in which the book was written. Fortunately, this book is rarely affected by either. Holl writes candidly about his role as an officer and soldier in the German Wehrmacht, an organisation that even to this day is still stigmatised. Holl's only 'attempt' to justify his role is this passage: *"...we were soldiers who had to carry out our orders. We had to fulfil our duty and be faithful to our oath for Führer, Volk und Vaterland! No-one asked whether it was right. We believed we were protecting our people from this concept of Bolshevism that was a danger to the entire free world. Had the English and Americans not once bitterly regretted supporting these 'Reds'?"*

As for accuracy, Holl's memoirs correlate almost perfectly to official records. Of course there are errors, but they are usually minor. Considering the fact that Holl was only able to use a few published sources to help him write his story, the level of detail and exactness in his recall of names, dates and places is remarkable. Naturally, three and a half decades after the events described, Holl wasn't able to get everything correct, but when one takes into account the amount of detail in this book, he can be excused. Only when you try to remember what you did a year ago, recalling all names, times and places, do you begin to understand.

Because reams of primary sources are now available, Holl's original text has been augmented by maps, aerial photos and footnotes. Apart from the correction of a few tiny factual errors, Holl's text is unchanged. All additional information is included in footnotes and captions in the hope that it will be beneficial to the reader. Maps and aerial photos have also been included so that the events can be more easily followed. Inclusion of documents from Armee and Korps war diaries back up many statements made by Holl. And finally, photos of people and places mentioned in the text have been added. Please note that because the Stalingrad battle passed into a crucial phase in November 1942, there is an almost complete lack of photos depicting the events from November 1942 until the surrender in late January / early February 1943. The decision has been made to only include photographs that show actual events - photos have not been relabelled. Many photos out there purport to show Stalingrad in the winter of 1942/43 but sadly for historians, genuine photos are few and far between. No photos seen by this publisher show events talked about by Holl in the latter half of the book. Unfortunately, this means that as the book progresses, the number of photos decreases. Hopefully, you – the reader – understand the position of this publisher. History should be fact, not fiction. And this too should apply to the labelling of photos.

First and foremost, I would like to thank Adelbert Holl for writing down his experiences in Stalingrad and thereby producing one of the great − if unknown − wartime memoirs. The German edition of this book, *'Als Infanterist in Stalingrad'*, first appeared in the 1970s. Its obscurity in the English-speaking world is due first of all, of course, to it being written in German, and secondly, to its scarcity because of a very limited printing. In no way is it because of the content of the book.

Heartfelt thanks go to Adelbert's son, Wolf-Theo, for kindly granting permission to produce an English version. Regarding the production of an English version, Wolf-Theo Holl said: "Please do it! In my opinion, this is a good opportunity to tell people about times and circumstances that should never happen again…"

I'm indebted to Tim Whistler for delving into the archives in Washington and locating quite a few personnel files that provided essential information for this book, including the crucial file of Holl himself. Thanks Tim!

My deepest gratitude goes to Neil Page for helping translate the original German text. The accurate and free-flowing nature of the translation is due to Neil's knowledge of the German language and his ability to convert the smallest nuance into English. And that's not always easy!

Many thanks to Malcolm King and Geert Rottiers for allowing me to use photos from their private collections.

And finally, my thanks go to you, the reader, for purchasing this book. It provides me with the incentive to keep producing original titles and translations of lesser-known German language books in a high-quality format.

Any comments, criticism, corrections or additions will be greatly appreciated. Write to info@leapinghorseman.com

Jason D. Mark
Sydney, Australia
January 2005

TABLE OF CONTENTS

From the GPU Women's Prison to the banks of the Volga in three days

23 September 1942

"Leutnant Holl reporting back from convalescence leave." I stood in front of my Battalion Commander, Dr. Zimmermann.

"My goodness Holl, you've been sent to me from Heaven!"

I looked questioningly into the strained, drawn face of my Major.

"Yes, I should tell you", he continued, "that all company commanders have become casualties in the past days. Your successor Oberleutnant Mehnert; Leutnant Jahnke from 5. Kompanie lost his right hand in the assault on Stalingrad-South, a nasty business, and for the time being 8. Kompanie is commanded by Oberfeldwebel Jacobs. Now at least I have you and my adjutant, Leutnant Schüler." This tall, lean man – he could've been my father – sat bent over a crate and looked at me seriously. The flame of the candle reflected in the lenses of his spectacles. "We've been waiting for replacements daily, as they're urgently required; they should already be on their way."

"On 8 July we left our winter positions in the Donets area near Nyrkovo to take part in the summer offensive. The attack on

Leutnant Adelbert Holl in 1941.

the Bastion, where you were wounded in April, brought us heavy casualties right from the start. Leutnant Riedel, 5. Kompanie, was killed, his successor was Leutnant Jahnke; Leutnant Mader[1], 6. Kompanie, was wounded, his successor was Leutnant Kraemer. We went through Voroshilovgrad in a generally south-east direction toward the Caucasus. After we crossed the Don, we continued into the Kalmuck steppe, always to the south-east. We met very hard resistance in the Katysheva Gully. After we had broken this, we received the order to wheel left and march in a north-east direction toward Stalingrad. On the southern edge of the city, we again had to overcome strong enemy resistance. Now we're stuck in the middle of this street-fighting."

I now looked more carefully around me. As I didn't know the city, the Battalion messenger had met me in the late afternoon somewhere in the southern suburbs. He had led me to this three-storey stone construction, bringing me to the battalion command post through a labyrinth of cellar passages. It was a bare, windowless cellar, and it smelt damp and musty. I was to learn that it had been a women's prison just weeks previously.

"Now tell us what happened to you after your wounding in Nyrkovo."

"That'll only take a few short sentences, Herr Major. After being operated on in Bad Schwalbach to remove the bullet from my right shoulder, I received marriage leave from the hospital. We were married on 20 June this year. Then my leave came to an end and I had to report to our Ersatz-Bataillon[2] 173 in Naumburg an der Saale. There I met a succession of comrades from our Division, including the present commander, Herr Hauptmann Scholz, my former company chief, Oberleutnant Ferstera, Leutnant Maletz and Leutnant Schirbel from our Bataillon and a few gentlemen from the other regiments. Herr Maletz offered me the chance to become an instructor of a tank destruction troop[3], but I turned down this invitation because I wanted to return to my comrades at the front. I was then given exceptional leave until my posting came through. On 20 August I was again in Naumburg and received the order to head for 134. Infanterie-Division, which was deployed on the central sector in the area of Orel. Despite the friendly reception that I received there from the command and troops, I wasn't happy. They weren't my old comrades. I know almost every man in the Bataillon here. I felt like a fish out of water. The fact that I'd been detailed as an infantry escort officer to the Commander of XXXXI. Panzerkorps, General der Panzertruppe Harpe[4], didn't change things. Under the pretext that I was still troubled by my last wound, a

---

1. *Major d.R. Franz Mader, German Cross in Gold (13 September 1942), Knight's Cross (12 December 1944). Born 28 January 1912 in Mitteldorf im Adlergebirge; died 24 October 1988 in Bielefeld.*

2. *Ersatz-Bataillon - 'Replacement Battalion'*

3. *Holl received two badges on 5 May 1942 for destroying two tanks with an anti-tank rifle on 8 August 1941.*

4. *Generaloberst Josef Harpe, Knight's Cross (418) with Oakleaves (55) and Swords (36), German Cross in Gold (295/2). Commanded XXXXI. Panzerkorps from 15 January 1942 to 15 October 1943. Born 21 September 1887 in Buer, Recklinghausen; died 14 March 1968 in Nürnberg.*

The headquarters of II./Infanterie-Regiment 276 was located in the GPU Women's Prison.

lung shot, I asked General Harpe that I be sent home to finish recuperating. Here is the march order. It's taken exactly 8 days for me to reach my old unit here."

The Major grinned: "The whole thing was just a ploy?"

"Jawohl, Herr Major."

"Now don't you worry about it. The Regiment will sort out the paperwork."

"I'm grateful, Herr Major."

"You can spend the night here at the command post and tomorrow you take over your old 7. Kompanie. Leutnant Schüler will arrive at the same time; he's going to the companies at the front to see whether everything's in order. Schüler will then put you in the picture regarding the current situation at the front. And how are things at home? Your wife and your parents?"

"Fine, Herr Major. They were naturally all happy and cheerful, especially since I recovered quickly from my wound and because of that, I was pampered by everyone during my 8 weeks of leave."

Malcolm King Collection

"I'm very happy for you, Holl. Who knows how long you'll have to wait for your next spell of home leave. Ah, here comes Leutnant Schüler[5]."

I turned around and saw the trusting face of my friend Joachim Schüler. He also recognised me right away. His face lit up. "Wow, Albert, it's great to have you back. Did you come straight from home?"

We grasped each others hands, looked at each other and then embraced.

"No, Jochen, I came directly from the Orel area on the central sector. The commander will tell you the rest. How's it looking at the front?"

His eyes were serious. "At the moment it's quiet at the front but we desperately need replacements because the last weeks have been hard on men and horses. Since launching the offensive from Nyrkovo after the winter pause, we've had considerable

Leutnant Hans-Joachim (Jochen) Schüler, Abteilung Adjutant II./Infanterie-Regiment 276.

---

5. Oberleutnant Hans-Joachim Schüler. Born 5 June 1918 in Mühlhausen. Conflicting reports about his fate; one source says he died 30 December 1942 in Stalingrad, another that he was captured late January 1943.

casualties. Helmut Riedel killed, Franz Mader wounded, Siegfried Pönigk's[6] horse stepped on a mine, both horse and rider being killed, and now in front of Stalingrad-South Oberleutnant Mehnert, your successor in 7. Kompanie, was wounded. Hans Jahnke, who took over 5. Kompanie after the death of our friend Riedel, lost his right hand. As for the men, it doesn't look any better; many of the old fighters are dead or wounded. It's high time we got some replacements."

I was brought back to harsh reality despite the reunion with friends. Just six months ago the Bataillon had had a well-balanced command structure: Kommandeur was Hauptmann Dr. Zimmermann, Adjutant was Leutnant Schüler, Kompanieführer[7] of 5. Kompanie Leutnant Riedel, Kompanieführer of 6. Kompanie Leutnant Mader, Kompanieführer of 7. Kompanie Leutnant Holl, Kompanieführer of 8. Kompanie Leutnant Weingärtner, Dr. Szcepanski as Bataillon doctor and Oberzahlmeister Knopp for supplies. We'd known each other since the formation of the Division in September 1939 on the troop training ground at Köningsbrück near Dresden. And now, just three years later, there were only a few of us still left.

"Come, you can lie over there and I'll take you to your company first thing tomorrow morning."

"Thanks, Jochen, I'm dog-tired." I lay down on a wool-blanket, made a 'pillow' from my march pack and tried to sleep. Half-consciously, I heard our commander talking to Regiment over the field-telephone. From outside, the muffled detonations of exploding light bombs penetrated the cellar vault, and the buzzing of a 'sewing-machine' – which is what we called the Russian Ilyushin planes[8] – told me that I was once again back home with my unit.

24 September 1942

```
Gen.Kdo. LI. A.K. – 0610 hours on 24. September 1942

During the night of 23./24.9., heavy enemy bombing attacks on the
city sector, as well as artillery and rocket fire, but no combat
activity...
```

A jolt on the shoulder woke me up. "Herr Leutnant, Herr Major would like to speak to you."

I jumped to my feet. A quick 'cat-wash', a tidy-up of my uniform, and then I was standing in front of my commander.

---

6. *Oberleutnant Siegfried Pönigk. Born 25 March 1914 in Leipzig; wounded and died 16 July 1942 in a first-aid post of Sanitätskompanie (medical company) 1./194 in Nishni-Krymskaya, Donets.*

7. *Kompanieführer - 'officer in charge of company' or 'temporary company commander'.*

8. *Polikarpov PO2 (or U2) biplane whose distinct sound came from its slow-running five cylinder engine.*

"Leutnant Holl reporting as ordered!"

"Danke, Holl, did you sleep well?"

"Jawohl, Herr Major, under the circumstances."

"Well, then we shall begin. Have a look at this situation map. We've been ordered to push through to the Volga from here either side of the Tsaritsa, this stream here, which flows into the Volga about 1000 metres from here, as the crow flies. The enemy has established positions in the ruins of the houses and is putting up stubborn resistance. We'll advance frontally here. It was at this point yesterday that our pioneers moved against the enemy's southern flank and tried to smoke him out with flamethrowers until darkness fell – but they were repulsed with considerable casualties. Your right neighbour – thus on the other side of the Tsaritsa – is Hauptmann Rittner's III. Bataillon. The left neighbour is the Aufklärungs-Abteilung of 71. Infanterie-Division[9]. The boundary with the left neighbour is this street, which more or less runs straight to the Volga. The remnants of 5. and 6. Kompanien will be placed under you,

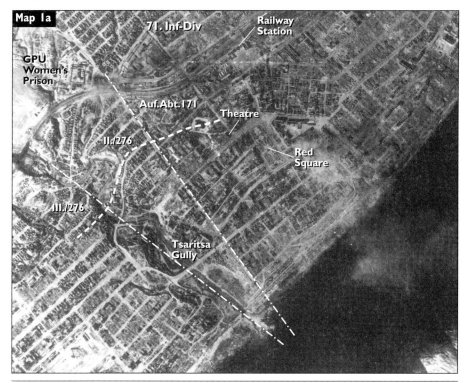

9. *In the original German text, Holl wrote that this unit was the Aufklärungs-Abteilung of 14. Panzer-Division.*
That is incorrect. Records show that the unit positioned to his left was Aufklärungs-Abteilung 171.

as well as 8. Kompanie that is under the command of Oberfeldwebel Jacobs for the time being. We received replacements from the Feldersatz-Bataillon[10] the day before yesterday, mostly 18 or 19 year-old Sudeten Germans without front-line experience. I await the arrival of officers any hour. I've yet to receive the exact time of the beginning of the attack from Regiment but I reckon it will be 0600 hours. Any questions?"

"Nein, Herr Major. I'm glad that Hauptmann Rittner is there, so that at least I don't need to worry about my right neighbour."

"Ja, Holl, Rittner's a pillar here at the front. It's because of the success he's had with his Bataillon that he's been recommended for the Knight's Cross[11]."

"I'm very happy for him. I've now got a better impression of Stalingrad from the map. Its situation is comparable to that of my home city of Duisburg. Both lie on a river; both have a north-south extension of about 30 kilometres and from west to east of 8-10 kilometres. Only, my birth city lies on the east bank of the Rhine, Stalingrad, however, is on the west bank of the Volga."

"Indeed, now you'd better go. Your messenger Marek will take you to your command post. Take care of yourself, and the best of luck." I saluted and left the room. Obergefreiter Marek was already waiting for me in the anteroom. I'd known him since I'd been in the company. He was from Upper Silesia[12], had a small farm and was reliability personified. His face lit up. I saw that his delight about my reappearance was genuine. I was glad to see his trusting old face again.

"Well, Marek, you old rascal, how's it going?" I reached out my hand to him.

"Good, Herr Leutnant, I've been dead lucky so far!"

"Have you had leave yet?"

"Nein, Herr Leutnant, the last time was from France."

"Then it's about damn time that you had it!"

"Ja, of course, but I'm not married and had to sacrifice it several times for the benefit of married comrades."

"Well, when this commotion is over, it'll be your turn. I'll see to it."

While we were chatting, Marek had led me outside through the labyrinth of passages under the former women's prison. Across the street from us – parallel to it, almost in a north-south direction – ran a railway line. I looked at my watch. It was almost 0400 hours. We veered to the east and went forward in the direction we were

---

10. _Feldersatz-Bataillon_ - 'Replacement Training Battalion'

11. _Major Artur Richard Rittner, Knight's Cross 27 October 1942, German Cross in Gold 13 September 1942. Commanded III./Inf.Rgt.276 from 1 November 1941 to 25 December 1942. Born 10 December 1904 in Biesendorf. He survived the war but his eventual date of death is not known._

12. _A large percentage of the non-commissioned officers and enlisted men were from Upper and Lower Silesia._

to take in the advance to the Volga. Sporadic machine-gun and rifle fire could be heard. It was coming from the left of us, from the centre of the city. The ruins of stone houses, silent and gloomy, were silhouetted against the slowly lightening horizon. The vacant area between them – a tangle of charred beams – was still smouldering and smoking. After nearly 100 metres, Marek led me into the cellar of a partially burnt out blockhouse. I had now arrived at my company command post. It was in a hole in the cellar, in front of which loomed the remnants of a brick wall from which we could observe the enemy. When I went in, the weak light of a Hindenburg lamp only allowed me to partially discern my surroundings. A figure stood to attention and reported: "Command post of 7. Kompanie. Feldwebel Grossmann with three messengers is glad to welcome you back to the Kompanie, Herr Leutnant."

I looked into the eyes of my trusted friends with some emotion. Unshaven faces, blackened with soot, showed the strain of the past few weeks. They were genuinely pleased to see me again. Words were superfluous – a handshake said it all.

"Danke, Grossmann, stand at ease. Guten Morgen, Kameraden."

"Morning, Herr Leutnant!"

"Marek, you stay here for the time being. Grossmann, you can show me, we have an order to attack in about two hours. Marek, you bring the commanders of 5., 6. and 8. Kompanien here and inform them that they've been placed under me for today by order of the Bataillon Commander. Do you know where their command posts are?"

"Jawohl, Herr Leutnant, everyone squats on top of each other here in the city."

After Marek had trotted off, Feldwebel Grossmann showed me where we were located on a captured map of Stalingrad. Looking up, I glanced into the mischievous smiling face of an Unteroffizier; he wore the Iron Cross First Class. My eyes widened with astonishment: "Good grief, Pawellek, Juschko, am I dreaming? You're an Unteroffizier and have the Iron Cross First Class! How'd you manage that?"

Feldwebel Grossmann answered for him: "Pawellek put a 'Ratsch-Bum'[13] battery out of action with a light mortar three days ago and was promoted to Unteroffizier and decorated with the Iron Cross First Class."

"Fantastic! Juschko, you have to tell me about it."

"Well, Herr Leutnant, we'd just forced our way into southern Stalingrad when I saw a whole battery, four guns, being manhandled into position right on a crossroads. Well, I set up the light mortar behind a wall, in next to no time – the second shot was already a direct hit, and then nothing but pounding them, always pounding, 20-30 shells, it was like a heavy downpour. Just like you did near Kanev on the Dnepr when

---

13. *Ratsch-Bum* - 'Crash-boom', a nickname for the Soviet 76mm gun whose muzzle velocity was so high that the discharge and impact of the shell were reputedly heard simultaneously.

Both photos: destruction along Krasnoznamenskaya Street, known to the Germans as the 'Lenia'.

The area north of the Tsaritsa that would be the area of operations for Holl and his men.

'Ivan'[14] approached to within 40 metres in the wheatfield and you gave them salvation from above with the light mortar. I haven't forgotten anything."

I thought back to the time in Oberlausitz and after that in France, when I was instructing these rough but honest men from Upper Silesia in infantry weaponry. Occasionally they would curse me under their breath, yet they knew that I pushed myself just as hard. Above all I'd shown them what counted. Here, I had to pass on what had been imparted to me by my instructors in the Reichswehr. Originally, my trainers had predominantly been Silesians and East Prussians.

"And what happened next?"

"Well, the entire Bataillon rushed forward; thanks to the blessing from above, 'Ivan' barely put up any resistance, and we'd taken another piece of this damned city."

I turned to Feldwebel Grossmann. He'd been in my 7. Kompanie since Kanev, a year ago in August (1941), when I. Bataillon had been completely shredded[15] and the remnants were distributed between II. and III. Bataillon. He came from Mecklenberg, and was tall, slender, blond, and blue-eyed – an archetypal Viking. His reliability was conspicuous. We could all recognise his North German origin by his accent. The sharply spoken 's' was his lingual characteristic, quite unlike the sharp, rolling 'r' of the Upper Silesians.

"Now, Grossmann, what's happened since my wounding in Nyrkovo on 19 April[16]? But please, only a rough outline."

"You now know we were assigned the assault on the Bastion on 8 July. Your successor was Oberleutnant Mehnert. He was wounded shortly before we reached the edge of the city at Stalingrad-South. That was about 10 days ago. Since then I've commanded the Kompanie. The frontal assault on the Bastion[17] of Nyrkovo was very

---

14. _Ivan_ - _German soldiers' nickname for their Soviet enemy. Although it is often thought to equate with the Germans being called 'Fritz' or 'Jerry' and the British 'Tommy', it is viewed as being racist and degrading by the Soviet people. However, most German soldiers seem unaware of the racial overtones of the term. It is only used here because it is the authentic language of the German soldier._

15. _The Bataillon was practically gutted of officers in this fighting. The Battalion commander Major d.R. von Heydbrand und der Lasa and his adjutant, Lt. Will, were wounded. Commander of 1. Kompanie, Oblt. Hahn, was killed when struck in the head by shrapnel; commander of 2. Kompanie, Hptm.d.R. Böge, was wounded, captured and died shortly after; commander of 3. Kompanie, Oblt. Meinhardt, suffered the same fate. The commander of 4. Kompanie, Oblt. Rittner, took command of the Bataillon until it was disbanded._

16. _94. Infanterie-Division had lain in its winter positions near Nyrkovo and Kamyshevaka since late 1941. These places, together with a string of other small villages that formed strongpoints in the front-line, would remain in the memory of every single man in the Division as symbols of a hard and brutally cold winter._

17. _The 'Bastion' was a dominating height called Hill 234.6, just north of Nyrkovo, upon which the Soviets had observation posts overlooking areas designated as starting positions for a major attack by 94. Infanterie-Division on 9 July 1942. A prerequisite for this attack was the capture of the 'Bastion'. Infanterie-Regiment 276 launched its attack on the hill on 8 July, captured it after heavy fighting and held it against repeated Soviet counterattacks. With the high ground under its control, the Division began its major attack as scheduled._

costly[18]. Leutnant Riedel was killed there. The entire southern front was in turmoil. For us, it mainly meant marching and yet more marching. We could barely keep up with the motorised units. Through Voroshilovgrad and Kalach, we had a general south-east march direction into the Kalmuck steppe, but then the Division wheeled to the east and we pushed into Stalingrad from the south. Leutnant Jahnke, successor of Leutnant Riedel in 5. Kompanie, lost his right hand shortly before we reached the edge of the city; Leutnant Pönigk rode over a mine near Voroshilovgrad and was killed. There are only a few of the original Kompanie members left. Our battle strength now, after your arrival, amounts to 1 officer, 2 Feldwebeln, 2 Unteroffiziere and 39 men: 44 men altogether. Feldwebel Cupal is close by and is commanding a platoon. The three squads are commanded by Unteroffizier Rotter, Obergefreiter Dittner and Obergefreiter Kowalski. Unteroffizier Pawellek is the Kompanietruppführer[19] and jack-of-all-trades."

A makeshift door opened from outside. Entering, the soldier stood to attention. "Oberfeldwebel Jacobs reporting as ordered."

"Danke, my good friend, it's good to see you again." We shook hands. Only if you've fought in the toughest combat, relying unconditionally on your comrades as we'd so often had to rely on Oberfeldwebel Jacobs and his heavy mortar platoon, could you comprehend the brief but heartfelt emotion in this greeting. It was reassuring for me to know that these combat-experienced men were in the forthcoming assault. Grossmann and Jacobs: they both had the stature of brothers; and Jacobs was also a North German.

I now awaited the appearance of my old friend Uli Weingärtner, who'd commanded 5. Kompanie since the wounding of Leutnant Jahnke. Weingärtner originally came from 14. Panzerjäger-Kompanie[20]. He'd experienced the end of the First World War as a young volunteer. He was the eldest of our comrades. He had time for everyone, was absolutely reliable and was thoroughly liked. I had also taken him into my heart, the age difference existing between us never being an issue. Only a few minutes passed before Uli appeared.

"Guten Morgen, gentlemen." His face beamed as he greeted me.

"Good grief, Bert, it's great to see you again! I'd already heard about your arrival and was glad to know one of the 'old men' was back with the Bataillon." We shook hands firmly. The presence of our fallen friends and men, who were still alive when I was wounded in April and were now no longer with us, could be felt – unseen – in

---

18. *Casualties suffered by 94. Infanterie-Division in the period from 8 to 11 July 1942:*
    4 officers killed and 18 wounded
    29 NCOs killed, 66 wounded and 2 missing
    120 men killed, 422 wounded and 8 missing.
19. *Kompanietruppführer - 'leader of company headquarters personnel'.*
20. *Panzerjäger-Kompanie - 'Anti-tank company'.*

the room. Our sorrow weighed on us wordlessly in this handshake.

"So, my dear Uli, you can tell me about your experiences over the past months later. Until Leutnant Fuchs arrives, can you report how the front looks here."

"Ja, my good friend, the last days have been damned hard and proved very costly for us. The Russians had been surprised by the thrust of our panzer and motorised units, who then constructed a so-called blocking position north of the city to ward off attacks from the north while expecting units to follow up and press into the city to take it. There was also a corresponding reaction when we fought our way into the southern part of Stalingrad out of the Kalmuck steppe. Leutnant Jahnke saw the city before he suffered his wound and I took over the company. The hardest fighting was around the Grain Elevator. Other brick and concrete buildings were also defended tooth and nail by 'Ivan'. It is a completely new way of fighting for us. You've got to expect a burst of fire out of every hole or gap in a wall. The fellows even come out of the ground. They know the sewer system: they suddenly lift up a man-hole cover, shoot at you from behind, a couple of your men are dead or wounded, and then they disappear like ghosts. Nothing is to be seen. It's a complete surprise. We've become more wary and now shoot at everything that moves. We've had to pay a high enough price in blood!"

The Grain Elevator: scene of some of the hardest fighting experienced by 94. Infanterie-Division.

I glanced at my watch. It was 0445 hours. We would soon be informed what time the attack would start. In the meantime, Leutnant Fuchs reported to me. He commanded 6. Kompanie, or more accurately, the remnants, because in terms of battle strength, we were only glorified platoon commanders. We introduced ourselves and I allowed him to explain the current positions of his Kompanie on a map (a captured city plan of Stalingrad). Accordingly, I placed my Kompanie on the left flank of the Bataillon, with a connection to the right flank of 71. Infanterie-Division's Aufklärungs-Abteilung, to the right of me was 6. Kompanie with a junction to III. Bataillon on the Tsaritsa, 5. Kompanie lay in reserve behind 6. Kompanie while 8. Kompanie with its four heavy mortars and four heavy machine-guns was positioned behind both forward companies.

"Gentlemen, we've been ordered to take the high-rise building drawn on the map here. You see that it's U-shaped, with both sides of the U pointing towards us. Now, you know better than I how strong enemy resistance is, since your attack floundered here yesterday. We'll learn shortly from the messenger when the attack will begin and whether we'll receive support from our artillery or 13. Kompanie with their howitzers. As you're not far from your companies I suggest you wait a moment for the runner to arrive."

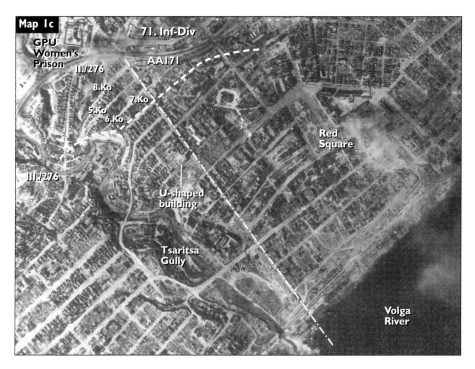

A scene of devastation: the battlefield in which Holl and his men fought on 24 September 1942.

We tried to peer through a hole in the wall at the battlefield lying in front of us. It began to get light. Smoke from the smouldering beams in destroyed apartment blocks lay like a shroud over the entire district. The breeze rekindled a fire here and there. Scattered haphazardly over the area, chimneys of burnt down wooden houses jutted up against the sky. In front of us – about 300 metres away – we could recognise the murky silhouette of the high-rise building. It was not yet light enough to make out details. Between it and us were only the ruins of bricks walls, bare chimneys and a smouldering tangle of wooden beams. We would need to work out how we could cross this expanse of ground and get into the apartment block. The central wing had been fairly well destroyed by direct bomb hits, but the machine-gun fire coming out of both side wings since the previous day was so heavy that our men could make no further headway.

"Jacobs, you must suppress enemy fire coming out of the side wings through aimed bursts from all of your heavy machine-guns, especially where 'Ivan' occupies the upper floors and can rake our men from above. You must smother ground objectives with your heavy mortars. If possible, we want to stay in verbal and visual contact. Herr Fuchs, you'll take the objective from the southern flank, therefore to the right of here; my company will take the northern, left wing. There, we will have narrow attack frontages and will be able to maintain visual and eventually aural communications.

Have any of you got any questions? No? Then everything is clear, except for the start time of the attack."

6. Armee HQ: – 1230 hours on 24. September 1942

Once the city sector up to the mouth of the Tsaritsa has been cleared, it is intended to transfer 94.Inf.Div. into the area north of Gorodishche, simultaneously positioning them to clear out the area around Orlovka.

With daylight slowly breaking, my old friend Marek appeared. "Herr Leutnant, order from the battalion commander that the attack will begin at 0600 hours[21] precisely. The Bataillon can initially expect no support from heavy weapons as these are supporting other units."

"Danke, Marek, report to Herr Major that we are attacking as ordered. See to it that Herr Major knows that we require artillery support as soon as possible."

"Jawohl, Herr Leutnant." Marek saluted, wheeled around and trotted off.

"Now, gentlemen, you've all heard that we won't have artillery support. Hopefully we'll have good luck: I wish it to all of us. Let's synchronise time: my watch now shows 0525 hours. Herr Fuchs, both of our companies will advance together at 0600 hours. We'll move as quietly as possible so we can take the area in front without alerting the enemy. The situation will then determine what we do. Uli, you'll stay here with your company, maintain communications with me and await further orders."

A handshake with my comrades, then I was alone with my Kompanietrupp[22] and Feldwebel Grossmann.

"Grossmann, you'll remain on the left side of the company along the street. You can see on the map here that this street runs past the left wing of the attack objective. Also tell your men that they should be careful. Because of our current battle strength, every casualty weighs twice as heavily."

"Jawohl, Herr Leutnant, it's fortunate that we received 20 replacements from the Feldersatzbataillon three days ago. They are 18 to 19 year-old Sudeten Germans. No combat-experience, cursory training, never thrown a live hand-grenade. I've already divided them up amongst the remnants of the Kompanie and entrusted them to our old, experienced hands.

"That means almost every second man is a newcomer without front-line experience! Well, then cheers!"

---

21. According to the war diary of 6. Armee, the attack began at 0700 hours, not 0600 hours.
22. Kompanietrupp - 'company headquarters personnel'.

"They'll soon have it, Herr Leutnant. They've generally made a good impression."

"I believe you, Grossmann, but without combat experience, and thrown into such a messy situation: that's a bit too much for the boys. We must be especially careful with them so that they're not put through a mincer. Right, it's about time they came forward. But as I was saying: you remain to the left of the street, and with that, I know where you'll be and where I can reach you. Take care of yourself."

"Danke, Herr Leutnant!"

There was still about 15 minutes before my comrades started their advance. Unteroffizier Pawellek, Obergefreiter Nemetz and Obergefreiter Willmann were near me. I had instructed these men myself after the French campaign when the Division was stationed for six months in Oberlausitz and around Zittau. There was not a light infantry weapon they couldn't master, and they'd also never failed as messengers. The past year at the front had melded us and each of us knew we could depend on the others.

"Juschko!"

"Herr Leitnant?"

"Do you still have our special weapons?"

"Jawohl, Herr Leitnant, the 'specials' are in the rear with the baggage-train, so we have to wait for them to be brought forward."

"That's good, think about it when Hauptfeldwebel[23] Michel comes with the field-kitchen tonight. How is Michel anyway?"

"Good, Herr Leitnant, he's as reliable as ever. When none of the others can find their companies, Michel always comes through."

I would've been happier if I'd had my arsenal with me now. The 'specials' included concentrated charges rigged from stick-grenades, a Russian submachine-gun, a Russian anti-tank rifle and the corresponding ammunition. After the first operations in Russia, we'd realised that Russian submachine-guns and anti-tank rifles were more robust than ours. Ours were good but temperamental when covered in dirt. Before long, I carried appropriate ammunition for use with the captured weapons – just in case – and several times in the past they'd proven useful when I'd brought them into action.

Two more minutes, then we would advance. I looked to the sky. Far and wide there was not a cloud to be seen, if you discounted the smoke coming from the fires all around us. The eastern horizon was getting brighter. With each passing minute, the silhouettes of the buildings in front of us – or rather, the ruins – became more distinct. Our attack objective also stood out more clearly from its surroundings. Sporadic machine-gun and rifle fire could be heard to the right and left of us. The discharge of

---

23. _Hauptfeldwebel_ - 'Master-Sergeant'. _More popularly know as 'Spiess' [literally means 'spear'] but also called the 'mother of the company'. A Spiess was a senior NCO that looked after the non-combat functions of a unit._

several enemy guns on the east bank of the Volga was also audible, their shells exploding some distance away from us. The day promised to be hot. My watch showed that our men had begun to move. The enemy had yet to notice anything since no shots fell in our sector. Hopefully it might be possible to move up close to the high-rise building undetected. My attention was now fully directed to the front. Unteroffizier Pawellek and both messengers fell silent and were likewise concentrating to the front. All of a sudden, Russian machine-gun fire shattered the quiet in our sector. Rifle fire was heard, followed shortly by bursts of fire from our machine-guns. From this point on an animated battle was under way. In the meantime, 8. Kompanie had opened fire with its heavy machine-guns. Ricochets buzzed through the area. Suddenly it was bright daylight. Through my binoculars, I could recognise the assigned objective with complete clarity. It was a six-storey

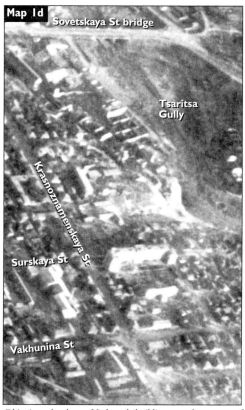

Map 1d

Sovetskaya St bridge

Tsaritsa Gully

Krasnoznamenskaya St

Surskaya St

Vakhunina St

Objective: the large U-shaped building on the corner of Krasnoznamenskaya and Surskaya streets. This photo was taken before the building had suffered any damage.

red-brick building with a total width of about 80 metres. On both the outer sides were the two wings, each about 20 metres long. The whole structure looked like an inverted, rectangular U. The central section had been battered by our Luftwaffe and our artillery. Large piles of rubble could be seen through the window openings. I could not locate the enemy in this section. However, defensive fire was coming out of both side wings. 'Ivan' was located in the upper floors. From up there, he had the entire foreground under control. Our attack was stopped about 150 metres from the objective. The squads had taken full cover and fired sporadically. Messengers from Feldwebel Grossmann and Leutnant Fuchs appeared at my command post and reported what I already knew myself. I gave them instructions to lay low for the time being and await further orders.

"Willmann!"

"Herr Leutnant?"

"Report to Bataillon: 'Attack under way at 0600. We've taken about 150 metres of ground and now remain lying up under defensive fire. The enemy dominates the battlefield with machine-guns from elevated firing positions. We cannot move forward without the support of heavy weapons. Urgently request support!' Have you written that down?"

"Jawohl, Herr Leutnant!"

I signed it and Willmann trotted off. The sun was now fully visible in the sky and it was getting warmer. I sent Obergefreiter Nemetz for Leutnant Weingärtner and Oberfeldwebel Jacobs. After a short time, both were with me. In the meantime it was already 0900 hours. You forget the time when your entire being is wide awake, in a frame of mind that enables you to react or reach a decision with lightning speed. I discussed the situation with both comrades. Thank God no casualties had yet been reported.

"Uli, is everything clear to you?"

"Jawohl, Bert."

"Jacobs, in this current situation, your heavy mortars cannot reach 'Ivan' situated in both wings of this block, but the heavy machine-guns can try to eliminate these nests."

"Herr Leutnant, we've established exactly where the Russian machine-gun nests are located, but those fellows are very nimble. They have alternate positions, firing irregularly aimed bursts from here and there before ceasing fire again. My men have to be on their toes."

"Yes, I've also seen that and reported it to Bataillon and moreover, I've urgently requested support from heavy weapons. With our relatively low combat strength, we must avoid every needless casualty. It's my assessment of the situation that we'll make no headway until we clean out those nests of resistance. There's also not much recognisable activity from our left neighbour. Their sector is also being lashed by machine-gun and rifle fire coming from the left wing of the building. From the sounds of the fighting, they're somewhere behind us to the left. Jacobs, go back to your company and keep the enemy down with your heavy machine-guns. Uli, you stay here with Unteroffizier Pawellek and stand in for me. Nemetz, you come with me. I want to pay a visit to our left neighbour and find out where we stand there."

"Alright, Bert. Come back safely."

I moved towards the rear utilising the available cover. Leaping and sprinting from ruin to ruin, I took care not to be seen, or at least only fleetingly by the enemy. After about 100 metres, a quick sprint took us across the street that formed the dividing line with our left neighbour. I had to ask several times for the command post of the unit, before I eventually found it. The sun, meanwhile, was burning down beautifully on the skin so that I was pouring with sweat. I reported to the Commander of Aufklärungs–Abteilung 171 and introduced myself as his right neighbour:

"Leutnant Holl, Kompanieführer 7. Kompanie Infanterie-Regiment 276."

"Von Holtey."[24]

"Herr Oberstleutnant, I would like to ascertain how far forward you are. We have to take the high-rise block whose upper section you can see from here. Our attack is stuck 150 metres in front of the block as we're coming under sporadic machine-gun and rifle fire from the upper floors and both side wings. We can't move forwards or backwards without suffering severe casualties. I've requested heavy weapon support for my Bataillon but I still haven't received any news. Your men are lying behind us. I would like to know why your units are hanging back."

Oberstleutnant Baron Arthur von Holtey, commander of Aufklärungs-Abteilung 171.

The well-groomed and good-looking Oberstleutnant – whose adjutant[25] was also well turned out – answered somewhat patronisingly: "Yes, my good man, we are not as far forward as we would have hoped. We are also waiting for support from heavy weapons. Hopefully, we will be getting two Sturmgeschütze in the early afternoon that we can employ here. Until they get here, I can hardly advance as my men on the right flank are having to keep their heads in the dirt because of that damn machine-gun fire coming from your attack strip."

"When does Herr Oberstleutnant expect the Sturmgeschütze?"

"In 1 or 2 hours."

"That means between 1400 and 1500 hours."

---

24. *In the original German text, Holl calls him 'von Winter'. There is no record of an Oberstleutnant (Lt.Col.) Winter commanding a unit in Stalingrad. Holl, however, is certainly referring to Oberstleutnant Baron Arthur von Holtey. Commanded Aufklärungs-Abteilung 171 from early 1940 to 31 October 1942. Commanded Panzer-Regiment 2 (16. Panzer-Division) in 1943 and Panzer-Regiment 24 (24. Panzer-Division) in 1944. Born 1904 in Kurland; died 1983 in Hannover.*

25. *Leutnant d.R. Alard von Rohr. Adjutant Aufklärungs-Abteilung 171 from 2 to 30 September 1942. Born 9 December 1920 in Stülpe; died 10 March 1945 in Karnitz.*

"Precisely, my good man, you can report here once again."

"If the situation hasn't changed by then, I'll come back." I saluted and walked back with my messenger. We exploited the available cover intuitively, just as we'd take cover if the heavy crump of artillery and the onrushing sound of an incoming salvo told you it was likely to explode in the vicinity. When I looked down at myself – I was caked with dirt and soaked in sweat – I understood the pompous manner of the gentlemen from the other branches of the service. They were not deliberately offensive and we didn't take it personally: we were infantrymen, or 'stubble-hoppers' as some mockingly called us. The infantry had covered thousands of kilometres on foot in this almost endless land; they had to firmly claw into the ground. They could not quickly mount up and be set down to assault the next position based on the tactical situation. Everything in these horse-drawn units had to be done on foot. In any case this attitude didn't perturb me.

When I arrived back at my command post, I informed my friend Uli Weingärtner of the situation with our left neighbour. Obergefreiter Willmann had returned from the Battalion command post. Major Dr. Zimmermann had made efforts to obtain heavy weapons for our sector. Hauptmann Rittner's III. Bataillon, on the other side of the Tsaritsa, had also suffered from the fire coming from the south wing of the building and could not make any progress. Unteroffizier Pawellek handed me a slice of bread and a cup of cold coffee. I gulped them down. I couldn't get the Sturmgeschütze out of my mind. Only with their support could we attack and take the high-rise building. But we didn't have them! And would this Oberstleutnant von Holtey put them at our disposal? Regardless of what happened, I was going to

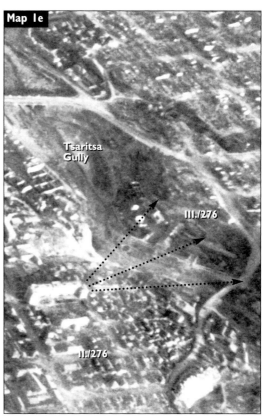

Map 1e

Tsaritsa Gully

III./276

II./276

Fire from U-shaped building affected the advance of Rittner's III. Bataillon on the other side of the Tsaritsa Gully.

see him again in an hour. Oberfeldwebel Jacobs appeared and wanted to know what happened with our left neighbour. Leutnant Fuchs was stuck up front with his men, along with Feldwebel Grossmann. Only a coup de main with the Sturmgeschütze or darkness could save my comrades at the front from their difficult situation. The sun beat down mercilessly on the city. The heat made the air shimmer and the sweet smell of decomposition was all-pervasive. Everything appeared to be dead in our combat sector. From the rear, I could recognise several comrades with the naked eye. They had selected a shady spot for cover. There was little movement to show that they were still alive. And I could sense the tension lying heavily over everything.

The adjutant to our Bataillon Commander, Leutnant Schüler, appeared at my command post with his messenger, Obergefreiter Marek. "Well, Bert, how's it look up front? The commander has ordered me to personally assess the situation here."

"Well, Jochen, nothing's changed since my last report to Bataillon. Our men are stuck fast in a mouse-trap. Fortunately, I've only had one slightly injured casualty up to now. Without support from heavy weapons, we won't be advancing any further in daylight today. Whether we can operate in darkness remains to be seen."

"I can tell you, from the commander, that he reckons we can't count on receiving any heavy weapon support today. The Division has concentrated every available gun on the right flank; even our 13. Kompanie must cooperate. They're determined to push through to the Volga there – whatever it takes – and destroy the enemy. You can hear the sounds of battle coming from there."

I had of course noticed that the loudest sounds of battle were coming from the right of us. It appeared that both protagonists had assembled all their guns in the same place. It was also very animated further to our left, in the area of the city centre. The sounds there, however, were coming from further afield than our 'concert', which was close by. It was being orchestrated by a pair of the enemy's lousy machine-guns and submachine-guns, in addition to single rifles. Their shooting was not particularly loud, so when they hit a target, it had much more of an impact. In such a critical situation, a front-line soldier only has eyes and ears for the enemy lying directly opposite him. Leutnant Schüler, observing the battlefield with his binoculars, turned to me with apprehension in his voice: "Bert, I'm worried about the commander, his appearance is yellowish, and he looks and acts apathetically. I think he's got jaundice."

"Bloody hell, that's all we need now, to lose 'Papa' Zimmermann! Hopefully he's not too bad. When it's possible, I'll come to your command post tonight. Report to Herr Major that I've been over to see our left neighbour, Aufklärungs-Abteilung 171. Two Sturmgeschütze are due to show up there. I'll see whether they can help us. So long, Jochen, look after yourself."

On my signal, Obergefreiter Nemetz stirred and followed me. The route to my left

A long-barrel assault gun of Sturmgeschütz-Abteilung 244 moves through one of Stalingrad's balkas.

neighbour was no longer unknown. As I crossed over the wide asphalt street, which was well suited as a boundary line, I could hear the deep rumbling of two engines and the squeal of tracks as they drove over solid ground. With delight, we both moved more quickly toward these sounds, which were like music to our ears. It was our comrades! I caught sight of them at the next side street. Two Sturmgeschütze, covering each other carefully, were rumbling toward us[26]. I waved my arms at them. The first vehicle – looking like a colossus – came to a stop. A head appeared through the commander's hatch. I saw a youthful mop of blond hair and two bright eyes looking at me questioningly.

"Leutnant Holl, Kompanie-Führer 7./276."

"Leutnant Hempel[27]."

---

26. *These two Sturmgeschütze belonged to Major Dr. Paul Gloger's Sturmgeschütz-Abteilung 244 and had probably been supporting Aufklärungs-Abteilung 171 on the previous day. The following extract for 23 September 1942 is from a report written after the war by a member of Aufklärungs-Abteilung 171: "The fighting continued bitterly. Two Sturmgeschütze on the 'Lenia' [what the Germans called Krasnoznamenskaya Street] supported 1. Schwadron as it moved through the park that lay behind the Theatre. The 3. Zug under Wachtmeister Gosche penetrated into the Theatre. Part of 3. Schwadron were up on the same level and tossed smoke-grenades and concentrated charges through the cellar windows…"*

27. *There is no record of a man called 'Leutnant Hempel' belonging to a Sturmgeschütz-Abteilung in Stalingrad.*

"Herr Hempel, you must help us! Can you come down for a moment?"

With two leaps the blonde Leutnant was standing next to me. He was approximately half a head taller than me. "Where's the fire?"

"We've been stuck here for a good eight hours. We can't move forward. In that high-rise building, whose upper section you can see through the gap here, the Russians are dominating the entire neighbourhood with machine-guns. You've been called for to bring some relief to Aufklärungs-Abteilung 171."

"Ja, that's right, I'm to report to Oberstleutnant von Holtey and I'm looking for his command post."

"Herr Hempel, you won't need to do that if you follow me with both your Sturmgeschütze and help us take that damned high-rise building and eliminate the enemy. When this nightmare is past, you can still report to Aufklärungs-Abteilung 171, but I believe that you'll then no longer be required today."

Leutnant Hempel appeared to be convinced by my remarks. "Fine, Herr Holl, we'll help you. What do you suggest?"

"If you follow me to the next intersection, we must then turn left on this asphalt street. You can see the high-rise about 400 metres ahead on the right side of the street. I'll follow your gun with three men, four others will follow the second gun. Keep the enemy in the left wing down with your cannon and shoot at everything you can recognise; the second vehicle will do the same on the right wing. The entire thing must happen so swiftly that the enemy doesn't realise what's hit him. Should anything unforeseen happen, we'll cover your rear."

"Jawohl, that's alright with us. When you move, I'll first of all drive up to the next junction. I'll give the second gun instructions in the meantime."

"Nemetz, you've heard our plan. Get to our command post as quickly as possible. Pawellek and Willmann will follow the first gun with you. I'll be there too. Oberfeldwebel Jacobs with three men from his unit will follow the second gun. Tell Oberfeldwebel Jacobs that we'll storm the left wing and he'll take the right wing of the building. Have you understood all that?"

As he trotted off, I heard him say "Jawohl, Herr Leitnant!"

"Herr Hempel, it'll be 15 to 20 minutes before my messenger reaches my men and they creep unnoticed up the street to link up with us. I'm going to get as close as possible to the intersection without being seen by those in the high-rise. Follow me slowly and stop on my signal. When I pump my fist in the air several times, that's the sign to 'march' and, without stopping, drive up to the objective."

"Everything's clear, Herr Holl. Good luck!"

<u>LI. Armeekorps HQ:</u> – 1645 hours on 24. September 1942

At 0700 hours, LI.A.K. launched its attack against the enemy bridgehead both sides of the mouth of the Tsaritsa...

<u>In particular</u>:

In hard house-to-house fighting, Inf.Rgt.267 has approached to within 300 metres of the Tsaritsa. Defence from the area of the Tsaritsa mouth, the railway area south-west of there and the north point of the Volga island.

71.Inf.Div. attacked after thorough preparation by VIII. Fliegerkorps. In the city sector north of the mouth of the Tsaritsa – consisting mostly of masonry buildings and numerous multi-storey structures – enemy resistance is noticeably stronger than in other areas of the city. Every house and factory must be fought for in the most stubborn combat.

I carefully worked my way forward using every scrap of cover. If possible, 'Ivan' should not notice anything. Both Sturmgeschütze slowly trailed behind me. When I reached the intersection, I gave the agreed signal to halt. Through my binoculars, I could see Unteroffizier Pawellek and Obergefreiter Willmann creeping along the street under cover. It would now be quite easy for them to link up with me as I passed by them behind the first Sturmgeschütz. I also saw that Oberfeldwebel Jacobs with three men was already in place, led by my messenger Nemetz. They had reached Pawellek and were waiting for us to appear. I once more surveyed this broad, straight asphalt street. Standing along the right side were several wooden poles with electricity cables hanging limply, others were snapped and lay partially over the street. The wires were still partly attached. We had to be careful that these did not hinder our advance. I clenched my right fist and thrust it upwards several times. Both Sturmgeschütze slowly rolled forward. Their commanders disappeared into the hatches. When Leutnant Hempel's gun rolled into the middle of the intersection, it spun around to the south and I leapt behind it. I followed it at a trot so that I had cover from the Russians and could give my men signals when we were level with them. A thunderclap threw me to my knees. Leutnant Hempel had recognised his target and loosed off a first shot. A second shot followed close behind. Now, the second Sturmgeschütz also began to fire on its objective, the right wing of the high-rise building. After the initial surprise, I became accustomed to the deafening blasts from both guns. Never before had I been so close to them. But they were bringing my comrades urgently needed help. We passed Jacobs, Pawellek and their men. In accordance with my orders passed on by Nemetz, they joined up with us. There were now four infantrymen following every gun. I shouted to Nemetz: "Nemetz, run to Leutnant Weingärtner! When we reach the block, he should move up across the entire sector with a coordinated charge. Stay with him until you also get to the high-rise building!"

"Jawohl, Herr Leutnant, understood!"

Everything happened with lightning speed as we followed the firing guns at the double. Surprise appeared to be complete. There was no defensive fire from the block that had been making it so difficult for us the entire day. We approached the building and had to keep dodging wire sent spiralling into the air by the tracks. There was still about 30 metres to the entrance on the left-hand side. The right-hand entrance lay about 100 metres further away.

"Jacobs, we're going to make a concerted push. I'll take the left-hand entrance, you take the right. Understand?"

"All clear!"

The Sturmgeschütze had

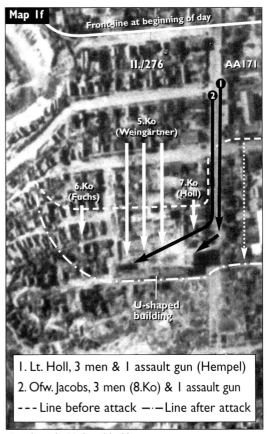

| Map 1f |

1. Lt. Holl, 3 men & 1 assault gun (Hempel)
2. Ofw. Jacobs, 3 men (8.Ko) & 1 assault gun
- - - Line before attack —·— Line after attack

Assault on the U-shaped building

come to a halt, their cannon ready to train their fire on both wings of the block.

"Hand-grenades ready! All okay? Let's go!"

We ran forward as quickly as we could. While storming forward, I saw that our line was now on their feet and running towards the apartment block. Now we were at the entrance. Nothing could be heard upstairs. A wooden staircase led down to the cellar. Noises were coming from down there. "Pawellek, you give me covering fire from above with Willmann. I'm going to see what's going on down there."

I held a primed hand-grenade and was at the bottom of the stairs in a few leaps. The open cellar door only let in weak daylight. I first accustomed myself to the diffused light in the cellar anteroom. Weak light was coming through the partly open door. I kicked the door open and suddenly stood in the door-frame, ready to throw the grenade and bring my submachine-gun into firing position. The room was crammed full of people. Women holding children in their arms, old men, old women, boys and girls, all with their eyes staring at me, full of the fear of death; everyone was crying and screaming in confusion.

I yelled into the room as loudly as I could: "Quiet!" The commotion abruptly stopped and all eyes were directed at me, full of fear.

"Can anyone speak and understand German?"

A brief whispering, then an old man worked his way forward through the throng and said to me: "I understand a little."

"Then tell all your people that they have nothing to fear. We're not fighting against women, children and old men."

He translated the general meaning into Russian.

I continued: "All soldiers that are hiding here in the room should come forward one by one and bring their weapons. Nothing will happen to you! The rest of you will remain in the cellar and await further directions!"

After the old man had translated, seven soldiers emerged from the furthest corner. They were sent upstairs and disarmed. In the meantime, Unteroffizier Pawellek had also come downstairs. Being born in Silesia, he also spoke Polish and was therefore in a position to tell these people what I wanted. I sensed the perceptible relief from these pitiful creatures when they realised that we German soldiers did not act in the manner in which we were depicted in their propaganda. Pawellek told the old man that he was responsible for maintaining peace and order. When we returned to the ground floor, I could see that we had captured a total of 17 Russians. About 20 had withdrawn to the next block of houses. Feldwebel Grossmann and Leutnant Fuchs had immediately secured the side of the building facing east. We were all relieved that there had only been three casualties through wounds and no fatalities.

It was almost 1700 hours. Both Sturmgeschütze waited in ambush positions and stood guard in the direction of the enemy. In the meantime, our left neighbour[28] had moved up alongside us[29]. Barely any battle noise could be heard in our sector. I went over to our marvellous helpers.

"Herr Hempel, on behalf on my men, I'd like to give you my heartfelt thanks for your excellent support. You can see for yourself what a miracle your intervention has provided."

"Herr Holl, we've only performed our duty, just as you and your men have."

28. *Aufklärungs-Abteilung 171*
29. *An extract from the Aufklärungs-Abteilung 171 report:*
    "House after house was taken as the Abteilung pushed on. On 24. September, a school used as a barracks – and obstinately defended by the Russians – was taken…"

"Well, you operated splendidly. But what about tomorrow? Making headway would be much easier with your co-operation."

"You're absolutely right. I'll report that to my commander and try to see whether we can help you tomorrow. If it's approved, we cannot be here before 0900 hours."

"Never mind, the main thing is that you come at all. Shall I report to your commander how well you and your men helped us?"

"That's not necessary. Our commander knows we're fulfiling our duty."

"Well, hopefully tomorrow then. All the best!"

"Danke, you too!"

The engines were gunned and both Sturmgeschütze slowly trundled off to the rear. Hopefully we would see them again tomorrow.

I went back to the apartment block and turned to Leutnant Weingärtner who, together with Unteroffizier Pawellek, was conversing with the Russian prisoners.

"Well, Uli, what do our prisoners have to say for themselves?"

"Not much actually, their understanding is poor. They were defending this building with about 40 soldiers. Their leader was a lieutenant. When the guns shot up their positions, the lieutenant pulled back with about half of his people."

"Then we must be particularly attentive tonight. Nemetz, you already know our left neighbour. Take three men – Feldwebel Grossmann will designate them – and lead the prisoners that way. We have no men to send on. Tell the Oberstleutnant that we require every man here."

Uli was pleased: "Fantastic Bert, it went like clockwork. I never thought we'd move another metre forward today. When you appeared with those two Sturmgeschütze – it was almost like a training ground exercise!"

"Ja, Uli, only with one small difference: we never had the opportunity to try it earlier and rehearse it a little. Hopefully, Leutnant Hempel will come back tomorrow. Right behind this block is a junction, and I don't know whether you've noticed: the closer we move toward the Volga, the more solid the buildings are getting; you don't see any wooden houses. For us, that means we'll have to be even more careful as the enemy may be hiding behind every wall, in every cellar or in the upper storeys. Make sure everything's in order at the front and that we don't get any unpleasant surprises. Unteroffizier Pawellek is at your disposal. I'm going to the Battalion command post with Willmann to file a report with the Major."

"Understood, take care of yourself Bert!"

While heading back to the Battalion command post with Willmann, I glanced at

6. Armee HQ: – 1945 hours on 24. September 1942

In Stalingrad, the attack to clear the city sector up to the mouth of the Tsaritsa gained ground in tough house–to–house fighting. About half the targeted area was taken. The district south of the Tsaritsa is basically in our hands. The attack will be continued tomorrow. LI. Armeekorps hopes that, despite company combat strengths dwindling to a few men, the clearing–out will be able to be completed tomorrow.

my watch. It was now 1700 hours. I made my way across part of the day's battlefield (and made sure that I checked all around, as one never knew whether or not 'Ivan' would turn up) where my comrades had been lying for hours. It was a desolate picture: dead bodies that were already partly decaying, single stoves and crockery lying next to extinguished fire-places. Smouldering timberwork was everywhere. This level of destruction could only have been the result of bombing attacks. It could not have been caused by artillery. It was still light when I reached the Battalion command post. It was still in the old GPU Women's Prison. I found my commander, Major Dr. Zimmermann[30], in exactly the same place as I had the previous day. I now felt that I'd never been away from the unit, and I had not even been back for a full 24 hour period. I was startled when I saw the Major. He was just as Leutnant Schüler had described when at my command post towards midday. My commander's face was as yellow as a quince, he appeared listless and obviously had a fever. I saluted: "I'd like to report that we reached our assigned attack objective with support from two Sturmgeschütze. Mission accomplished!"

He forced a smile; I noticed that he had difficulty speaking.

"Danke, Holl. Make your report."

I described the course of the past day. He listened attentively. "Schüler's already reported how bad your situation was after returning from your command post. Messengers were here several times. We tried everything to get some support for you and our requests for help were constantly turned down. To the south of us is an encirclement that extends to the banks of the Volga, and it just had to be eliminated today. Hopefully this is what has happened because that then means the heavy weapons will be placed at our disposal tomorrow."

"I hope so too, Herr Major. It's still very important for us to have both of those Sturmgeschütze again tomorrow. There is no more effective help in house-to-house fighting. Leutnant Hempel was going to try to come again tomorrow. I

---

30. *Major d.R. Dr. Wolfgang Zimmermann, commander II./Infanterie-Regiment 276, was awarded the German Cross in Gold on 23 October 1942.*

regard it as essential that the Regiment or Division understands the importance of securing this support."

"I'll do everything possible, Holl."

"Danke, Herr Major!"

"Ja, Holl, it's hit me very hard, as you may have already realised. In addition to jaundice with fever, I feel completely exhausted. On doctor's orders, I must leave the Bataillon tonight for a short time. Major Professor Dr. Weigert[31] will replace me. You already know him from the formation of the Division in Königsbrück. He's in the Führerreserve[32] for the time being and will hopefully bring a few officers with him."

"We certainly need them, Herr Major. Allow me, Herr Major, to talk with Leutnant Schüler?"

"Yes, go ahead."

I went into the adjoining room, which was as poorly illuminated as the room I'd just left. This was where Bataillon staff was located. Leutnant Schüler was compiling the daily report for the Regiment. A man was trying to obtain a connection on the field-telephone. There was as much activity as there would have been in any peacetime office, except that external appearances were so completely different.

I greeted Feldwebel Rupprecht, who had been the soul of the staff for years, and other comrades I had not seen the night before. Our friendly greetings were sincere. We all knew what one another had to endure.

"Jochen, fetch me something to eat, I'm almost dying of hunger." My stomach was asserting its rights. I had neglected it during the events of the past day.

"No sooner said than done, Bert! We're trying to get a connection to Regiment so the commander can get the Sturmgeschütze tomorrow. At the moment, the line's not working."

The 'Strippenzieher'[33], as our communications people were irreverently known, reported to the adjutant that they had established a connection to Regiment. Leutnant Schüler took the receiver: "Command post II. Bataillon here, Oberleutnant Krell[34] please." I listened with surprise. My old friend Rudi Krell was back with the Regiment?

This old Breslau 'Lerge'[35] was the divisional O2. I was going to ask Jochen when Krell had returned to the Regiment.

---

31. *Major d.R. Dr. Professor Weigert, Führer II./Infanterie-Regiment 276. Commanded 14./Inf.Rgt.276 in 1941 as a Hauptmann. Took temporary command of II./Inf.Rgt.276 on 9 August 1941.*

32. Führerreserve *- A reserve of officers maintained by larger units, such as Division, Korps and Armee. Officers would be called upon from the Führerreserve to replace active officers that had become casualties.*

33. Strippenzieher *- 'Cable guys' or 'cable-layers'.*

34. *Hauptmann d.R. Rudolf Krell. Born 10 May 1911 in Breslau; died 9 January 1970 while on holiday in southern Austria.*

35. Lerge *- a nickname for people from the city of Breslau in Upper Silesia.*

```
                    Noch Generalkommando LI.A.K.

Verwundet: 1.10.42  Lt.d.R.   Stein,      2./Pi.Btl.635  (  --  )
                                          Chef

Vermisst:  1.10.42  Oblt.d.R. Tilsen,     1./Pi.Btl.71   (  --  )
                                          Chef

           1.10.42  Lt.d.R.   Schröder,   1./Pi.Btl.635  (  --  )
                                          Zugfhr.

Erkrankt:  21.9.42  Major d.R. Waitl,     III./I.R.211   ( 71.I.D.)
                                          Kdr.

           22.9.42  Oblt.d.R. Bulgrin,    A.A.1/1        ( 71.I.D.)
                                          Adj.

           25.9.42  Lt.       Kraus,      3./A.R.171     ( 71.I.D.)
                                          B.-Offz.

           30.9.42  Lt.d.R.   v.Rohr,     A.A.1/1        ( 71.I.D.)
                                          Adj.

           24.9.42  Major d.R. Zimmermann, II./I.R.276   ( 94.I.D.)
                                          Kdr.

           25.9.42  Oblt.d.R. Knop,       Dinaffl 295    (295.I.D.)
                     (w)                  M.Offz.

           26.9.42  Hptm.     Busch,      II./I.R.517    (295.I.D.)
                                          Fhr.

           29.9.42  Lt.d.R.   Zander,     I./I.R.546     (389.I.D.)
                                          Adj.

           29.9.42  Lt.d.R.   Baetz,      14./I.R.544    (389.I.D.)
                                          Fhr.

           30.9.42  Lt.d.R.   Grün,       4./I.R.544     (389.I.D.)
                                          Fhr.

           21.9.42  Hptm.     Jaquet,     Verb.Offz.z.   (100.Jg.D.)
                                          kroat.I.R.369

           22.9.42  Lt.d.R.   Klever,     1./Na.Abt.100  (100.Jg.D.)
                                          Zugfhr.

           22.9.42  Hptm.     Walther,    I./Jg.Rgt.54   (100.Jg.D.)
                                          Kdr.

           26.9.42  Hptm.     Witte,      III./Jg.Rgt.54 (100.Jg.D.)
                                          Fhr.

           26.9.42  Lt.d.R.   Wohlsdorf,  Jg.Rgt.54      (100.Jg.D.)
                                          Zugfhr.

           29.9.42  Oblt.     Dieckmann,  2./A.R.616     (  --  )
                                          Chef

           30.9.42  Lt.d.R.   Hatvom,     2./Jg.Rgt.54   (100.Jg.D.)
                                          Zugfhr.

Berichtigungen:
     Der am 3.10. als verwundet gemeldete Lt.d.R. Wolf,
6./I.R.577 , ist am 30.9. verwundet worden.
     Der am 1.10. als erkrankt gemeldete Lt.d.R. Korbel,
10./I.R.264 , heißt richtig " K ö r b e l ".
     Der am 26.9. als verwundet gemeldete Oblt.d.R. Gentz-
lin, 4./I.R.203, heißt richtig " G a n t z l i n ".
```

A 6. Armee casualty list showing the names of officers who fell ill between 21 and 30 September 1942. Eighth from the top is Major d.R. Zimmermann, Kommandeur II./Infanterie-Regiment 276.

Leutnant Schüler spoke again: "Guten Abend, Herr Oberleutnant, is Herr Oberstleutnant Müller around? Major Dr. Zimmermann would like to speak to him. How does it look here? Better now, which was something that couldn't be said a few hours ago. But the messenger will be there any moment to see you with the daily report. Wait a moment, I've got someone here that wants to speak to you."

Schüler had understood my signals and handed me the receiver.

"Greetings to you, my dear Rudi!"

A short silence on the other end, then a happy voice replied: "Wow, Bert, we heard last night that you were back. I've already told Oberstleutnant Müller a few things about you. With the complement of officers being seriously depleted over

Leutnant Rudolf Krell, O2 of 94. Infanterie-Division.

the past days, we're glad for every new arrival, particularly when they're old experienced comrades."

"How long has Oberstleutnant Müller[36] been with the Regiment?"

"About two weeks. Oberst Grosse[37] and his adjutant, Oberleutnant Kelz[38], have taken home leave. Oberstleutnant Müller was sent from the Führerreserve as a relief commander and I was assigned as his adjutant because I came from the Regiment."

"Who else is with you?"

"Oberleutnant Polit[39] and Leutnant Dr. Hofmann[40]."

"I know them both. Rudi, we must stop because our commanders will want to talk.

36. *Oberstleutnant Julius Müller. Born 19 June 1897 in Neu-Brandenburg; listed as missing in action in Stalingrad 23 January 1943; died April 1943 in Soviet captivity.*

37. *Generalmajor Erich Hugo Richard Grosse. Born 23 June 1885 in Barmen-Rittershausen; severely wounded on 28 November 1942; died 1 December 1942 in a hospital in Elshanka, a suburb of Stalingrad.*

38. *Oberleutnant Erich Kelz. Born 25 February 1904 in Meiningen; died 7 January 1943 in Stalingrad.*

39. *Hauptmann Ewald Polit. Born 11 February 1908 in Kreuzburg; died 2 October 1942 in Stalingrad.*

40. *Leutnant Dr. Horst Hofmann. Born 13 January 1912 in Chemnitz; died 30 November 1942 on Hill 135.4, about 3km east of Orlovka, Stalingrad.*

But look after yourself, old boy. I'll see you soon."

The receiver was passed to the commander. Unteroffizier Jersch, who had also been with the Bataillon since its formation, brought me some coffee and a sandwich.

"Danke, Jersch, I'll enjoy this." I consumed the sandwich with great relish. The warm coffee was good. I turned to my messenger:

"Nemetz, have you already had something to eat?"

"Jawohl, Herr Leutnant, I've already been taken care of. The Hauptfeldwebel will be at the front soon with his 'Gulaschkanone'[41], so we'll get a warm meal."

Oh well, I would see my old Spiess, Hauptfeldwebel Michel, and both the cooks with the driver, later. I'd left the Kompanie five months ago, so I wondered whether they were still the same people. I asked Nemetz. "All of our old people are still with the baggage train, Herr Leitnant, even your horse 'Mumpitz' is there." My old four-legged friend Mumpitz was still alive, how splendid! Hopefully I could ride him again soon. I wondered if he would recognise me? We had become good friends, me and this small stocky white gelding from the former Czechoslovakian army. His name was not ill-suited[42], as many riders had already been thrown off him. But we both liked and understood each other well.

I had now been at the command post for two hours. It was about time that I returned to my comrades at the front. Leutnant Schüler, who had been in with the commander, came back into the room. "Bert, Herr Major wants to speak to you again." I went into the next room and announced my presence.

"There you are, Holl, I've spoken with the Regiment Commander. He'll do everything possible to ensure that we have both Sturmgeschütze again tomorrow. The enemy in the pocket to the right of us has been compressed into the narrowest possible area, so he's confident that artillery will be deployed in our sector tomorrow. Inform your men so that they're not surprised."

"Jawohl, Herr Major. Since the enemy will probably not reply, something will be in store for us tomorrow."

"I believe that too. And now you should go back to your people. I will be replaced tonight. My dear Holl, I wish you all the best and may God be with you." His eyes looked at me earnestly as he proffered his hand in farewell. I stood to attention, returned his handshake, and had to swallow several times before replying: "I also wish you all the best, Herr Major, for a speedy recovery and a healthy reunion." A salute, about face, and I left the room. Would fate ever again re-unite me with this man whom I revered and respected? Despite his exactitude he was still a father figure to all of us.

---

41. _Gulaschkanone_ - _German nickname for their mobile field-kitchen._
42. _Mumpitz_ - _'rubbish' or 'nonsense'._

My train of thought was short-lived. The new commander due that night was Major Professor Dr. Weigert, known to us all as 'Papa' Weigert. He was the archetypal university professor. He had been a Hauptmann in World War One, after that a lecturer at the University of Breslau and an authority on German art history. Like his predecessor, he was about 45 years-old, however, his character was different from Major Dr. Zimmermann. Major Dr. Zimmermann gave his orders concisely and in a soldierly manner; Major Professor Dr. Weigert could also give orders, however, he spoke as if talking to his university students. Men and officers alike valued and respected both of these father figures.

I said goodbye to my friend, Leutnant Schüler, and the other members of staff, and made my way back to the front with my messenger Willmann. After a short distance my eyes became accustomed to the darkness. Signal flares rose into the night sky here and there. They indicated the approximate course of the front-line. Ivan's 'sewing-machines' buzzed overhead, dropping light bombs. To make it easier on ourselves, we used the broad asphalt street that the Sturmgeschütze had proceeded down several hours earlier. Our sector was quiet. Combat-proven men knew that sentries on both sides would be straining their eyes, looking out to the front, pricking up their ears, senses alert. If they noticed anything suspicious, they would immediately raise the alarm. A failure could have disastrous consequences and would mean both their own death and that of many of their comrades. Because of the short distance to the enemy – at the most they were only 30 to 50 metres from the apartment block – twice the vigilance was called for. The challenge 'Halt, who goes there? Password?' demonstrated this. After we repeated the password, the sentry allowed us to approach. There was nothing of significance to report.

> **Ic of 6. Armee HQ:** – 2030 hours on 24. September 1942
>
> **Disposition of enemy forces:**
> **Mouth of the Tsaritsa:** 92nd Rifle Brigade, identity of 111th Rifle Brigade is newly confirmed.
> **North of the mouth of the Tsaritsa:** Combat groups from destroyed units of 10th NKVD Division, 244th Rifle Division, 115th Fortified District, 42nd Rifle Brigade, in addition to city civil defence of around 80 men drawn from workers and Communists.

A gentle clanking could be heard from the high-rise building. Hauptfeldwebel Michel was there with his field-kitchen and the squads were getting warm rations and enough supplies to last until the next hot meal. If any mail had arrived, then this would also have been brought forward.

Our Spiess saw me, came over and reported in a low voice. I thanked him and extended my hand. "Well, Michel, how's it going? Everything alright at the baggage train?"

"Jawohl, Herr Leutnant. We're glad that you're back with the company."

"Likewise. I'm just sorry that there are so few oldies still with the company. We could put them to good use now."

"Unteroffizier Pawellek has already prepared rations for Herr Leutnant."

"That's good, but I'd rather eat my soup from the field-kitchen."

Three old, trusted faces grinned at me, without letting themselves be distracted from their work. They understood my friendly slap on the shoulder. It was as if I'd never been away. The barley broth with beet was delicious, as always. There was no extra wurst here. Whatever rations we received from either cook – one was a butcher and the other a baker – they always managed to concoct something good.

I turned to Michel and told him that he should come to my command post after he had finished distributing the rations.

At my company command post, I met my friend Uli Weingärtner as well as Pawellek and Nemetz. Uli reported to me that everything was in order at the front. It was quiet for the moment. I turned to Pawellek: "Juschko, I want Leutnant Fuchs and Feldwebel Grossmann to come to the command post, along with Oberfeldwebel Jacobs." Then I turned to Uli again and advised him of the change in commanders and that I wasn't at all happy about the state of the Major's health. Hauptfeldwebel Michel appeared and reported that he was leaving with the field-kitchen crew.

"Very good, Michel, see to it that you return intact with the men and our 'Gulaschkanone'. You'll know our approximate position tomorrow. If we are fortunate, perhaps already on the Volga, if not, somewhere between here and there. Well, take care of yourself."

Michel saluted smartly and disappeared. Feldwebel Grossmann arrived soon after with Oberfeldwebel Jacobs, followed a short time later by Leutnant Fuchs.

<u>LI. Armeekorps HQ:</u> – 2230 hours on 24. September 1942

    The enemy bridgehead both sides of the Tsaritsa was cleared of the enemy in its southern section with the exception of the west bank of the Volga and in several places in the Tsaritsa Gully itself...
    <u>In particular</u>:
    94.Inf.Div. succeeded in cleaning out the city sector south of the mouth of the Tsaritsa up to the housing district on the Volga bank and the bend in the Tsaritsa projecting to the north-east. The enemy still holds the remaining riverbank with strong forces.

(cont.)

In laborious, difficult fighting, 71.Inf.Div. reached the
following line on 24.9.: Tsaritsa bridge 35a1 – oval plaza – street
to north–east – south edge of Theatre Square – Theatre (excl.) –
north edge of the square of the Party buildings – bank of the Volga
46c2. Enemy fights doggedly for every house. According to prisoner
statements, the groups of resistance are led by experienced
officers and commissars. Active assistance by the population is
repeatedly detected. Due to the severity of the fighting, prisoners
are rarely taken. The bloody casualties of the enemy are high...

Casualties on 24.9.:
    94.Inf.Div.: Killed – 1 Offz, 19 Uffz and men
                  Wounded – 54 Uffz and men
    71.Inf.Div.: Killed – 1 Offz, 18 Uffz and men
                  Wounded – 2 Offz, 52 Uffz and men

Prisoners and captured materiel on 24.9.:
    398 prisoners
    2 tanks destroyed, 25 machine–guns, 2 anti–tank guns,
    11 anti–tank rifles, 14 mortars, 85 submachine–guns,
    3 aircraft shot down

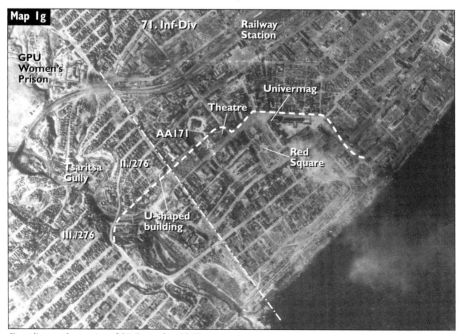

Front-line on the evening of 24 September 1942.

"Well gentlemen, a short situation conference: you know as well as I how thing's went today. My company had two light and one badly wounded. The lightly wounded men remain with the company. How many casualties did your company take, Herr Fuchs? None? Excellent! Before we discuss tomorrow, I'd like to give you all regards from our commander. I was at Bataillon. Herr Major Dr. Zimmermann has jaundice[43] and will be replaced by Major Professor Dr. Weigert tonight. Herr Weingärtner and I have known Dr. Weigert since Königsbrück. When the Division was established, Leutnant Weingärtner was even a platoon commander in 14. Kompanie of Hauptmann Weigert, as he was then. I believe it's a stroke of luck. Who knows how a strange commander would have gone down both with us and the troops."

Uli said happily: "'Papa' Weigert will take good care of us. He's a fine fellow!"

"And now, tomorrow: the two Sturmgeschütze will most probably return. The Regiment has also requested them to be brought in. In addition, we'll also be supported tomorrow by our artillery as well as 13. Kompanie[44] with its heavy field howitzers. We therefore have more firepower behind us and will not be left to fend for ourselves, as we were at noon today. When I spoke to the commander of the Sturmgeschütze, Leutnant Hempel, he said – if he comes – that he won't be here before 0900 hours. For us that means we won't be able to commence before then. When it gets light, we'll have to carefully observe the terrain and the ruins and leave them to be bombarded by our heavy weapons. When the Sturmgeschütze are here, my company will go into action alongside them. Grossmann, you'll go with two squads to the right and left of the street with the second gun, I'll go with the rest, also to the right and left of the street, with the first gun under Leutnant Hempel. You, Herr Fuchs, will follow with your company somewhere to our right and rear. According to how the enemy reacts, you'll then be aware of what to do, and be able to provide my company with covering fire from the right. Uli, follow the situation and deploy behind both companies as a reserve. You'll hear from us when we need you. And maintain communication. Jacobs, you'll employ your heavy machine-guns and heavy mortars to keep the enemy down. Any recognisable targets are to be eliminated as quickly as possible. Easier said than done, gentlemen! We must be hellishly attentive and may possibly have to fight to all sides, as we never know where 'Ivan' will be hiding in this confusion of ruins. Any questions? No! Until tomorrow then, hopefully without trouble. Grossmann, a moment please."

My three comrades left the command post.

"Grossmann, when the two Sturmgeschütze actually arrive, you'll stay with the second

---

43. *Yellow jaundice (later known as hepatitis A) took a heavy toll on German forces in Russia, but it was rampant among the 6. Armee troops at Stalingrad. The Soviets were aware that many German soldiers were falling ill to an unnamed infectious disease, and in such large numbers, that they called it the 'German sickness'.*

44. *Commander of 13. Kompanie was Hauptmann Walter Israel. Born 19 January 1894 in Bernstadt; died 29 November 1942 in Orlovka, west of Stalingrad.*

gun. The commander is a Wachtmeister. We must both remain within earshot of the commanders as much as possible and – if necessary – shout over the noise of the engine, so that we can bring obstacles to their attention. And you must make it very clear to your men to always keep away from the vehicles! They're magnets for our people because they believe they'll find cover behind them. Exactly the opposite is true: the vehicles are easily recognised by the enemy. Their light weapons are not effective against the armour plating but anyone outside the vehicle is a first-rate target. Our main assignment is to screen both guns from surprises and provide the crews with a feeling of security. If we cannot reach the commanders through sign language, then we'll fire a signal flare in the direction of the objective. Have you liaised with our left neighbour?"

"Jawohl, Herr Leutnant!"

"Is there anything else?"

"Nein, Herr Leutnant, everything's clear."

"Then I wish you a trouble-free night."

"Danke, Herr Leutnant!"

I looked at my watch: still half an hour until midnight.

"Pawellek!"

"Herr Leitnant?"

"I'm going to get some sleep now. Check whether the sentries outside are correctly posted, and if something happens, wake me at once."

"Jawohl, Herr Leutnant, Gute Nacht."

"Danke."

On the floor of my current command post – it was a corner of a corridor in the ground floor of the wing that we had stormed in the afternoon – I pushed aside the rubble, placed a map-case as a pillow and spread out a Zeltbahn[45] as a blanket. My steel helmet was kept ready at head level, my submachine-gun next to me. As I tried to think over whether I had forgotten anything, tiredness overwhelmed me.

25 September 1942

<u>Gen.Kdo. LI. A.K.</u> – 0620 hours on 25. September 1942

>   During the night, numerous heavy aerial attacks in the city sector of Stalingrad and the rear area...

---

45. <u>*Zeltbahn*</u> – *a camouflaged tent-quarter that every soldier carried to protect himself from the elements. When combined with three others, it could make a small tent. Its saddest use was to wrap the body of its owner if he was killed.*

A shaking on my shoulder jolted me wide awake. My Kompanietruppführer had awoken me. For a moment I had to think where I was, then I regained my senses. I looked at my watch; it was 0615 hours on 25 September. I stretched and yawned.

"Herr Leutnant was sleeping like a log."

"You're right, Juschko, I was dog-tired. Anything special?"

"No, Herr Leutnant, otherwise we wouldn't have allowed you to sleep so long."

"Bring some water so I can freshen up a bit."

"At once, Herr Leutnant."

I went outside and relieved myself. It was still dark. Along the entire line, only a few sounds of fighting could be heard. There was not a cloud in the sky, therefore it was going to be another hot and sunny day. I went back into the ruins. Ah, the cold water was good. There was only enough for a brief wash but the cool liquid was invigorating.

Our Spiess[46] had sent forward the field-kitchen driver with two canisters of hot coffee. Every one of us now had something hot to drink with our morning rations and we were able to fill up our canteens. It is only in situations such as this that you realise how important it was to have a responsible man as 'the mother of the company'.

My Bataillon messenger Marek appeared. "Herr Leutnant, report from Bataillon. Herr Major Weigert has taken over command. The objective – to reach the Volga – still applies. The Sturmgeschütze are coming. Forward observers from the artillery will be employed in your sector, and Herr Major wishes Herr Leitnant and your men all the best."

"Danke, Marek. Report to Herr Major that everything is in order at the front and the attack will commence as soon as the Sturmgeschütze arrive."

"Jawohl, Herr Leitnant. Ah yes – I almost forgot: Leutnant Weingärtner will be replaced by a new officer. He arrived last night with Herr Major Weigert; his name is Hauptmann Funke. I have to take him to Leutnant Weingärtner, show him around, and return with Leutnant Weingärtner to the Bataillon staff."

"Did any other officers arrive?"

"Nein, Herr Leitnant."

"Then report to the Herr Major that we're glad to have him as commander and that everything is in order here at the front. I will inform the commanders of 6. and 8. Kompanie that Hauptmann Funke has assumed command of 5. Kompanie."

Marek trotted off.

Thus a single officer had been deemed sufficient for our Bataillon. When would replacements for our non-commissioned officers and men be likely to arrive? We

---

46. <u>Spiess</u> – popular nickname for a company's senior NCO who looked after non-combat matters.

couldn't keep on attacking with such a low combat strength. We were lucky yesterday. But what would today bring? What a situation to be in. I wasn't against my friend Uli Weingärtner being detached to the staff and this Hauptmann Funke taking over. Uli was not much younger than our commander but he did at least know what we were faced with at the front.

An officer could not make up for an urgently required combatant in the forward line. Hopefully, someone higher up was conscious of this fact and would try to put things right.

Before it got light outside, I requested that the commanders of 6. and 8. Kompanien, as well as Feldwebel Grossmann, come to me. I informed them of the change of command in the Bataillon, as well as the change of command between Leutnant Weingärtner and Hauptmann Funke, with whom we were soon to be acquainted. Leutnant Fuchs was in touch with the left flank of Hauptmann Rittner's III. Bataillon, my company with the right flank of Aufklärungs-Abteilung 171.

"Gentlemen, the most important thing today is the fact that both Sturmgeschütze from yesterday will be here again to support us. In addition to that, forward observers from our artillery will be in our sector, as Herr Major Weigert communicated via my messenger. I wish you all the best. Auf Wiedersehen!"

My comrades went back to their units. Now I just had to wait until Leutnant Hempel and his two guns arrived. Waiting can put a hard strain on your nerves. Without me noticing, it was suddenly bright daylight. Together with the three men of my Kompanietrupp, I observed the terrain in front of us from our positions under cover. To get a better overview, Pawellek and I crawled up the staircase – which was completely covered in rubble – to the first floor. With our binoculars, we searched through the buildings opposite, looking for signs of the enemy. They must have been well-camouflaged, however; we still couldn't see anything. One thing was clear; it would not be as straightforward as yesterday's surprise tactics. First of all, we had almost only large houses or ruins in front of us – the individual wooden houses had been burnt down; secondly, 'Ivan' had been warned in advance yesterday and thirdly, we had to carefully work from one block of houses to the next if we didn't want to fall into an ambush. In the meantime, the hands of our watches slowly moved around to 0900 hours. Leutnant Hempel must appear soon. The sun appeared as a red sphere behind the Volga. It was going to be a hot day, in every respect. Artillery on both sides had been blasting out their 'music' for a good hour. The report was heard first, then the whooshing of the shell high over us on its trajectory and then somewhere, far in front or behind us, the detonation as it impacted. We recognised these battle noises only too well. As they did not directly affect us, we weren't unduly perturbed. The impact of the heavy mortars, with their recognisable hollow 'plop' discharge, were much worse. Or the shells from the 'Ratsch-bum' (crash-boom), because you never

An after-the-battle photo taken by a PK photographer shows the terrain and buildings along the 'Lenia'.

knew what you heard first: the discharge or the impact.

I heard the rattle of tracks from behind. Thank God! It must be Leutnant Hempel. We carefully worked our way down the staircase. As we climbed down I could see both Sturmgeschütze wheeling around the corner. They stopped behind my command post a few moments later. Leutnant Hempel and his Wachtmeister, the commander of the second vehicle, climbed out. Hempel smiled at me: "Well, we managed it, Herr Holl. I reported to my commander how well we cooperated with you yesterday and that you also urgently needed us again today. It was therefore easy for him to deploy us here because he received an order from Armeekorps[47] to help your Division."

"Then my urgent requests to my Bataillon Commander had the desired effect. And now to business! Do you have a map or can we dispense with it and just give you the facts?"

"I think the latter is better. You have to reach the bank of the Volga. Your right boundary is anchored on the Tsaritsa. The left boundary is this asphalt street. We've been scheduled to take the area lying between these. When the street splits into two or

47. *LI. Armeekorps of General der Artillerie Walther von Seydlitz-Kurzbach.*

a junction appears, my second gun will veer to the right. It's important that the men covering the guns stay with the vehicle they've been assigned to, either left or right along the street."

"That's clear. I've already thoroughly discussed that with the platoon commander, Feldwebel Grossmann."

Feldwebel Grossmann had overheard our conversation because he had left his position as soon as he noticed the Sturmgeschütze.

"Grossmann, take the Rotter and Kowalski squads with you. I'll take the Dittner squad and the Kompanietrupp. And take care to always keep your distance from the Sturmgeschütze, but at all times remain in visual contact with the commander. When can we move out, Herr Hempel?"

"We're ready now."

"Good, then we go in ten minutes. We'll go inform the men. Grossmann, you know what's happening. I'll follow the first gun, you go with the second. Our neighbours to the right and left of us will likewise follow. Oberfeldwebel Jacobs' 8. Kompanie and 5. Kompanie also know their mission. All the best, Grossmann!"

He nodded and went back to his men.

"Juschko, bring Gruppe Dittner here, but carefully, as we don't want 'Ivan' to notice."

"Jawohl, Herr Leutnant!"

Both commanders climbed back into their hatches, the engines idling gently.

Obergefreiter Dittner arrived with his squad. I gave him the order to at all times stay roughly parallel with the Sturmgeschütze on the left side of the street. I'd stick to the right-hand side of the street with my Kompanietrupp. Ten minutes was up. A short sign of agreement between Leutnant Hempel and I – and with the engine already howling – the tracks rattled into motion. Another day of fighting had begun. As Leutnant Hempel's gun turned towards the asphalt road, Gruppe Dittner rushed to the left side of the street and I followed it, utilising the available cover. I remained with my Kompanietrupp on the right side of the street. In the first block of houses, which lay behind the high-rise building, there were no signs of movement. The Sturmgeschütze cautiously drove up to it. On the left, Dittner worked his way forward with his squad. We were still probing because we didn't know where our adversaries were. With a concerted charge over 30 metres, we reached the first house, secured it, and tried to find the enemy. Nothing.

Hempel carefully moved up to the house with his vehicle. The second gun came forward and turned right into the side-street behind us. Feldwebel Grossmann and both squads followed up to the right and left. On my command, both squads leapt over to our side and searched through the forward side of the building. We paused for a few moments, until our comrades had turned left into the parallel street. I could see a squad running back to the other side of the street. Well done, boys! Then our gun set off again. Since both commanders were able to communicate over the radio, nothing was left to chance. Behind the building ran another side-street. We now stalked up to this junction while covering the blocks of houses to our right and left and securing to all sides. A discharge from the gun on the right, where Feldwebel Grossmann was, showed that the enemy had displayed his colours. Machine-gun and rifle fire was heard, continuing further to the right. Kompanie Fuchs had also now made contact with the enemy. Nothing had yet happened near us. When we reached the crossroads, however, we came under machine-gun fire. A spray of bullets struck the Sturmgeschütze. A carefully aimed riposte silenced the machine-gun. We took complete cover. We were now coming under rifle and mortar fire from the next house ruin. From the impacts on the enemy's side, I saw that Oberfeldwebel Jacobs and his men were replying. Enemy targets that were visible to me and were causing us trouble were passed on to Leutnant Hempel by shouting over the noise of the engine. I remained in the vicinity of the gun without neglecting my own cover. In the meantime, the enemy had come to life along the whole sector. Artillery from both sides had suddenly opened up. It was

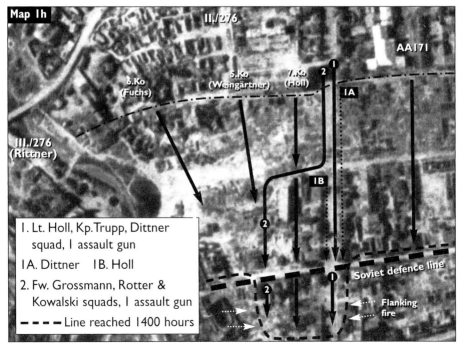

The course of the attack on the morning of 25 September 1942.

such a racket that it was hard to know from which side the blessing came, but the turmoil of battle did not make us forget our mission. The enemy nests in our attack sector were eliminated one by one. Because of the two guns, we were suddenly the spearhead of the assault. Our right and left neighbours were lagging somewhere behind us. This was perhaps why we suddenly received flanking fire out of our neighbour's area from enemy rifles and machine-guns. Our escort also helped here. One shot was generally sufficient when it was machine-gun fire. The lightly wounded scurried back to our dressing station located in my last command post. Two heavily wounded men were given emergency first-aid and then taken back at the next opportunity.

My voice was already completely hoarse from shouting to Leutnant Hempel when I recognised targets. When I tried to speak normally, all that came out was a croak.

Leutnant Hempel called out to me that both Sturmgeschütze had to drive back: their ammunition was getting low[48]. They had to regroup and refuel[49] and would return in about an hour.

I looked at my watch. It was 1410 hours. Where did the time go?

I gave the order to remain under cover and wait for the guns to return. Now I had time to file a written report to the Bataillon Commander. Nemetz would deliver it to the battalion command post. Gruppe Dittner had rounded up seven Russians hiding in the cellar of the building we'd taken. They offered no resistance to our men and surrendered immediately. They were brought to me. The men were between 20 and 40 years of age. Through Pawellek, I asked two of the younger prisoners where they came from. They answered: "We are from Polish Ukraine near Lemberg."

With Pawellek translating, I asked whether any more of their comrades were hidden in the nearby ruins. They answered in the affirmative and added that some of them no longer wanted to fight. I let the prisoners smoke. They were surprised and happy. They could see that we were men just like them. What had Soviet propaganda told them about us!?

I turned back to the two young Ukrainians and asked them whether they were prepared to return to their comrades, without weapons, and urge them to come over to us. I gave them the option of staying with us and continuing to fight.

They conferred amongst themselves and after considering briefly, they agreed. They

---

48. *Standard ammunition capacity for the Sturmgeschütz III Ausf. F and Ausf. F/8 used by Sturmgeschütz-Abteilung 244 was 44 rounds for the 7.5cm StuK 40 main gun, although some crews carried more by stacking them on the floor of the fighting compartment. In addition to these, 600 rounds of 7.92mm were carried for the MG-34 mounted in front of the loader's hatch.*

49. *Fuel capacity was 310 litres, giving an on-road range of 140km and 85km for cross-country. The refuelling point was close to the command post of Sturmgeschütz-Abteilung 244 near Gumrak, a village 13km west of the Tsaritsa battlefield in Stalingrad.*

stressed that they would return no matter what. I was keen to see whether my assessment would be proven correct. If they returned with others who were unwilling to fight, then that would make our job easier. If I was mistaken, then the loss of two prisoners would not be too great. At that moment, it seemed as if the entire line had taken a breather. The infantry fire was desultory, a shell exploding now and then. The sun beat down, oblivious to anything. In order to better get my bearings forward and to the left, I crept along the wall to the corner of the house. I looked carefully around the corner and saw how the street continued and what obstacles awaited us there. In the blink of an eye I pulled my head back, then I looked again at the spot. No, I had not been dreaming. No more than three metres away from me, I could see a human head. A man's head and nothing else! The rest of the body was missing and could not be seen anywhere.

Had we been attacking at that moment, I would perhaps have only given it a cursory glance. But now, while we were awaiting the return of the Sturmgeschütze, I had time to worry about it. The head had been cleanly separated from the body. But where was the body? I involuntarily thought about Salome, who had the head of John the Baptist brought to her on a platter.

The street fell away gently towards the Volga. We still couldn't see the river because houses and ruins obstructed the view. Nothing could be seen of the enemy either. I returned to my Kompanietrupp. Had the Ukrainians returned? The five remaining prisoners squatted in a corner of the entrance. They were being guarded by one man. Once Leutnant Hempel returned with his guns, I would have them taken to the rear. Then, both Ukrainians emerged from the field of rubble to the left of us. I couldn't believe my eyes: they were accompanied – appearing one after the other through a gap in the rubble – by one, two, nine, thirteen, twenty-two men! Christ, I hadn't reckoned on that! They were both grinning and were proud of their success. Unteroffizier Pawellek exchanged a few words with them and said to me: "They've had enough!"

"Ask them if they've got any heavy weapons."

They answered in the negative. Only rifles and a few machine-guns. The artillery had been firing from the other side of the Volga, and heavy mortars were dug in along the bank on this side of the river.

After questioning them, I learned that the strength of their unit was only about 100 to 150 men fighting on my sector. They had a lieutenant and a junior lieutenant, as well as several sergeants and corporals. The staff with the higher officers and a commissar had their command post on the banks of the Volga.

The prisoners were taciturn and suspicious. I told them through Pawellek that they had nothing to fear, that they would be treated properly and would be taken to the rear. Two men from Gruppe Dittner received the order to deliver the prisoners to the

Battalion command post and then immediately return to the squad.

I took both Ukrainians aside and had Pawellek ask them: "The Leutnant wants to know if you want to stay with us. You will not be required to fight. When we have wounded, however, you'll help them and carry them back. You'll receive the same food as us and will be treated well."

They discussed the offer for a moment and asked: "What will happen later?"

"The Leutnant will give you a form stating you've helped wounded German soldiers and that you should be treated well."

Another short conversation between them both, then Pawellek translated: "We are agreed. But we will not fire a weapon under any circumstances."

"Tell them that I don't expect that from them. Ask them their names."

The small, stocky one with the dark eyes was called Pjotr, the thin and somewhat taller one was Pavel.

I told Juschko to look after both of them.

Where were the Sturmgeschütze? An hour had passed long ago. Aha, I could hear them! My neighbour had also heard the clatter of the tracks and knew that the fighting would soon start up again.

When the vehicles arrived at our positions, the commander's head popped out of the hatch. In the meantime the second gun had driven up on the right to Feldwebel Grossmann.

"It took me a little bit longer but now we can press on. Has anything happened at the front?" asked the commander of the first gun.

I reported to him briefly what had happened in the past hour. I also reported my observations about the further course of the street as well as the statements made to me by the prisoners about the enemy's strength. Leutnant Hempel then said: "The second gun reports that everything's ready over there."

"Then let's go!"

The engine was gunned, the tracks began to turn, the heavy colossus – without which it would have been very difficult for us – started to move off. We waited until Hempel's gun turned into the street that led to the Volga. Then, just as we did earlier, we followed to the right and left of the gun in loose formation. We were greeted by rifle fire. The enemy now had something to aim at. Hempel stopped his vehicle because he had noticed we couldn't keep up. My men on both sides of the street returned fire at recognisable targets. Even the heavy mortars and a heavy machine-gun from 8. Kompanie joined in. We could not make any progress because the enemy was firing from all directions. We were being shot at from the upper storeys, then came under fire from the right, then again from the left in front of us. The apparent peace and quiet that reigned a few moments earlier had all at once become the complete opposite.

The enemy had not let this opportunity slip. Suddenly, soldiers came panting up from behind. A Hauptmann squatted near me and said breathlessly: "Funke, I'm in charge of 5. Kompanie and have been ordered by Bataillon to support you!"

I could tell from his demeanour that he had no combat experience[50], or as good as none. I answered: "Holl, commander of the seventh."

"I know. Why aren't we advancing? We should be up with the Sturmgeschütz and carrying on the attack!"

What was I now to say to this man in such a situation, in the presence of our men, some of whom were nearby?

This man was a Hauptmann and I was a Leutnant.

"Herr Hauptmann, you must keep your distance from the gun. If you don't do that, you'll be a goner!"

This idiot wasn't going to take advice from me: he ordered the squad from his 5. Kompanie to follow him, and in the next instant, a bunch of 8 to 10 men were clustered behind the Sturmgeschütz. The enemy immediately concentrated his fire on this target. We returned heavier fire from our side in an attempt to eliminate the enemy that we recognised. We were not entirely successful. A soldier was already lying motionless on the ground. Another cried out; holding his shoulder, he ran back to us. Then the Hauptmann caught it: he held his right thigh and was bent double in pain. Two soldiers grasped him and the entire squad came back to us as quickly as possible. This nightmare had only lasted a few minutes. I was furious. This 'hero', who until this moment had not experienced a single moment in the front-line of the entire war, had been trying to prove his courage. The result: one killed, one severely wounded, two medium wounded, and the man himself had been shot through the thigh. This stupid Heini would have been better off staying at home or wherever he'd been up to now.

He only got a short breather from me, then I laid into him: "See what you've done now! But you didn't want to take advice from a simple Leutnant!"

He was crestfallen and in a subdued voice said: "You're right, I should've listened to you."

I turned away. The Hauptmann, supported on both sides by helpers, limped away to the rear. His guest appearance with the fighting troops had not even lasted a day. In any case, I would accurately report this incident to the commander. We could dispense with replacement commanders such as this in battle. No battle experience in this street-fighting was almost a death sentence.

---

50. *Funke actually had been in combat before. He was lightly wounded in Stalingrad-South on 17 September 1942 while commanding 12./IR276, the heavy weapons company of Hauptmann Rittner's III. Bataillon.*

```
              Noch Generalkommando XIV.Pz.Korps

Erkrankt:  22.9.42  Oblt.d.R.  Glaeser,      3./Na.Abt.66    ( -- )
                                             Zugfhr.

                    Generalkommando LI.A.K.

Gefallen:  25.9.42  Lt.d...    Grünewald,    1./I.R.191      ( 71.I.D.)
                                             Fhr.

           26.9.42  Lt.       Heuser,        11./A.R.171     ( 71.I.D.)
                                             B.Offz.

           27.9.42  Lt.d.R.   Hirn,          7./Jg.Rgt.54    (100.Jg.D.)
                                             Zugfhr.

           27.9.42  Lt.d...   Eggermann,     13./Jg.Rgt.54   (100.Jg.D.)
                                             Fhr.

           27.9.42  Lt.d.R.   Kürz,          1./Jg.Rgt.227   (100.Jg.D.)
                                             Zugfhr.

           27.9.42  Oblt.d... Jimel,         II./Jg.Rgt.227  (100.Jg.D.)
                                             Adj.

           27.9.42  Lt.d.R.   Henné,         13./Jg.Rgt.227  (100.Jg.D.)
                                             Zugfhr.

           27.9.42  Lt.       Franjik,       kr.I.R.369      (100.Jg.D.)
                                             Fhr.

           27.9.42  Oblt.     Viertel,       2./Pz.Pi.Btl.46 (16.Pz.D. )
                                             Chef

Verwundet: 25.9.42  Oblt.d... Krüger,        1./A.R.171      ( 71.I.D.)
                                             B.Offz.

       x)  26.9.42  Obstlt.   Roske,         I.R.194         ( 71.I.D.)
                                             Kdr.

           25.9.42  Hptm.     Funke,         5./I.R.276      ( 94.I.D.)
                                             Fhr.

           25.9.42  Oblt.d... Scheffler,     I./I.R.267      ( 94.I.D.)
                                             Adj.

       x)  25.9.42  Oblt.d.R. Kutzner,       III./I.R.267    ( 94.I.D.)
                                             Fhr.

           27.9.42  Oblt.d... Jahn,          5./I.R.267      ( 94.I.D.)
                                             Fhr.

           27.9.42  Oblt.d.R. Fock,          2./I.R.267      ( 94.I.D.)
                                             Fhr.

           25.9.42  Lt.d.R.   Klimm,         III./A.R.295    (295.I.D.)
                                             Fhr.AVT.

           25.9.42  Lt.d.R.   Schreck,       A.R.295         (295.I.D.)
                                             Verpfl.Offz.

           25.9.42  Lt.d...   Gessert,       7./I.R.516      (295.I.D.)
                                             Fhr.

           25.9.42  Oblt.     Geissler,      6./I.R.517      (295.I.D.)
                                             Chef

           25.9.42  Lt.d.R.   Körner,        7./I.R.517      (295.I.D.)
                                             Fhr.

       x)  26.9.42  Lt.d.R.   Bayer,         3./A.R.295      (295.I.D.)
                                             B.Offz.
```

A 6.Armee casualty list showing the names of some of the officers killed and wounded on 25, 26 and 27 September 1942. Thirteenth from the top is Hauptmann Funke, Führer 5./Infanterie-Regiment 276. The 'x)' next to some names indicates that that officer stayed with the troops.

Meanwhile my company had made further headway. The guns had also pushed forward. If we could take the next block, we would be able to see the Volga. With satisfaction, I saw that our left neighbour had almost moved up to our level. My view to the right, where Feldwebel Grossmann was located, was blocked by houses and rubble. There was also violent fighting there.

I reached the Sturmgeschütz again. It fired – as on the previous day – only at recognised targets, which were effectively dealt with by direct hits from the shells. We had to finish off what remained.

The next intersection was reached. Hempel fired a shot into the left-hand side-street when he recognised enemy movement there. His comrade in the second gun moved up on the right of us. My men there reached the houses on the other side after a sprint over the street. Both guns were now in the thick of the action. It required nerves to remain steady and not lose sight of the bigger picture. We offered up thanks to our comrades who were hammering away with everything they had from both barrels. The men recognised the current situation and exploited it. They knew that 'Ivan' was now nervous. He was pulling back – slowly, while offering fierce resistance. Even the enemy artillery, whose shells were exploding at intervals in the battle sector,

The course of the attack on the afternoon of 25 September 1942.

could not delay the inevitable. As they had no precise clues about our location, most impacts were landing too long or too short. After we advanced in this way metre by metre and reached the centre of the last large block of houses, Leutnant Hempel signalled to me that he had no more ammunition and had to return for today. He was not able to say if he would be employed here again tomorrow. I raised my hand over my head as a sign of thanks. Our valiant allies were soon out of sight.

We couldn't let up now and had to try to reach the next corner of the block before the Russians noticed the changed situation. As we worked forward another few metres covered by our heavy weapons, a messenger rushed over from our right flank. Lying prone, he was nonetheless within earshot and called out to us: "Herr Leutnant! Feldwebel Grossmann[51] is dead, Unteroffizier Rotter has taken over command."

For a few seconds I was stunned. The news hit me like a thunderbolt. But I did not have time to think about it. We had an assignment to carry out, if possible without stopping a bullet ourselves.

With gritted teeth I raced to the next corner. Running to meet me, crying, were two of the young and inadequately trained Sudeten Germans. Horror was etched all over their faces: "The Russians are coming! The Russians are coming!"

One received a kick in the backside, the other a box around the ears. I then turned them around, shouting: "You can count yourselves lucky that you're going back to the front!"

Obergefreiter Dittner had returned to the front with his upper arm bandaged; he'd just had a near miss.

"Dittner, look after both of them. They've lost it."

Dittner nodded and led them off.

Had I not had my Upper Silesians, then I would have been much worse off. They were the backbone of the unit, able to give as good as they got. But they also knew that no-one should be left in the lurch. I'd drummed it into them again and again over the past years. It had been repeatedly proven: they and their comrades from Middle and Lower Silesia were still the framework of the Regiment. The new replacements were mainly men from other regions of our Fatherland, and only several of the 'old men' came back.

Thank God! I had reached the crossroads. We'd made good progress on almost the entire sector. Twilight was setting in. Soon after, everything fell silent. The quiet was only broken now and then by single rifle shots and the occasional burst of machine-

---

51. *Oberfeldwebel Karl Grossmann. Born 1 January 1914 in Klein Wangelin, Landkreis Parchim, Mecklenburg; died 25 September 1942 in Stalingrad. In 1939, Klein Wangelin had only 91 inhabitants, and Karl Grossmann was the fourth soldier from the village to die during the war.*

gun fire. The watching and listening had begun again. Countless pairs of eyes on both sides peered to the front, checking to the right and left. There could be a deadly surprise from around every corner. Having made sure the necessary security measures had been carried out, I went over to the right flank. Unteroffizier Pawellek came with me. I wanted to bid farewell to my platoon commander, the irreproachable Feldwebel Grossmann. Unteroffizier Rotter made the report with a grave face.

"Where's Grossmann?"

"To the rear here, about 100 metres back."

We silently followed Rotter. My platoon commander was lying in a recess in a wall. The burst of fire from a Russian submachine-gun had killed him instantly.

"How'd it happen?"

"The men with him reported that suddenly, out of a manhole – you can still see the cover – he was shot from behind. Feldwebel Grossmann was killed instantly, without uttering a sound."

We went to the manhole and opened the cover. There was nothing to be seen down there. Iron rungs made it possible to climb down into the sewer.

"Our men immediately fired at the opening, but the raised lid was dropped down in a flash. Our men tossed hand-grenades in but without effect. The entire thing was like a ghostly manifestation."

"Juschko, take Feldwebel Grossmann's personal effects with you and make sure Hauptfeldwebel Michel takes them back with his field-kitchen. Unteroffizier Paul will look after the other wounded and dead."

My Kompanietruppführer was visibly affected by the death of our comrade. Instead of answering, he simply nodded. He searched Grossmann's pack, placed the few meagre possessions into a bread-bag and then covered the lifeless body with a tarpaulin. We gave a final salute as a mark of respect. With clenched teeth and stony faces, we stood still for a moment, before the present – with its relentless call to duty – once again intruded.

"Rotter, you'll now command the Grossmann platoon until further notice."

"Jawohl, Herr Leutnant!"

"How high are your casualties?"

"As far as I have seen, we've three dead and five wounded, two of those seriously. Feldwebel Grossmann is amongst the dead."

Damn! That was almost an entire squad! We had registered four casualties on my side; that made twelve altogether. If we wanted to reach the banks of the Volga tomorrow, Leutnant Weingärtner's 5. Kompanie would also need to be deployed.

"Listen, Rotter, when your men have been supplied from the field-kitchen and things are quiet, come and review the situation with me. Bring Leutnant Fuchs from 6. Kompanie with you. Your messenger knows where we are. Let's say an hour after the field-kitchen arrives here."

"Jawohl, Herr Leutnant, understood!"

We parted and I went to my command post, exercising caution on all sides. It was just a short distance to the rear of the junction. We reached it as darkness was falling. It was an area of flat ground cleared out of bomb-wrecked rubble and ruins. Still, it protected us from shrapnel and was not visible from the enemy's side.

Behind a camouflaged tarpaulin, by the light of a Hindenburg lamp, I made out my daily report to Bataillon. When the Spiess arrived, he could take it to Bataillon.

I ran over the street and was soon at Gruppe Dittner.

"Well, Dittner, have you calmed the two boys?"

"Jawohl, Herr Leitnant! They've been straightened out, they just have no experience. They're not cowards. It was just a bit too much for them."

"You're right, but we must watch out they don't crack up again. How strong is your squad now?"

"Including myself, we're eight strong."

"5. Kompanie will come forward tomorrow. I've reported to Bataillon that we won't be able to complete our mission without reinforcements. We're too weak after the casualties we suffered today. Have you managed to establish a connection with our left neighbour?"

"Jawohl, Herr Leutnant, we're in touch."

Nemetz appeared and told Obergefreiter Dittner that the field-kitchen had arrived and we were receiving provisions. Dittner allocated two men, one of the 'old guards' and one from the last replacements. I didn't need to tell the old hands to be on their guard because, like me, they'd learned this much over the past months. Our youngsters would also quickly learn the same thing.

When I arrived back at my command post – how quickly I crossed that short stretch! – I came across Marek, our messenger from Bataillon.

"Herr Leitnant, Herr Major wants to know what the situation is at the front."

I gave him my written report. "It's all here, Marek. Tell Herr Major that I urgently need the units of 5. Kompanie for tomorrow. Otherwise, we're in no condition to attack. And I would like Herr Major to point out to Regiment that we require strong support from our heavy weapons because the Sturmgeschütze won't be coming tomorrow. The commander, Leutnant Hempel, told me as much."

Leutnant Weingärtner again took over 5. Kompanie, as I suspected. Marek told me that he would arrive shortly.

I dismissed him; a short while later, he disappeared into the darkness. The field-kitchen had driven up and stood some 100 metres to the rear in the protection of a house. Like the previous evening, its bustling activity took place in almost total silence. There was soft talking, and now and again the rattling of mess-tins could be heard. Men came up quietly, others went away. Everyone made an effort not to stay any longer than was necessary.

When I saw Hauptfeldwebel Michel, he saluted and made a report. I nodded. "Michel, Pawellek is shortly bringing in Feldwebel Grossmann, who was killed this afternoon. Take him with you to the rear. Pick up his personal effects. You'll be given the effects of the others killed so that we can send them on to relatives. – Anything else to report?"

"Jawohl, Herr Leutnant! We received mail today, but it'll be better to hand it out when this racket is past."

"That's alright. What've you cooked today?"

"Pea soup."

"Then let's have some!"

While eating this tasty soup, it occurred to me that I'd had nothing to eat throughout the whole day, not even a bite. At one point, my Kompanietruppführer had handed me his field-flask and I'd gulped down a few mouthfuls of luke-warm coffee.

Now, under the cover of darkness, every one of us was able to fill up, even the sentries made it after they were relieved.

It was no different with the enemy, as was evident by the 'Tretminen'[52] which we found during the attack. Men's vital needs could be postponed for some time but not switched off indefinitely. While spooning up the rest of the soup, my friend Uli Weingärtner arrived. I had missed his usual roguish smile. He had already heard about the day's casualties. He also took the death of Grossmann very hard. Not so hard was his short guest appearance at the Battalion staff.

'Papa' Weigert regretted Hauptmann Funke's quick wounding. The anger I felt around midday towards the higher ranks had almost passed. Things couldn't be changed now.

I told Uli how it had occurred and that I'd already recorded it in my report to the commander. "Uli, because of today's casualties, your company must be employed alongside us tomorrow. Later, in about half an hour, Leutnant Fuchs and Unteroffizier Rotter, who has taken over Grossmann's platoon, will arrive for a situation conference. Oberfeldwebel Jacobs will also be here. We must consider how we're going to reach the

---

52. _Tretminen_ – _literally means 'anti-personnel mines' or 'mine canisters', but in this case, it is the German soldiers' nickname for Soviet mess-tins that bore a strong resemblance to the German S-Mine._

Volga tomorrow. I reckon this'll be the hardest nut we've ever had to crack.

"It was clear to me that we'd be employed with you tomorrow when I heard of your casualties. Thanks to your progress, Hauptmann Rittner's III. Bataillon has also managed to push the enemy back to the Volga. The commander already knew at midday that the Sturmgeschütze would not be at our disposal tomorrow. As the main effort is in our sector – together with our left neighbour Aufklärungs-Abteilung 171[53] – the Division has promised us heavy weapons. Your progress has earned the Regiment's recognition."

"Well, hopefully, we'll also have the necessary good luck tomorrow."

Our Hauptfeldwebel arrived and reported that he was leaving with the field-kitchen. We watched the vehicle as it disappeared into the darkness, taking our good comrade – who merited our appreciation – with it.

At my command post, my comrades from 6. and 8. Kompanien were already waiting for me. A brief handshake, then our thoughts were immediately focused on the forthcoming mission.

I asked the commander of 6. Kompanie: "Herr Fuchs, how many casualties have you had, and how strong is your unit?"

"My company had two killed, four wounded. I'll have a total of 44 men fit for action for tomorrow."

"Herr Jacobs, how's the situation with your company?"

"We were fortunate: only two lightly wounded. Battle strength totals 38 men."

"And you, Uli?"

"No casualties, battle strength 48 men all told."

"Then you have four squads at your disposal?"

"No, five, I've made five squads out of four."

"That's good. Send two squads to me and a squad to Herr Fuchs. With the two remaining squads, you'll follow up approximately in the centre of the battle sector so that you can be deployed for all eventualities, wherever it hots up. And what tactics should we use tomorrow? What are your thoughts, gentlemen?"

After some consideration, Leutnant Fuchs said: "As we can no longer count on the two Sturmgeschütze, we must carry it out tomorrow as we've already learned: attack, keep the enemy down with heavy machine-gun and mortar fire, and take the area in front. Before the enemy realises that we're attacking, we should've already taken the

---

53. *The following extract for 25 September 1942 is from a report written after the war by a member of Aufklärungs-Abteilung 171: "The street fighting also continued to rage bitterly on 25.9. along the 'Lenia'. The street gently climbed to a rise and then fell away again. In position behind this crest were Russian guns crewed by female gunners, and they caused us a great deal of trouble. They were eliminated by the Sturmgeschütze…"*

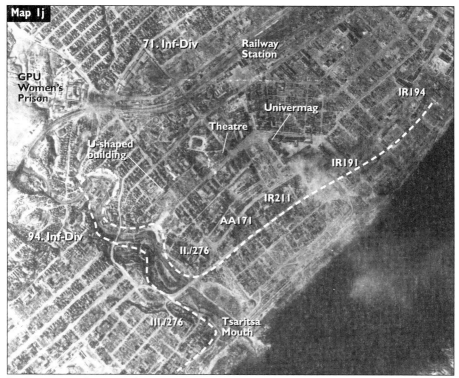

Final positions on the evening of 25 September 1942.

<u>Gen.Kdo. LI. A.K.</u> — 1725 hours on 25. September 1942

LI. A.K. has continued the attack against the enemy bridgehead around the mouth of the Tsaritsa by making local gains of ground...
    <u>In particular</u>:
    In front of 94.Inf.Div., enemy forces still hold the bank of the Volga with railway sheds and jetties, both the housing districts hard south—west of the Tsaritsa mouth and both northern loops on the south bank, defending themselves with great toughness.
    71.Inf.Div. set off again at 0730 hours to clean out the city sectors lying north of the Tsaritsa and slowly gained ground in hard fighting. The Party buildings[54] were taken...

---

54. *Party buildings* — *the German name for what they supposed were the most important buildings on Stalingrad's main square. In fact, the main so-called 'Party building' was actually the Univermag Department Store.*

The Univermag Department Store, one of the buildings referred to in German reports as 'the Party buildings'. This same building also contained the Narkomtorg CCCP (People's Commissariat for Foreign and Domestic Trade).

piece of ground. In addition, we'll be receiving artillery support. Their fire must be directed at the nearest enemy targets."

After we had argued all the pros and cons, we decided to stick with the suggestion of comrade Fuchs. We set the time for the beginning of the attack for 0745 hours and synchronised our watches.

"Herr Jacobs, bring your heavy machine-guns into position so that they can effectively support the attack, as well as the mortars. I'll see the Bataillon Commander with a personal report."

After my comrades left, I turned to Pawellek: "Juschko, you've followed everything. I'm going to the Battalion command post now with Nemetz. Should anything happen here, send Willmann to me so that I can return immediately. I think I'll be back in an hour. Is everything clear?"

"Understood, Herr Leitnant!"

I made my way to the Battalion command post without incident. Our commander was satisfied with the day's successes since progress had again been made. He was worried by our low battle strength and the lack of replacements. He agreed with our plan of action for the coming day. He left it up to our experience and promised that we would receive all the support he could organise for us. As junior commanders, we had great appreciation for our commander. Given our concern for him, we hoped he would stay to the rear until we reached our assigned objective – the Volga. In this situation, he could do more for us from his command post than if he ran unnecessary risks in this street-fighting.

I was informed about the general situation in the greater scheme of things and then departed.

When I returned to my company command post, my Kompanietruppführer reported that there were no significant occurrences.

It was fast approaching midnight.

I crouched down in the corner of the half-collapsed room and tried to get some rest. There was no chance of sound sleep in these situations: it was more like sleeping with one eye open. You always had to be alert if you wanted to avoid any unpleasant surprises.

The nights had already become cooler. Since there was no possibility of warming up, limbs grew stiff, uniforms were cold and damp. For the enemy, lying somewhere in the vicinity opposite us, things would not be much better. Nights like this seemed to drag on forever. We longed for daylight with its warming rays of sun. We'd had good luck so far with the weather.

Gen.Kdo. LI. A.K. – 2220 hours on 25. September 1942

LI. A.K. continued the destruction of enemy forces in the bridgehead both sides of the mouth of the Tsaritsa – with success.
In particular:
Around 1830 hours, Inf.Rgt.267 of 94.Inf.Div. took by storm both the remaining housing districts hard south–west of the Tsaritsa mouth that were being obstinately defended by the enemy. Violent enemy counterthrusts – still continuing at the present time – were repulsed. The 600 metre long docks are still occupied by strong enemy forces supported from the east bank of the Volga. In both loops of the Tsaritsa, the enemy still stubbornly holds out in gullies and houses.
71.Inf.Div. continued its attack at 0730 hours to clean out the city sector north of the Tsaritsa. With the same tenacity as on the previous day, individual mounds of rubble had to be fought for. In several particularly hard fought–for cellar positions, only the use of flamethrowers and explosive charges led to the abandonment of resistance. On 25.9., the Division took about 600 prisoners, including 8 Komsomols.

Front–line on 25.9.:
> 94.Inf.Div.: Row of houses on the high edge of the Volga from south–east of the Theatre to south–west of Tsaritsa mouth – south bank of Tsaritsa up to the loop in Tsaritsa south–east of the railway
> 71.Inf.Div.: South–east Tsaritsa bridge – park north–east of there – south corner of sparse housing district south–east of Party building area – waterworks on the Volga

Casualties on 25.9.:
> 94.Inf.Div.: Killed – 9 men
> (w/o IR276) Wounded – 2 Offz[55], 3 Uffz and men
> 71.Inf.Div.: Killed – 10 Uffz and men
> Wounded – 1 Offz[56], 42 Uffz and men

Prisoners and captured materiel on 25.9.:
> 741 prisoners, 17 guns, of those five 12.2cm, 13 AA guns, 89 machine–guns, 19 anti–tank guns, 56 mortars, 96 anti–tank rifles, 159 submachine–guns, 1 gunboat sunk by a direct hit, 1 gunboat damaged.

---

55. *Hauptmann d.R. Gustav Kutzner, Kdr. III./Infanterie-Regiment 267 and Oberleutnant d.R. Scheffler, Abteilung Adjutant I./Infanterie-Regiment 267.*
56. *Oberleutnant d.R. Krüger, Batterie Offizier 1./Artillerie-Regiment 171.*

26 September 1942

Towards 0400 hours, hot coffee was brought to us at the front. Our Spiess knew exactly what we needed. The hot coffee raised our spirits, stilled our hunger pangs and made the world seem a little rosier. We still had almost two hours ahead of us before the attack began. Several thoughts ran through my mind. They would preoccupy me for the next few hours. The utmost was required of our men and ourselves. The objective simply had to be reached today because we couldn't stand the strain much longer. We had to do everything physically possible.

Dawn began to break. I saw the first bright rays on the eastern horizon on the other side of the Volga. Our immediate surroundings slowly became more recognisable. I now had Gruppe Dittner in sight.

"Willmann, go to Unteroffizier Rotter and tell him once again that Gruppe Dittner will attack right at 0745 hours and his squad will commence no later. Immediately cross into the next block on the other side of the street."

Willmann repeated the order and moved off. He was back several minutes later and reported: "Order carried out, everything is clear!"

I gave Dittner a sign to attack. With a leap, and being careful to avoid every possible noise and with no shouts of command, Gruppe Dittner was over the street. We slowly

A street branching off the 'Lenia' shows the complete destruction wreaked by artillery and bombs.

followed the squad and kept watch on all sides for any sign of the enemy. Rotter and his men also carried out their move unnoticed.

Suddenly, all hell broke loose: from the left as well as from the front, there were bursts of heavy machine-gun fire, frantic rifle fire and mortar detonations. The attack came to a standstill.

Our squads took complete cover. I had not crossed over the street with my Kompanietrupp. We were on the other side and found cover in the ruins of a building.

The heavy machine-guns of 8. Kompanie had picked out enemy targets and brought them under fire. The heavy mortars of Oberfeldwebel Jacobs were also in action. In the meantime, our left and right neighbours had also made contact with the enemy. From the sounds of fighting, I saw that progress was better on the right wing. On the other hand, there appeared to be no progress to be made on the left. Exploiting the heavy machine-gun fire, I worked my way back with the Kompanietrupp and in a rearward detour via the building taken yesterday, came across Gruppe Rotter. With a co-ordinated charge, the four of us crossed the street utilising our own cover-fire.

To the right of us, towards the slope down to the Tsaritsa Gully, 5. Kompanie was moving forward. About 50 metres away to the left was a transformer building standing between Gruppe Rotter and 5. Kompanie. It was a massive three-storey construction. The enemy that had been located there had been overpowered. There would be a great view from there.

"Rotter, give us cover-fire, we've got to get inside that transformer!"

Rotter understood my bellowing.

"Listen up, men. When I say 'let's go', we'll run hell for leather to that building there!"

We readied ourselves.

"Let's go!"

We got there out of breath and immediately disappeared into the building: the sound of lively fighting could be heard from outside. Grenades exploded nearby.

After a short breather, we looked around. The large transformers stood on the ground floor. There was no cellar. We carefully climbed the staircase to the first floor. Various pieces of equipment were also installed here.

From up here, we could look to the front – to the Volga – and to the left, precisely along the last side-street that ran parallel to the Volga. From a height of about five metres, we had a view over the enemy's terrain. Diagonally to the left of us was a large, vacant square. It was about 200 square metres in size. Approximately in the middle of the last third of the square, towards the Volga, stood a monument. Behind that, on the banks of the river, were several one-storey masonry houses. I could not make out what was on the other side of those houses. From this position, however, I could see the river the Russians call 'the

Map 1k

Attack on the morning of 26 September 1942.

mother of the people', right across to the bank on the far side.

Violent Russian defensive fire came across to us from the left from roughly the same level at which we now found ourselves. Defensive fire was also coming from the riverside embankment, directed at 6. Kompanie and my right flank.

Cautiously, so that we remained undetected, we observed all that we could survey through our binoculars.

Pawellek called over to me: "Herr Leitnant, there are Russians to the left of us, about 150 to 200 metres away, on the first floor!"

I looked through my binoculars in the direction indicated: he was right. Through a large hole in the wall, I could see Russian soldiers carrying ammunition boxes upstairs. They were in my field of vision for just a few seconds. Apparently there was a staircase located there and they were going up and coming down again.

Presumably there was a group of soldiers offering resistance from there and giving our left flank a great deal of trouble.

"Juschko, a rifle!"

I cautiously leant forward to get a clear field of fire from my covered position. It was time to do my duty. And now to keep cool. I took careful aim, my right finger applied pressure to the trigger, a target appeared, I squeezed the trigger, a crack, bulls-eye! Reload, continue observation.

In the meantime, my men from Kompanietrupp kept their eyes on the square. After the initial surprise, it would now be more difficult for me. From time to time, I caught sight of the enemy for fractions of a second through the hole in the wall before they disappeared.

As I only fired a single shot each time, the enemy could only guess where I was holed up. I was successful on three or four occasions. Suddenly, five or six enemy soldiers appeared from upstairs. Another shot and one hit. Then no more movement could be detected.

Where had all these men come from all of a sudden?

Leutnant Weise[57], a platoon commander of 13. Kompanie, suddenly showed up to act as a forward observer for our artillery. The Bataillon Commander had ordered him to report to me.

We had the best observation possibilities from this transformer building. It stood on its own but was on the same axis as the facades of the houses bordering the square to the west.

I agreed with Weise's opinion that he would be able to direct the fire of his guns from here. Soon, the first impacts from shells landing behind the river embankment showed that the forward observer had given them exact co-ordinates at which to shoot. The shelling was directed over the radio set. The results could not be seen because they were in the dead-angle behind the river embankment. The enemy unleashed aimed machine-gun and mortar fire from this direction when he recognised a target on our side. His mortar fire was still proving effective. He was somewhere behind the embankment and was laying down a barrage of shells on our forward line. The enemy artillery on the other side of the Volga was not entirely in the picture as their impacts were heard far behind us. They were apparently shooting at our heavy weapon emplacements.

Despite all the fire conjured from our side, we had not advanced a metre forward in the last hour.

The sun was now almost in the south-west; its rays glinted in the currents of the Volga. They were dazzling when observed with binoculars.

---

57. *Leutnant d.R. Alfred Weise, platoon commander 13./Infanterie-Regiment 276. Born 23 June 1902 in Dresden; missing in action 21 January 1943 in Stalingrad*

Map II

III./276

II./276   AA171

Transformer

Square

Embankment

Tsaritsa Mouth

German bombardment shown thus

Area below the river embankment targeted by German artillery, 26 September 1942.

Our commander had also sent a forward observer from the Heeresartillerie[58] to me and a short time later he radioed his battery to join the 'concert'. In breaks between the fire we observed attentively. Suddenly, I saw a Russian soldier, apparently a messenger, run over the open expanse from the other side of the large square. He wore an unbuttoned green overcoat that was flapping behind him.

I grasped my rifle. From up here, I could work out his track from my side-on perspective. The distance amounted to about 200 to 250 metres. He had crossed almost half of the square. He seemed to be heading for the place where I had been fighting his comrades with partial success a little while ago (had it been hours already?). My hand remained steady as I took aim and crooked my index finger. It had to be a clean head or heart shot: the force of the impact lifted him off his feet and threw him to the ground. "That was for Grossmann!" I said to myself, yet I was glad that this anonymous enemy soldier had not suffered.

Unless there was a miracle, then we were likely to remain stalled here despite all efforts. The enemy was putting up stiff resistance. We, the attackers, had to advance. The enemy could not afford to abandon his positions. It would be crazy to attempt

---

58. Heeresartillerie – Army-level artillery

to get across this gigantic, empty square during daylight. However, that meant it could only be done in darkness. The reflection of the setting sun in the west bathed everything in a rosy glow. Pawellek pointed to the left: "Herr Leitnant, what's our left neighbour doing?"

I looked to the left. Our neighbours from Aufklärungs-Abteilung 171[59] had fought their way forward and ignited the first smoke candle. Several of these candles suddenly emitted a thick, smoggy smoke, the entire cloud moving slowly – carried by a breeze – into my sector and obscuring the enemy's view. Now we were in business!

"After me!"

We rushed down the stairs disregarding any precautionary measures.

"Juschko, run to Dittner! He must immediately prepare to move. I'll go with Gruppe Rotter!"

It was not a moment too soon. We were enveloped in a thick fog for which we had to thank our comrades to the left of us. We had to exploit it.

I yelled to the right and left: "Men, let's go, marsch, marsch!"

We stormed forward as fast as we could. We fired our rifles and submachine-guns on the run. Our sudden forward charge dragged some of our left neighbours with us. Also from the right, where Leutnant Fuchs was located, sounds of movement could be heard. We couldn't see a thing!

Under cover of this wall of fog, which was gradually thinning but was fortunately being driven in the desired direction, towards the Volga, we reached the edge of the embankment. We were literally running into the unknown.

The Russians were rattled. Perhaps they thought it was gas. After some hand-to-hand fighting around the small house ruins, in which we used hand-grenades, we were the masters of the upper edge of the embankment.

How glad I was that our left neighbour had used those smoke candles. We were happy enough to be able to lug our weapons with the appropriate ammunition; we never even thought of smoke candles. The man who came up with this idea should be awarded a medal!

Now we had the upper hand. Our adversary was sitting somewhere below us between the embankment and the shore. We now had to establish ourselves here so that any surprise attack was impossible.

In the meantime, it had become completely dark. How very mistaken we were:

---

59. *The following extract for 26 September 1942 is from the post-war Aufklärungs-Abteilung 171 report:*
   "At the end of Leninskaya, 1. Schwadron reached the last row of houses in front of a square with garden lay-outs. On the square was a monument to a pilot, whose upper part had already been seen during the earlier fighting on the Leninskaya…"

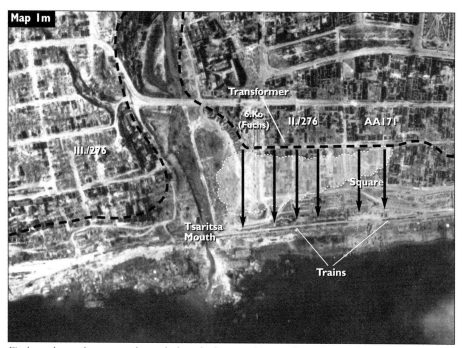

Final assault over the square and towards the embankment under cover of a smokescreen, 26 September 1942.

between us and the river bank ran a stretch of land approximately ten metres deep, which I estimated to be between 80 and 100 metres wide. Running directly alongside the embankment was a railway track. I realised this as I could see wagons below us loaded with guns, tanks and other war material. I could not see how long this train was. I supposed that this stretch of rail had been put out of action by our Luftwaffe.

<u>Gen.Kdo. LI. A.K.</u> — 1800 hours on 26. September 1942

On 26.9., LI. A.K. cleared the enemy from his bridgehead both sides of the Tsaritsa mouth with the exception of the 600-metre long enemy-occupied quay wall south of the Tsaritsa mouth and several enemy nests north of the mouth...

<u>In particular</u>:

94.Inf.Div. cleaned out the south bank of the Tsaritsa, including both loops. Enemy continues to hold the quay wall.

71.Inf.Div. reached the Volga shore but several enemy nests are still holding out.

<u>Aim for 27.9.</u>: Continue clearing out both sides of the Tsaritsa mouth.

<u>Gen.Kdo. LI. A.K.</u> – 2300 hours on 26. September 1942

LI. A.K. finally succeeded in taking the city sectors both sides of the Tsaritsa mouth firmly into its hands after hard combat, except for enemy remnants in the docks. This success was obtained by operations of 71. and 94.Inf.Div. despite both already suffering heavy casualties...

<u>In particular</u>:

After a systematic preparation, an assault with stormtroops of 29.Inf.Div. and 94.Inf.Div. in the afternoon of 26.9. against the enemy behind the quay approached to within 20 metres; every further approach was rendered impossible by heavy enemy fire after the loss of a flamethrower.

71.Inf.Div. continued the attack on 26.9. to gain the Volga shore. At midday, the last resistance nest in the city centre was destroyed and the Reichs war flag was hoisted on the Party buildings and the Theatre.

71.Inf.Div. will now take over security along the Volga.

94.Inf.Div. will be pulled out and sent north.

<u>Front–line on 26.9.</u>:

94.Inf.Div.: Volga shore to 600 metres south–west of Tsaritsa mouth – north–west edge of railway

71.Inf.Div.: North–west edge of railway to 600 metres north–east of Tsaritsa mouth – Volga shore to divisional boundary

<u>Casualties on 26.9.</u>:

94.Inf.Div.: Killed – 3 Uffz and men
Wounded – 23 Uffz and men

71.Inf.Div.: Killed – 1 Offz[60], 10 Uffz and men
Wounded – 35 Uffz and men

<u>Prisoners and captured materiel on 26.9.</u>:

789 prisoners, 8 tanks destroyed, 2 guns, 38 machine–guns, 4 anti–tank guns, 27 mortars, 30 anti–tank rifles, 38 submachine–guns, 1236 rifles, 1 aircraft shot down

---

60. *Leutnant d.R. Horst Heuser, Batterie Offizier 11./Artillerie-Regiment 171. Born 18 August 1921 in Wilhelmsthal; died 26 September 1942 in Stalingrad.*

Ic of 6. Armee HQ: — 2100 hours on 26. September 1942

<u>Disposition of enemy forces</u>:
<u>Tsaritsa mouth</u>: 92nd Rifle Brigade, 244th Rifle Division
<u>North of Tsaritsa mouth</u>: 10 NKVD Division (remnants of 270 and 272 Regiments), 42nd Rifle Brigade and 13th Guards Rifle Division, which received 550 replacements on 21.9. from Rifle Regiment 680 of 196th Rifle Division.

Final positions on the evening of 26 September 1942.

My company command post was now located in a massive house lying directly in the front-line. Early tomorrow morning we'd have to carefully clean out the enemy in the area ahead of us as quickly as possible. The forward observers returned to their units. Our comrades to the right and left of us also settled in on the upper edge of the embankment.

My friend Jochen appeared. Marek was with him.

"Guten Abend, Bert."

"Guten Abend, Jochen. Good job you've come. It'll save me from having to write up a report for the commander. Just jot down any necessary notes."

"With pleasure, my good man."

I described the events of the day in my sector to the adjutant. I related how the large square appeared to be an almost insurmountable obstacle and that the completely unexpected smokescreen created by our left neighbour had literally enabled us to snatch victory at the last possible second.

"Listen, Jochen, I've never had such numbers of guns at my disposal; 13. Kompanie, our heavy artillery and towards midday Army artillery. The men immediately recognised what was at stake and radioed energetically between them. We'll find out first thing tomorrow what damage was wrought in the so-called 'dead angle' below here."

"Well, Major Weigert dispatched all of those men to you because you've been the focal point of the attack for three days and have virtually made regular headway day by day, according to plan."

"But with what casualties! At the moment, we company commanders are glorified squad commanders. If replacements don't arrive soon, I don't know how I can go on with my mob. And we need a couple of days of absolute rest so that we can look like men again. – Juschko!"

"Herr Leitnant?"

"Have we got the total casualties from today?"

"Jawohl! Rotter had two men wounded, Kowalski had one severely wounded man, Dittner also had two men. We now have 32 men altogether."

Leutnant Schüler made some notes and then asked: "Can you give me a messenger to take me to 6. Kompanie?"

"Of course. Willmann, take Herr Leutnant to Leutnant Fuchs."

"Jawohl, Herr Leutnant!"

"Right, take care of yourself, Jochen. When the situation is straightened out here tomorrow, I'll report immediately."

"Danke, Bert, until tomorrow then."

The field-kitchen was as reliable as always. It was driven up to the square and was under cover there. Nemetz fetched rations for us. He soon appeared with our Hauptfeldwebel.

"Well, Michel, is everything alright with you?"

"Jawohl, Herr Leutnant, everything is in order with the baggage train."

"Have we received mail?"

"Jawohl, the mail's arrived."

"I believe we'll finish up things here tomorrow. Should the Bataillon be pulled out from here, then I reckon we'll have a couple of days of rest. Prepare everything so that we can wash and shave. Tailors, repairers, and barbers will all have their hands full. Well, that's nothing new for you!"

Michel grinned, as if to say: "You reckon we're old camels."

I realised this and grinned.

It was reported from outside that the field-kitchen was ready to depart. Michel took his leave.

Silence had once again descended on the large city – apart from the isolated bursts of fire from machine-guns or submachine-guns that could be heard somewhere.

The room in which we spent the night had no home comforts. The window panes were missing. Our medics had also gathered here.

After I had eaten, I lay down on a stretcher. As usual, my steel helmet lay alongside my head, as well as my submachine-gun. I even had the use of a blanket. I was soon deep asleep.

A dull blow on my head, that I felt subconsciously, awoke me. I did not know how long I had been asleep. Something was happening somewhere, but what?

Around me, everything was still, the room was dark. Overhead, I could hear the engine noise of a 'sewing-machine', which as usual were indiscriminately dropping their cargoes of light bombs.

Now I could think more clearly. I felt a pain on my head and reached up there to feel it; a laceration!

I stood up, waking my comrades. We lit a lamp. Everything was now clear to me: a bomb from one of those Russian machines had hit our quarters. The detonation had dislodged some debris from the ceiling about four metres above me. A piece about thirty centimetres in diameter landed at head level near the stretcher where I'd been lying. A fist size piece landed on my head.

Our Sanitäts-Unteroffizier Paul cleaned the wound[61] and bandaged my head. My comrades congratulated this lucky beggar. Despite everything, I'd had a stroke of luck. The large piece could have easily crushed my skull. After that, I couldn't sleep any more. My head buzzed, but it was still there, so I had to go on.

Those damned 'sewing-machines' took liberties at night. They weren't airborne

---

61. This wound, regarded as being very light, was still recorded in Holl's personnel file and counted as one of the five or more wounds needed to be awarded the Wound Badge in Gold.

during the day, but at night, these slow machines flew low over the front-line area dropping their bombs haphazardly. I had just seen for myself that they occasionally had some success.

I lay down on the stretcher and reflected on how, at times like these, destiny was hanging by a thread. I was convinced that every man's final hour was decided by the Lord. In the meantime, I had also realised what Friedrich the Great had meant when he said: "It is not necessary that I live, but only that I do my duty!"

> Gen.Kdo. LI. A.K. — 0535 hours on 27. September 1942
>
> Along the front—line of LI.Armeekorps, the night of 26./27.9.1942 passed with incessant sorties by the enemy airforce and lively harassment fire...

27 September 1942

Coffee arrived. The new day would soon dawn. Hopefully it wouldn't be too difficult because all of us required rest and recuperation. My friend Uli Weingärtner, Leutnant Fuchs and Oberfeldwebel Jacobs appeared one after the other. They had heard about my misfortune and were glad that, nonetheless, I'd had so much good luck. We all had the same opinion that the enemy could now inflict little damage since we'd have him on a platter when it got light. Nevertheless, caution was the order of the day.

It was getting brighter. I was no longer on the stretcher. I took my binoculars and tried to get an overview of the shore terrain lying below me. The freight train, which I had seen yesterday evening, was incredibly long. I couldn't see the head of it from here. It was impossible to assess the amount of booty on this train. Tanks, trucks, tractors, guns and other equipment were loaded on the flatbed cars. I tried to look further on and glanced towards the edge of the bank.

Wait, there, behind the small spit of land jutting into the river. Something was moving.

"Juschko, take a look down at that spit. What do you see there?"

Pawellek peered through his binoculars: "They're Russians, Herr Leitnant, an entire group!"

Exactly my thoughts.

"Let's go, Juschko, come with me! Nemetz, Dittner and Rotter will provide covering fire with the machine-guns."

We scrambled down the embankment, ducked under the wagons and moved towards the spit.

The final stage of the battle: Soviet units – who had been offering stubborn resistance in the many ravines and dug-outs in the Tsaritsa Gully – pull out of the pocket and assemble on the spit, hoping to be picked up.

Soldiers of Infanterie-Regiment 276 (probably Leutnant Fuch's 6. Kompanie) in position above the embankment. On the left is the statue of pilot Viktor Stepanovich Kholzunov, visible to the Germans many days before they reached it. Kholzunov, born in Stalingrad, was awarded the title 'Hero of the Soviet Union' for his actions during the Spanish civil war. The statue survived the battle and still stands today.

I could barely comprehend what I saw: a group of Russian soldiers had crowded together at the outermost tip of the sandbank. I estimated at least 100 men. They were unarmed. They saw us coming towards them and spontaneously raised their hands.

Soldiers of Inf.-Rgt. 276 move about openly above the embankment after the complete destruction or capture of the Soviet units facing them.

Thirty metres of ground lay between us. The flowing waves of the Volga lapped over my boots. I only noticed it when my socks and feet were wet.

"Ask if there are any officers here."

Pawellek called across to the Russians. A man detached himself from the crowd and said he was an

<u>Ia Abt of 6. Armee HQ:</u> – 1040 hours on 27. September 1942

From 000 hours on 28.9., Pz.AOK4 will temporarily take over security for the Volga sector to the north, up to the city power station (exclusive). 71.Inf.Div. will be tactically subordinated to it.

Boundary between XXXXVIII. Panzerkorps and LI. Armeekorps will be agreed upon by the Korps HQs involved...

<u>Gen.Kdo. LI. A.K.</u> – 1810 hours on 27. September 1942

Along the front–line of LI. A.K., the final enemy resistance both sides of the Tsaritsa mouth was broken and the enemy bridgehead eliminated...

<u>In particular</u>:

94.Inf.Div. pushed through to the quay wall with assault troops at 0600 hours, destroyed the enemy that had entrenched behind the wall, and reached and cleaned out the Volga bank along their entire front–line.

71.Inf.Div. eradicated artillery resistance nests along the Volga in the morning hours and through that, took over 400 prisoners. The Volga bank was reached along their entire front–line before 0700 hours. The Division set itself up here for defence...

<u>Casualties on 27.9.</u>:

94.Inf.Div.: Killed – 4 Uffz and men
Wounded – 2 Offz[62], 20 Uffz and men
71.Inf.Div.: (No figures available)

<u>Prisoners and captured materiel on 27.9.</u>[63]:

896 prisoners, 29 tanks, 10 guns, 106 machine–guns, 9 anti-tank guns, 60 mortars, 58 anti–tank rifles, 10 lorries

---

62. *Oberleutnant d.R. Fock, commander 2./Infanterie-Regiment 267 and Oberleutnant d.R. Jahn, commander 5./Infanterie-Regiment 267*

63. *A large proportion of this tally resulted from the major attack to the north carried out on 27 September 1942 by 24. Panzer-Division, 389. Infanterie-Division and 100. Jäger-Division.*

officer. I let him come over to us. When questioned about his rank, he answered that he was a junior lieutenant and that he was a teacher by profession. He appeared to be about 30 years old and struck us as being calm and composed. Pawellek translated my question as to whether there were any other officers: "Four officers and two commissars crossed the Volga in a boat during the night."

With Pawellek's help, I made it clear to the junior lieutenant that as the highest-ranking officer, he was responsible for his fellow prisoners. The men would come to us in rows of three and would march off under his command. The junior lieutenant spoke to his comrades; they came over and formed up. The head of the column was already moving when I spotted a man lying on the ground. Pawellek called the last four men back to take along the wounded man.

The Russians had not yet reached the first house behind the square when artillery started firing at us from the other side of the Volga. The explosions of the shells were not difficult to detect for those doing the firing because they landed right next to the column of prisoners.

"Those mongrels are shooting at their own comrades!" cursed Pawellek, and I could only agree with him. Fortunately, none of them were injured. There were 124 prisoners.

We all breathed easier. Now we could move about freely because our immediate enemy had been completely vanquished[64]. They had put up stiff resistance. The scattered artillery impacts from the other side of the Volga worried us much less. I gave my Kompanietruppführer the order to remain at the command post while I returned to report to the Bataillon Commander.

I had just crossed the empty square that held us up for so long when I caught sight of 'Papa' Weigert. Accompanied by a messenger, he came straight towards us. Before I could report to him, he called out: "Congratulations, Holl! You and your men have performed outstandingly. I'm nominating you for the Knight's Cross[65]!"

The Major greeted me with a handshake and nodded to my messenger Nemetz. He inspected yesterday's battlefield. I gave the desired answers to his questions. Together, we then went to my command post.

---

64. *The following extract for 27 September 1942 is from the post-war Aufklärungs-Abteilung 171 report:*
   "On 27.9., after overcoming the last resistance, the Abteilung stood on top of the steeply sloping Volga bank. On the Volga shore, a train loaded with anti-aircraft guns was captured. Proud and moved, the few remaining men of the Abteilung stood in front of the great river. The objective of this merciless battle was reached…"
65. *There is no mention in Holl's personnel file of a Knight's Cross recommendation, so it is likely the proposal was not forwarded by either 94. Infanterie-Division or, more probably, by LI. Armeekorps.*

CHAPTER 2

Infanterie-Regiment 276 is subordinated to 24. Panzer-Division

28-29 September 1942

<u>Gen.Kdo. LI. A.K.</u> — 1645 hours on 28. September 1942

     94.Inf.Div.: Inf.Rgt.267 was relieved by elements of 71.Inf.Div. before 0530 hours. Inf.Rgt.276 was returned to the command of its Division...

The two days of rest were rest days in name only for us infantrymen. In contrast to the days of operations, where at any moment we could make contact with the enemy, we now had other priorities, 'operations' that were necessary if we didn't want to go to the dogs. First of all, there was personal hygiene, bathing or washing, shaving, hair cuts. If possible, we changed our underwear and had our uniforms mended. Above all else, because it was important for foot-troops, we had to clean our weapons and replenish our ammunition. For these purposes, the proper men from the baggage train were used because they were skilled people: tailors, shoemakers, barbers, armourers, etc. Mail from home was distributed, mail to home was collected and forwarded. Paperwork that couldn't be completed on operations — such as strength reports, requisitions etc. — were also now taken care of. It was up to the Hauptfeldwebel, the 'mother of the company', to ensure that everything was carried out according to regulations.

    Enemy fire from the other side of the Volga rarely fell on our sector. There was little sign of the enemy air force, not counting the 'night-time coffee-grinders'. And the

<u>Gen.Kdo. LI. A.K.</u> — 2320 hours on 28. September 1942

     On the morning of 29.9., 94.Inf.Div. will set in march to XIV. Panzerkorps without the elements already near XIV. Panzerkorps and without Inf.Rgt.276, which is still with LI. Armeekorps...

Malcolm King Collection

A soldier of 94. Infanterie-Division uses a quiet period to write a letter home. The insignia of the division (crossed Meissen swords) is clearly visible on the lorry door.

Malcolm King Collection

94. Infanterie-Division soldiers get their mess-tins filled.

The ever-present black cloud that covered Stalingrad's eastern horizon.

weather gods were still being kind to us. The sky had not been darkened by clouds for days, if the man-made clouds created by our machines of war were not taken into account. These clouds were enormous black-grey hazes shrouding the city. They were at their thickest north of us, from where the sounds of battle could be heard. The main operations of our Luftwaffe were also being flown over that sector, dropping bombs with their destruction-bringing loads. From approximately six kilometres away, we could see iron girders tossed through the air like broken matchsticks.

At the company commanders conference held by our Bataillon Commander yesterday, we made it absolutely clear that with the present company combat strengths, we were too weak to be used as attack troops. This was just as evident to our commander and we really hoped we'd receive replacements before we were deployed again.

I sat under the razor of 'Figaro', as our company barber was facetiously known. He had just finished cutting my hair when Marek handed me an order from Bataillon which stated that the Regiment would be pulled out tomorrow and assigned to another sector. The Bataillon Order included further details about the time of departure, the order of march for the battalions as well as the positions to which the companies would be allocated.

After I had finished freshening up, I went to the Battalion command post with Nemetz, my messenger. First, I sought out our adjutant, my friend Joachim Schüler.

"Greetings, Jochen!"

"Servus, Bert!"

"What's this about 'taking over a new sector'? You yourself heard last night at the conference – and know from your reports to Regiment – how weak we are. For Christ's sake, we couldn't conquer a flower-pot with the handful of men we have! Can you see any rhyme or reason in it?"

Jochen tried to placate me: "You're right in principle, Bert. We've also made strong representations to Regiment along those same lines. However, we've been assured that we'll only replace another division that's occupying positions in the Barrikady housing settlement. We'll only be holding positions. There's no intention to attack with our weak units. Our Regiment will be placed under 24. Panzer-Division for this period. 389. Infanterie-Division will be pulled out of there and employed elsewhere."

I was sceptical. If we were out of the divisional structure – of which we were a considerable element – who would be concerned whether we would or wouldn't later be in a position to mount an attack, should we be assigned to another unit? I expressed these doubts to my commander, Major Dr. Weigert. He listened attentively, nodded in agreement and, while looking at me fixedly, finally said: "Listen Holl, don't criticise the decisions of your superiors. We've received the order and we'll carry it out like Prusso-German soldiers. Is that clear?"

I stood to attention: "Jawohl, Herr Major! I'm only concerned about my men."

He said with a smile: "We all have these worries, Holl."

After I had been informed about the general situation at large – as far as the Bataillon staff were in a position to do so – I reported my departure and went back to my company.

Hauptfeldwebel Michel, who was there with his Gulaschkanone, was already aware of the departure order for the coming day. The baggage train would follow later and be assigned its area somewhere behind our operational area by Bataillon. Responsibility for this lay with our Bataillon paymaster Knopp. From there he would re-establish links with the companies.

"Michel, send two panje wagons to the company as early as possible tomorrow. I don't want our men to cart too much unnecessary kit. They should only carry the most essential things because we want to be prepared for any surprises; everything else will go on the vehicles."

It was a good job we had these small wooden flatbeds that we called panje wagons. They were each pulled by a pair of shaggy ponies. When they bogged down, four to six powerful fists grabbed the spokes, and the wagon was back on the road again. How difficult it had been in such instances for our company battlewagon. They were perfect in central and western Europe with their good road network, but here in extreme eastern Europe, they were not at all suitable. The condition of our well-nourished horses was noticeably deteriorating because we were not always able to give them the fodder they needed to remain strong. It was a different matter with the small panje ponies: they were

undemanding yet continued to perform well. We didn't have much trouble procuring fodder for them; in addition, 'the little comrades' required less of it.

According to the map, the distance – as the crow flies – from our present strongpoint to the Barrikady housing settlement amounted to just under nine kilometres. However, to get into our new operational area and avoid being harassed from the rear, we had to make a large detour, which effectively meant a march of at least twenty kilometres. I surveyed the map again. Located in the extreme south of the city was Elshanka, where my comrades had first entered Stalingrad. Currently, we found ourselves at the mouth of the Tsaritsa, and now we were to go to the northern part of Stalingrad, to Barrikady. It would be bloody hard for us 'stubble-hoppers'.

30 September 1942

It was still dark when the two drivers arrived with the panje wagons. We had plenty of time and it allowed us to begin peacefully. Everything that we absolutely did not have to carry would go on the vehicles. Two of the three squads were allocated one wagon, the third squad with my Kompanietrupp, the other. My special weapons – concentrated charges, Russian anti-tank rifle and Russian submachine-gun – would now be at hand.

Our two Hiwis, Peter and Paul, were each assigned to a wagon. They were happy to be with us. They were especially impressed that we all received the same rations.

Pjotr said to Pawellek: "In the Red Army, there are five different levels of rations."

I couldn't believe it. The Communists were supposed to be an 'army of workers and peasants'!

We were now ready to march, moving off to the ordered rendezvous in dispersed formation to lessen the risk of aerial attack. Our panje wagons were in the first and second thirds of the small column. Despite our small battle strength, our gang stretched for about 100 metres. Along with my messengers and Pawellek, I was in the vanguard, while Unteroffizier Rotter was at the rear of the column. Waiting near the former GPU women's prison was Jochen, ready to brief us.

"Morning, Bert."

"Morning, Jochen."

"You can continue marching. 5. Kompanie has just passed. Leutnant Weingärtner has a guide who knows the exact road we have to take."

"Who's behind us?"

"Next is 6. Kompanie with Leutnant Fuchs and then Oberfeldwebel Jacobs with 8. Kompanie. We'll join up with 8. Kompanie. When everyone is moving, the Commander will drive with me to the head of the column."

"Well, see you later then."

"Ja, take care."

I hurried to get back to my company. For the moment we were moving along the railway line in a northerly direction towards the centre of the city. The sounds of fighting grew louder. The large dark mushroom clouds of smoke were at their thickest there. Looking at the railway embankment to the left of us and the ruined houses to the right, our march route could almost be described as being a cutting. An ideal target for attack from the air. Fortunately, we hadn't seen the enemy air force in our sector at all during daylight hours. We maintained visual contact with the tail of 5. Kompanie in front of us and in so doing, were relieved of the burden of paying particular attention to our route.

Major Weigert, with Leutnant Schüler, drove past us on a motorcycle-sidecar combination. Coming towards us were some supply lads with their vehicles; they were not from our 94. Infanterie-Division. Several trucks were also trying to move to the rear in low gear.

There, what was that? In front of us, the column split apart to the right and left. Machine-gun and cannon fire from airplane guns hammered down along our march route. I yelled as loud as I could: "Enemy planes attacking from the front! Take cover!"

My comrades had become aware of the aircraft at the same time, however, and had already – as far as was possible – dived for cover, even as I had screamed out my order.

The entire episode lasted for only a few seconds. It was like a nightmare. We came out of it with two comrades struck by shrapnel from the onboard weapons. Fortunately, their wounds were slight and only required a field dressing. The men stayed with the unit. After a short break, we continued on. Had it been any worse for our other units?!

Our march direction changed: from the north we now turned and headed in a north-west direction. The railway embankment was a long way behind us; our field of vision widened. Only now and then did we pass stone buildings. The western edge of the city consisted almost entirely of wood and clay huts. Isolated ones were still standing but most of them could only be recognised by their chimneys, everything else having been flattened.

Around noon we crossed a large, deep trench with rampart-like walls which dated

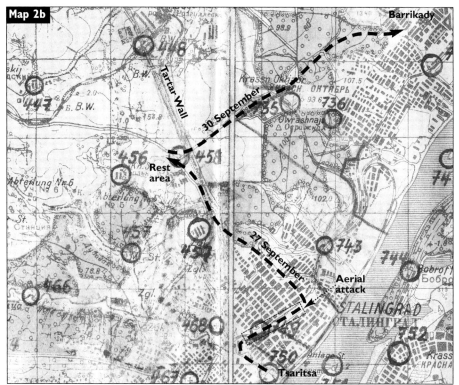

Working from the map, it seems the sequence of events of this march in Holl's account are incorrect. He states that his unit started their march from the Tsaritsa, but according to 6. Armee records, Inf.Rgt.276 was resting "south-west of Reference Point 458, 4km south of Razgulyayevka". This is a considerable distance from the Tsaritsa. It is likely that the first stage of the march – including being attacked by the enemy aircraft – took place on 27 September, when Inf.Rgt.276 was sent from the Tsaritsa to its rest area. As can be seen on the map, the Tartar Wall was just north of the rest area and so was probably the first obstacle crossed when marching to the Barrikady on 30 September.

from an older era. This trench was marked on our maps as the 'Tartar Wall'. I did not know which historical period it was from but if I had the opportunity, I would find out something about it.

One of the numerous chimney graveyards in Stalingrad.

We now crossed another railway line that ran roughly in an east-west direction. It appeared to come from the centre of the city. In front of us now there was another chimney graveyard with a few partially destroyed huts. It must have been the 'Red October' housing estate. Our march direction was now almost exactly northward. The noise of battle echoed from the direction of the Volga – thus to the right and behind us to the right[1]. Even counting the lightning-like surprise raid by the Russian ground-attack aircraft, we had been lucky.

As the terrain here fell away slightly to the city and the Volga, we were able to make out the carpet-bombing of our Luftwaffe while we were marching. Their principal targets were mainly the Red October and Barrikady factories.

Despite the severity of the enemy resistance, I was convinced that our 6. Armee would take the city. We had to seize it before the weather shifted.

The Bataillon Adjutant, Leutnant Schüler, came up to me in the motorcycle-sidecar.

"Hallo, Jochen, what's new?"

"Hallo, Bert, I've brought you the order detailing the take-over of your new positions. We've reached the western edge of the Barrikady complex. We'll be there in close to quarter of an hour. A messenger from 3. Kompanie of Infanterie-Regiment 544[2] is waiting to brief you. The relief will take place after dusk." Driving off to the rear on the motorcycle, Leutnant Schüler went to the following company.

Taking into account the breaks in marching and involuntary delays, we had now been on the road for eight hours. In the ruins of this former housing estate, the few

---

1. *These sounds of battle were from both a Soviet attack then in progress against 100. Jäger-Division and 24. Panzer-Division and the countermeasures of both those divisions.*
2. *Holl is incorrect: Inf.Rgt.544 was much further north. According to 6. Armee records, he would have been relieving a unit from Jäger-Rgt.54 of 100. Jäger-Division. On 30 September, 6. Armee war diary states that "Inf.Rgt.544 has pushed forward covering parties into the area north of the Gorodishche Brook (36b – 37d and b)..." This meant that Inf.Rgt.544 was a long way from the Barrikady housing estate.*

The ruins of the Barrikady housing estate. In the distance is the Barrikady Gun Factory.

men of 7. Kompanie had quickly 'become invisible', in other words, gone into cover. My Bataillon Commander was nearby. I reported to him.

"Now, Holl, is everything alright with you?"

"Jawohl, Herr Major. Apart from the aerial attack this morning, there's nothing to report."

"We were just as fortunate, Holl. Shortly after we passed your company, we heard aircraft strafing the column behind us. We came through unscathed."

"It could have been different, Herr Major. Our Bataillon really did have good luck."

Major Weigert signalled to a messenger who had been waiting somewhere aside under cover. "This Gefreiter will lead you with your men to his company, but we must first wait for darkness. The enemy should not notice that there is a relief taking place opposite them. The entire operation to replace Infanterie-Regiment 544 in the line as well as the occupation of their positions by our Regiment must be carried out during the coming night. You'll receive further details about the course of the front-line, the enemy situation and your sector from the company commander of 3. Kompanie, Infanterie-Regiment 544. More orders will follow later. Stay in your positions until further notice."

I saluted and returned to my company. The guide followed me. The squads, as well as my Kompanietrupp, had in the meantime unloaded ammunition, machine-guns, light mortars and anything else needed for operations from the panje wagons. We now had everything we required. At the onset of darkness, we marched off in a column. The men were cautioned not to make any noise and to speak only when necessary.

> **Gen.Kdo. LI. A.K.** — 1735 hours on 30. September 1942
>
> 24.Pz.Div repulsed enemy attacks in battalion strength from 0200 to 0600 hours... Inf.Rgt.276 has taken over a sector on the right flank of the Division...

This district was about one square kilometre in size and pressed fairly close to the western edge of the city of Stalingrad. The unsealed roads ran at right angles from south to north and from west to east. Green bushes still grew in the gardens of almost every wooden house, even those lying in ruins. We had almost reached the edge of the housing estate when our guide turned to the right. We moved through a patch of garden to a seemingly almost undamaged wooden house located behind the front. My men stopped on my order and waited for instructions. My Kompanietrupp followed me. The command post of 3. Kompanie of Infanterie-Regiment 544 was in the cellar of this wooden house. After brief introductions, we immediately got down to business. Oberleutnant Bäumle[3] spoke first: "Herr Holl, the Russians have snipers here. We've been here more than one week and over the first few days we had quite considerable losses. Mostly head shots. Warn your men to be extremely careful so that you don't come out like us."

I thanked him for this advice. Then I asked: "Herr Oberleutnant, can you give me a rough situation plan that will enable me to orient myself when it gets light?"

"I've already done it, here it is. Right: we're here, on this street corner. It's the central street of the complex. It runs directly into the city via the Barrikady factory. In front of the factory – I've drawn it here – is the Bread Factory. Over here to the left is the Silikat Factory. Our front-line's about 30 metres from here, directly in front of us. It's on a roughly 40 metre wide unsealed road that separates the city and the complex. The Russians are in

---

3. *There is no record of an Oberleutnant Bäumle belonging to either Inf.Rgt.544 or Jäger-Rgt.54. There was a Leutnant d.R. Artur Bäumle (born 4 September 1906) who belonged to Inf.Rgt.576 of 305. Infanterie-Division. However, 305.Inf.Div. would not arrive in in Stalingrad-North for another fortnight.*

The Barrikady and Krasny Oktyabr housing estates.

the houses on the other side. They're about 80 metres away. Our sentries are on the edge of the street about 40 metres opposite. The sector boundary is the street you arrived on. The boundary on the right flank is about 200 metres from here. I placed my command post here because this junction required particular attention."

Pawellek and both my messengers had attentively followed the conversation.

"Willmann, I want the squad commanders here."

Willmann repeated the order and hurried off.

"Herr Oberleutnant, do you have men ready to guide us?"

"Of course, my men are impatiently waiting for you. We've got to cover several kilometres tonight."

My squad commanders were assembled. I informed them of the situation and showed them Oberleutnant Bäumle's sketch.

"Dittner, you bring your men here and take over the positions in front of the command post. Kowalski, you'll replace the comrades in the centre, and you, Rotter, will take over the right flank, linking up with Leutnant Weingärtner's 5. Kompanie. And be extremely careful during daylight. The enemy's using snipers."

The squad commanders went with the guides.

"Herr Oberleutnant, how has it been here in general during the last few days?"

"Apart from the casualties due to sniper fire in the first three days, we've been fortunate. 'Stalin Organs' plaster this sector once or twice a day. They vary between 12 and 24 impacts. The enemy has had zero success. We've had no casualties so far from their shells. It's more of an area bombardment; Ivan can't aim them. The projectiles only have low penetrating power and explode immediately on impact. We got used to them quickly. Their firing positions are varied because the 'Organs' are motorised and the Russians immediately change position. The projectiles can be seen roaring through the air. It's just the explosions of the shells that weaker nerves can't stand. You believe the world's going under, especially during a 24 piece salvo. Over time, you get used to it."

Oberleutnant Bäumle said good-bye with a handshake and wished me and my men all the best. I thanked him and returned his good wishes.

After we had set up in the cellar, I climbed up the wooden stairs, through a hatch, into the living area above. Under the cover of darkness, I could go to the window without risk and look out towards the enemy in the night. There was little to be seen. Here and there, a couple of signal flares climbed into the sky. It was quiet on our sector.

The wooden house consisted of a single room. The oven in the centre divided it into two halves. The room had four windows in total, two overlooking the street front while the other two were on the sides of the gable. The door opened to the rear. The windows were boarded up but slits had been cut out for observation and shooting. Our predecessors had covered the floor with a layer of sand about 15 to 20 centimetres thick. The command post was, to some extent, protected against bombs or artillery shells as well as mortars. If nothing special was likely to happen for a while, our time here would be bearable. But who knew what the morning would bring?

I went back into the cellar and lay on a plank-bed that my predecessor had used as a cot in the past nights. As I did not have a precise overview and the enemy was very close by, I lay down as I always did in such a situation, with just my steel helmet and belt next to me. I took nothing else off; one never knew.

<u>Gen.Kdo. LI. A.K.</u> — 2200 hours on 30. September 1942

    Along the front of LI. Armeekorps on 30.9., there were strong enemy counterattacks in the Krasny Oktyabr and Barrikady city sectors. After repelling these attacks, 100.Jäg.Div. was able to reach the railway line in the Krasny Oktyabr sector at two places and 24.Pz.Div. won city sector 74c in Barrikady.

    <u>In particular</u>:

    On 30.9., 100.Jäg.Div. attacked on its northern wing and reached the railway line in Krasny Oktyabr at two places against stiff enemy resistance. Because of an enemy attack on the left flank, some of the ground won on this northern wing had to be relinquished. Connection to 24.Pz.Div. has been established.

    With Inf.Rgt.276, 24.Pz.Div. made contact with 100.Jäg.Div. by attacking. In tough house—to—house fighting against strong enemy forces, rifle squads gained a bridgehead north of the gully in 74c as a prerequisite for an intended advance to the north—east...

<u>Casualties on 30.9.</u>:

    100.Jg.Div.: Killed — 15 Uffz and men
                      Wounded — 2 Offz[4], 68 Uffz and men
                      7 men missing
    24.Pz.Div. : Killed — 5 men killed
                      Wounded — 30 men
    94.Inf.Div.: Wounded — 2 Offz[5]
                      (No other figures available)

---

4. *Leutnant d.R. Kuhnfels, Zugführer 3./Jäger-Regiment 54 and Leutnant d.R.z.V. Pichler, Kompanieführer 2./Jäger-Regiment 54.*

5. *Major d.R. Dr. Prof. Weigert, Bataillonsführer II./Inf.Rgt.276 and Leutnant d.R. Westernhagen, listed as Kompanieführer 6./Inf.Rgt.276 (see next page). Holl states that Leutnant Fuchs was commanding 6. Kompanie at this time. Major Weigert was only lightly wounded and remained with the troops. Leutnant Westernhagen suffered wounds that required treatment in a rear-area hospital.*

```
          beim Generalkommando XIV.A7.-Korps

Verwundet: 17.10.42  Oblt.      Fils,          1./Pz.Gr.Rgt.64   (16. . .)
                                               Kp.Fhr.
           17.10.42  Lt.         Waassen,       II./Pz.Gr. .79   (16. . .)
                                               . . ffz.
           4.10.42   Hptm.       v.Pogrell,     1./Pz.Abt.160    ( 6 . . .)
                                               Chef
           6.10.42   Lt.d.R.     Wilde,         . .tl.16         (  . . .)
                                               . . .
           9.10.42   Lt.d.R.     Auras,         . ./1. .         (  . . .)
                                               . . . .
           . .  .42  Lt.d. .     Krohnenb . . r, . . . .         (  . . .)
                                               Zugfhr.
        x) 12.10.42  Lt.d. .     Christoph,     5./1. .          (  . . .)
                                               Zugfhr.
        x  . . . .   Maj. . . .  . . rt,        . ./1. .276      (  . . .)
                                               Btl.Fhr.
           . . .42   Lt. . .     v.West . . .-  6./1. .276       (  . . .)
                                ven,           Fhr,
        x) 1.10.42   Oblt.d. .   Krüger,        . ./1. .         (  . . .)
                                               Fhr.
           1. .42    Oblt.d. .   Kahlmeier,     5./1. .274       (  . . .)
                                               Fhr.
           . . .42   Oblt.d. .   Keßler,        6./1. .276       ( 94.I.D.)
                                               Fhr.
           . . . .   Oblt.d. .   Dr.Pickert,    . ./4. . .       (  . . .)
                                               Chef
           . . . .   Lt.d. .     Scholz,        7./1. .74        ( 94.I. .)
                                               Zugfhr.
           . . . .   Lt.d. .     Müller,        15./1. .74       ( 94.I. .)
                                               Zugfhr.
           . . .42   Lt.d.R.     Jendulan,      5./1. .74        ( 94.I. .)
                                               Fhr.
        x) 2.10.42   Hptm.d. .   Rittner,       III./1. .276     ( 94.I. .)
                                               Fhr.
           . . .42   Lt.         Czichy,        15./1. .276      ( 94.I.D.)
                                               Fhr.
           . . .42   Lt.d.R.     Kehrer,        14./1. .276      ( 94.I. .)
                                               Fhr.
        x) 5.10.42   Oblt.d. .   Harzgen,       4./1. .74        ( 94.I. .)
                                               Fhr.
        x  7.10.42   Lt.d.R.     Röder,         I. .274          ( 94.I. .)
                                               Zugfhr.
        x) 10.10.42  Lt.d.R.     Klette,        3./Pi.Btl.194    ( 94.I.D.)
                                               Kp.Fhr.
           12.10.42  Oblt.d. .   Frhr.v.See-    Div.Stab         ( 94.I.D.)
                                bach,          Offz.(Ing.)
           14.10.42  Lt.d.R.     Schmidt,       14./1. .276      ( 94.I.D.)
```

A 6. Armee casualty list showing some of the officers wounded on the final day of September and during the first half of October 1942. Eighth from the top is Major d.R. Weigert, Bataillonsführer II./Infanterie-Regiment 276. Ninth from the top is Leutnant d.R. Westernhagen, Kompanieführer 6./Inf.Rgt.276. Seventeenth from the top is Hauptmann.d.R. Rittner, Bataillonsführer III./Infanterie-Regiment 276, who was lightly wounded on 2 October.

1 October 1942

The night was trouble-free. If I was not mistaken, today was 1 October.

Hauptfeldwebel Michel brought rations and hot coffee for the company. As it was quite bright, I'd already shaved and washed.

Unteroffizier Pawellek sent Obergefreiter Willmann upstairs to observe the enemy's positions. Since I hadn't heard anything from my squad commanders, everything seemed to be in order.

I went upstairs to get an idea of the situation with the help of the sketch drawn by my predecessor.

Nemetz continued to stare through his binoculars.

"Seen something, Nemetz?"

"Jawohl, Herr Leutnant! With the binoculars, enemy positions in the front gardens of those houses can be seen. And behind the houses are covered trenches with entrances that open to the rear. I've already seen several 'Ivans' flash past but it's only been a very brief glimpse of their heads."

I looked to where Nemetz had described. He was right. The enemy had dug in opposite us and was well camouflaged. During the coming night, our men would have to do likewise, in case it was required.

My gaze again strayed towards the Volga, where sporadic anti-aircraft fire could be heard. The white explosion clouds were clearly visible. Our Luftwaffe comrades were once again in the thick of the action as yet more strikes went in. They droned through the sky calmly and unhurriedly. The falling bombs could also be seen with the naked eye since the skies were clear, as they had been over the past days. Objects were then seen whirling through the air. Only afterwards could the detonation of the bomb be heard. When you see something like that from a few kilometres away and have no involvement, then you're glad not to be stuck in the middle of it. With bigger gardens and shrubbery that offered protection against being seen, our side had better possibilities for camouflage. Here, on the city's outer edge, the 'fury of war' had not struck so mercilessly. Small trees, bushes, shrubs and sparse grass were a pleasant diversion for the eyes.

The bitter fighting, however, allowed no time for idle contemplation. We had to be on our guard every second here because carelessness could mean death or a severe wound. The apparent peace was deceptive. Several aimed shots from the enemy's side confirmed the presence of snipers. What they can do, we can do too. I would look for a suitable spot at dusk so that I could give them an answer tomorrow. Even if I did not have a rifle with telescopic sights, I would prove that I had not worn my 'Schützenschnur'[6] after my first year of service for nothing.

---

6. _Schützenschnur_ = _marksmanship cord._

Midday was already approaching. In the meantime, I had turned to the rear and, with extreme caution, noted everything of importance. I pricked up my ears at the howling of an organ and glanced in the corresponding direction. The shells of the Stalin Organ, known to the Russians as 'Katyusha', were already hissing upward. I had barely taken cover when they arrived: boom, boom, boom, boom... It was neverending. From all sides, sometimes closer, then further away, was this boom, boom, boom. For anyone who had not experienced it, it really did seem like the world was going under. And then it was suddenly silent. Only the thinning plumes of smoke from the detonations revealed where the shells had impacted. It was lucky that our predecessors had warned us. By my estimation, it was 24 rocket salvo. Only a few had landed on us; most of them exploded behind us. The Russians knew where the forward line ran, and the risk of causing casualties to their own people by this scattergun fire was too great. The impacts from the heavy Russian mortars were more dangerous because they were aimed.

And now quickly over the street! I crossed the street in one bound and took cover in a garden. I then moved toward the enemy where, standing about 50 metres in front of me, was a battered wooden house that looked as though it would serve my purpose as a sharpshooter. My instincts had not deceived me: parts of the walls of the house gaped open but were still standing. From the loft, which was about four or five metres above the ground, I had a good view over the enemy terrain. The layout of the trenches could be easily seen. The hatch door was hanging on a hinge. The shortest distance from the course of the trench directly in front amounted to 100 metres at most. To the right, I had a view of at least 300 metres. My view to the left was obstructed by the hatch. This would be my lying-up position for tomorrow. I carefully made my way back.

When I arrived at my command post, Pawellek handed me the first mail from my wife that had been addressed to my last unit on the central sector. Oh well, at least it was something. With joy and emotion, I read the lines from my beloved. The field-post was the only way for us soldiers to maintain a link with our loved ones back home. It enabled us to record all our impressions and emotions for our next of kin.

The boom, boom, boom was again heard outside. I counted 12 impacts.

Nemetz said laconically: "That was the afternoon blessing, Herr Leitnant!"

Marek appeared. He stood to attention in front of me and reported: "Order from the commander; there will be a conference at 1800 hours at the battalion command post."

"Danke, Marek, understood. Otherwise, anything new?"

"Nope, Herr Leitnant, just that the salvo this morning caused some confusion. We'll just have to get used to it."

We both smiled in understanding. Years of being with my comrades had produced an atmosphere that outsiders or non-soldiers would have had difficulty understanding. On the one hand I was their superior – that was a fact – but on the other hand I was their comrade in battle, employed just as they were, because everyone knows: you're nothing without your comrades. Such a relationship can only be built when you're in constant contact with death – as we now were. Whether an individual felt more or less fear was unimportant: duty linked us together in success and failure, whether we wanted it or not.

I went to the battalion command post at 1800 hours with Willmann. As always, Major Dr. Weigert greeted us in a dignified and serious manner. The commanders of the other three companies were also there.

"Gentlemen, I have invited you all here, firstly, because the enemy situation has allowed it, and additionally, I would like to shed some light on the enemy situation outside the Regiment's area. At the moment, our Infanterie-Regiment 276 has been detached from the divisional units and subordinated to 24. Panzer-Division. This was the former 1. Kavallerie-Division from East Prussia. We've taken up positions here in the northern part of the city, approximately two to three kilometres in front of the Barrikady Gun Factory, which we must hold until further notice. Compared to our last days of fighting, it will be a period of recuperation for us. To the right of us is Infanterie-Regiment 203 of 76. Infanterie-Division[7], to the left is Infanterie-Regiment 544 of 389. Infanterie-Division[8]. We –Infanterie-Regiment 276 – are employed in the area of 24. Panzer-Division. I've said it before, gentlemen: positions must be held. No reconnaissance with scouting patrols because our present manpower just does not permit it. We can't count on stocking up with replacements at the moment, at best, we'll get our lightly wounded and sick returning from the rear hospitals. I am not able to say how long conditions will remain like this. It depends on how the attacking divisions progress. Attacks mounted by our bombers show us that at the moment, the focal point is located in the Red October and Barrikady factories, which lie directly east of us. If there are no special occurrences, situation reports will be forwarded daily to Bataillon at 1800 hours."

We were all glad that we were getting a breather. Attacking always had greater risks for the attacker. In defence, one is allowed to take cover from the enemy. The attacker must never show any signs of weakness. It was good for my young comrades from the Sudetenland. After the inferno of the Tsaritsa, they could get acclimatised in these quiet positions for the first time.

---

7. *This is incorrect. On 1 October 1942, the right neighbour was Jäger-Regiment 54. Inf.Rgt.203, together with the rest of 76. Infanterie-Division, was many kilometres away, on the northern blocking position between the Don and Volga rivers.*

8. *Inf.Rgt.544 was the left neighbour of 24. Panzer-Division – to which Inf.Rgt.276 was subordinated – but the Regiment's direct left neighbour was Pz.Gren.Rgt. 21 of 24.Pz.Div. (See map on next page).*

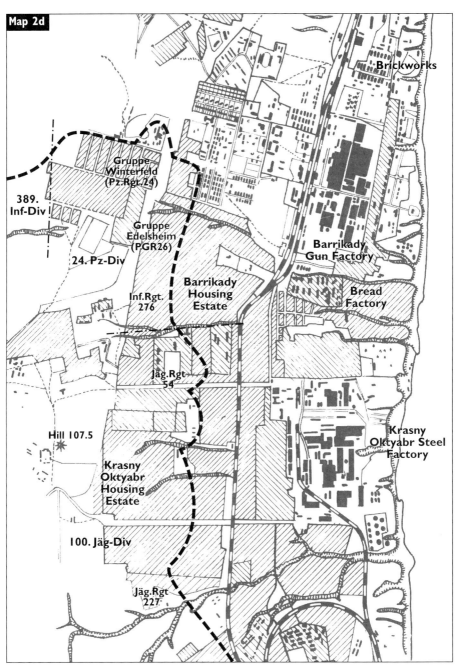

Front-line and position of units on 1 October 1942.

We company commanders exchanged our experiences and were then dismissed by the commander. After we arrived back at the company command post, Hauptfeldwebel Michel reported. The company had already been supplied. It was quiet along the front-line. Buzzing over the line – like almost every other night – were the Russian 'sewing-machines'. The night was clear and we were all hoping that it would remain peaceful. Sporadic noises of fighting rang out south-east of us, from the direction of the Red October factory.

> **Gen.Kdo. LI. A.K.** – 1740 hours on 1.October 1942
>
>   ...24.Pz.Div. held its positions. All attacks were repulsed. The enemy in front of the Division's front–line is in bunkers and has tanks in strong emplacements...

2 October 1942

How long had I been sleeping? Someone shouted out 'Alarm'! I leapt to my feet. The word 'Alarm' could immediately drag any experienced soldier from the deepest slumber. Rifle shots could be heard right in front of the command post, then a machine-gun opened up, hand-grenades exploded, followed by short bursts of fire from Russian submachine-guns. The sentries outside reported: "There was shooting going on near Gruppe Dittner, apparently an enemy patrol to the right and left, but nothing's happening now ."

He must have been right because as suddenly as the gunfire started, it just as suddenly died away. The brooding silence was felt twice as keenly.

A glance at my watch told me that it was already 0600 hours. I went forward to Dittner with my messenger Willmann. We had a good two hours left before it got light. Attention was still called for in the darkness because the enemy might still be nearby.

Dittner was furious and cursing in his Upper Silesian accent. As I listened to what happened, I could understand.

"Shit, it cost him his life. He didn't want to listen to his comrade, Gefreiter Cuballa. They were both in a foxhole observing their sector. Suddenly, Cuballa noticed that something was moving towards him. Next to him was the young rookie from the Sudetenland. When he also noticed it, he leapt from his cover to snatch the Russian, who dropped a grenade in front of his nose and it was curtains for him."

"Who was it?"

"Schütze Körner."

"Have you retrieved the body?"

"Jawohl, he's lying behind the ruins there. Sanitäts-Unteroffizier Paul is looking after his removal."

"How many Russians were there?"

"Four or five, Herr Leutnant. Cuballa said he hit one of them but it was too dark to recognise anything."

I was pensive. Inexperience had cost this young man his life. Ten days earlier, two of them had succumbed to panic and ran away. This was not cowardice. These youngsters were having to confront the unfamiliar, and it was unacceptable that they were thrown directly into battle with only eight weeks experience of soldiering. And here, one of them lost his life through his inexperience, trying to prove his courage, abandoning the protection of his foxhole. Every old hand, that is, everyone who had enough front experience – age had nothing to do with it – knew that in such instances, you must let the enemy approach and then fight him from cover; even more so in darkness. It was imperative that the young ones be warned about this.

> **Gen.Kdo. LI. A.K.** – 0600 hours on 2.October 1942
>   There was generally only light combat activity along the
> front-line of LI. Armeekorps during the night of 1./2.October...
> 24.Pz.Div. repulsed individual patrols...

I had to hurry if I was to carry out my plan as a sniper in an ambush position. I would take up position before daylight so the enemy didn't notice. Pawellek and both messengers were warned only to disturb me if something out of the ordinary happened. Equipped with binoculars, rifle and ammunition as well as two egg hand-grenades, I set off and soon made myself comfortable in my observation post.

Positioning myself in the darkness about three metres back from the loft door, I began to observe. I rigged up a support for my rifle to enhance accuracy. Should a worthwhile target be seen, the first shot must hit.

One of the most unsettling things for every soldier is the call: "Look out, sniper!" One shot, the target goes down, and nobody knows a thing. Where had the shot come from? Every soldier on both sides is then rattled.

As I had plenty of time, I observed the terrain in peace. My binoculars dwelled for a longer time on places where I saw the most movement. I had already spotted the individual outposts in the trench on the other side of the street. Straight ahead of my observation position, about 200 metres away, that is, about 100 metres beyond the Russian forward line, was an enemy command post.

I was able to see into about 10 metres of trench that led to the dug-out. Russians came and went at varying intervals. The position lay in a garden area and was well camouflaged. That would be my Number 1 target. The distance amounted to 200 metres.

As my Number 2 target, I chose a machine-gun post 100 metres away that was

```
Ic of 6. Armee HQ: — 2100 hours on 30. September 1942
        Disposition of enemy forces:
        A. Newly established:
        1.) West edge of the Barrikady: 193rd Rifle Division with
            Rifle Regiments 893, 895. The Division was pulled out
            near Voronezh in July and sent to Kogan (Chelyabinsk) to
            be brought up to strength. After replenishment, crossed
            the Volga in companies near the Tractor Factory on 28.
            September. Division commander: Generalmajor
            Semshatvorov⁹...

        B. Confirmed:
        1.) ...
        2.) Krasny Oktyabr: 95th Rifle Division
        3.) East of Gorodishche: 112th Rifle Division (Rifle
            Regiment 416). 6th Guards Tank Brigade. On 28.9., still
            has 8 T—34, 3 T—70, awaits 4 to 5 new tanks out of the
            Tractor Factory. 38th Motorised Rifle Brigade.
            Replenished mid—September by replacements from Rifle
            Regiments 178, 190, 390 out of Leninsk, however, was
            again severely hammered on 29.9. by German panzers...
```

directly opposite Gruppe Dittner. Further to the right – about 300 to 350 metres away – there must a well. Most of the movement was there. It was in the sector of my right neighbour and I designated it Target Number 3.

With my 98K rifle – it had never let me down – I practiced my aim and after some adjustments, was satisfied with my makeshift support. After adjusting for distance, I could then begin.

Having observed the area for some while, the enemy appeared to feel secure because they were moving at a pace we soldiers call the '08:15 trot'. It would not be very difficult to hit with the first shot because the entire body was visible in that ten metre stretch.

Here comes one! Not on, he moved out of the zone too quickly. But he surely had to come back. I was now completely focused. Had it been 10 or 20 minutes? I didn't know. His return run from the command post was slower. Pressure was applied, my finger slowly pulled back, the shot struck home, hit...

Target Number 2: I adjusted the sight for 100 metres. The observation post for the machine-gun position was well camouflaged. Only after observing the spot for a long

---

9. *Major-General Fedor Nikandrovich Smekhotvorov.*

A Stuka starts to pull out of its dive after dropping its bomb on the distant Red October factory.

time with my binoculars could I see a slight head movement. I carefully marked the position and looked with the naked eye. I could still see it. I again practiced my aim; it would have been easier with a telescopic sight. Over my head I could hear the howling of the Stukas as they plunged headlong down on the Barrikady and Red October factories, unleashing the destructive force of the payloads. All this, combined with the noise of fighting from near and afar, could not distract me. The only thing that mattered to me now was to take out the designated target with a single shot. Even the daily 'afternoon-greeting' from the impacting shells of the 'Stalin-Organ' landing in our sector could not deflect me from the task. A deep breath, take up pressure, calmly exhale, hold my breath and gently pull back my index finger. I looked through my binoculars: the target had vanished. Despite the battle noise going on outside, I was certain the shot had hit.

A gulp out of my canteen did me good, and although it was already 2 October, it had got warm up here. The weather was again being kind to us.

For a change, I looked through my binoculars in the direction of both factories. Massive dark mushrooms of smoke climbed into the blue sky.[10] With raids like that, something devilish would have to happen to prevent us from taking this city, this city that bore the name of the Red Dictator himself. I did have to concede one thing to the enemy: he was

A plume of smoke from the burning oil reservoir marks Chuikov's HQ.

damned obstinate, otherwise our troops would have long ago cleaned up the two or three pockets here in the northern part of the city. It was not my concern to worry myself over it. We received our operational orders and had to carry them out for our homeland as best we could.

My watch told me it was time to head back to my command post. Before I moved out, I wanted to have a crack at Target Nr.3. It was clear to me that targets at a distance

10. *In preparation for an assault on 3 October, the Luftwaffe was bombing selected targets, concentrating in particular along the Volga. Without knowing it, one of the German bombers crews almost left the Soviet 62nd Army leaderless when they dropped their bombs on an oil reservoir located above the cliffside command post of General Ivan I. Chuikov. A massive plume of oily, choking smoke rose into the sky where it was then spread by a westerly wind.*

of 300 to 350 metres would be difficult to hit – but I'd still try. The well I had spotted in the sector of my right neighbour obviously couldn't be seen from there because the Russians would not be moving about so brazenly. Wait, there were two people coming. They were carrying buckets in both hands and heading towards the well. Now they were standing still, filling their buckets. It was a favourable opportunity for my third shot. Sights were set for three hundred metres, centre of target lined up, pressure applied, pull through silently. Terrified, both Russians threw themselves to the ground, then in one move they were under cover, without their buckets. I'd missed my target. Oh well, I couldn't always knock them off with the first shot! I reflected that my luck was good, however, and the weapons of the enemy were not to be taken lightly. Carefully, I left my elevated hide and realised that my stomach was grumbling: I was hungry. When I arrived back at the command post, my Kompanietruppführer Pawellek had nothing to report. He asked me about the results of my morning's work. I tried to explain to him and the other comrades from our observation point in the command post. It was puzzling how completely different the enemy positions looked from here. With sketch in hand – which I had drawn in my hide – we compared it with the enemy positions as best as we could see them from here.

"Juschko, draw up a sketch like this for every squad commander so they can compare it with their own observations."

"Jawohl, Herr Leitnant!"

"Have you got anything to eat? I'm as hungry as a horse!"

I was soon chewing with relish, completely satisfied with the day's events. Later, once it was dark outside, I went to the Bataillon command post. I took the sketch with me. Nemetz escorted me. I reported to my Bataillon Commander, Major Weigert, who greeted me with a handshake. My friend Joachim, his adjutant, was also present.

"Well, my dear Holl, how's it going, what do you have to report from the front?"

"I immediately filed my report to Herr Major about the failed Russian scouting attempt early this morning, ."

The commander nodded in agreement.

"The death of the young soldier Körner can be attributed to his inexperience. His comrade, Gefreiter Cuballa, never imagined that Körner would leave the protection of his foxhole. By the time he'd noticed, it was too late. Herr Major, we do urgently require replacements, but not youngsters like that who've had no contact with the enemy."

Major Weigert looked at me seriously. "We've told them that. Unfortunately, we can do nothing else other than continue to point it out to Regiment. I'm just grateful that for the time being we only have to hold the positions here."

"Herr Major, I too don't know how we can be expected to attack with these few men!? As long as we stay in our positions, the impacts from the rocket-launchers are relatively ineffectual."

With the aid of the sketch, I now reported my observations and successes as a sniper to my commander. He listened attentively. When I told him that I planned on doing the same thing the next day, he warned me to be careful. On reflection, I felt his concerns about me were unwarranted. I had no intention of paying with my life. My motto: Men think and God guides. Nevertheless, it paid to be careful.

My friend Joachim Schüler threw some light on the general situation, as best he could under the circumstances. From both north and south, other army units increased pressure on the encircled enemy. Having pinned them back into the large factories and surrounding districts along the Volga, they were now attempting to eradicate these enemy pockets. Enemy resistance, however, was so stubborn that our comrades there only made headway with difficulty.

I could well imagine what was taking place there since virtually the entire arsenal of heavy weapons from both sides had been concentrated in this area over the last few days – and with good reason. On top of that, our bombers flew over in daily attacks.

I left my commander and his adjutant and headed back to my command post with Nemetz. It was all quiet in my sector.

10 October 1942

We had already been in our positions for a full ten days. It was possible to believe that this inferno in the centre of the northern part of the city, about 3 to 6 kilometres away, barely concerned us. Thinking back over the past week, I had to admit that very little had happened in our sector. The Stalin Organ salvoes, morning and afternoon, on occasion with 12, on others with 24 impacts, were already a regular feature. In reply, the enemy command post which I'd pinpointed from my elevated hide received a barrage – 'Kapow'! Leutnant Weise, commander of a platoon of heavy infantry guns, sent me a forward observer. I briefed him on the target. Weise was reluctant to bring down his '15-cm luggage' – as these 15cm shells were dubbed – too close to the front-line. He believed the risk was too great but I convinced him that it would be effective. Prior to him giving the order to fire, my men were informed. With the thundering approach of the heavy shells, they took complete cover in their foxholes. When you knew a shell was incoming, its flight could be followed with the naked eye. Shortly after Leutnant Weise transmitted the command to his emplacements over the field-telephone, the discharges could be heard, followed a few moments later by the roar of the shells. They were visible for a fraction of a second and then, right after that, the 'bbooomm' of the detonation was heard. In the same instant, shrapnel, shards of wood

```
24. Panzer-Division                    Einsatz: Sowjetunion 1942

                    Verleihungsliste Nr. 1
für E.K. 1. Klasse

                    Infanterie-Regiment 276
```

Lfd. Nr.	Zuname	Vorname (Rufn.)	Ort	Geburts-		Dienst- grad	verliehen am
					Tag		
1	Schreiber	Edm.	Jägerndorf	11. 8.11		Uffz.	12.10.42
2	Richter	Max	N.-Würschwitz	17.10.13		O.Gefr.	12.10.42
3	Weise	Alfr.	Dresden	23. 6.02		Lt.	22.10.42

Generalmajor
m. d. F. d. Div. beauftragt

For his excellence in providing artillery support to Infanterie-Regiment 276 and other units of 24. Panzer-Division, Leutnant Alfred Weise, 13./Inf.Rgt.276, was awarded the Iron Cross First Class on 22 October 1942.

and bits of debris showered down throughout the area and over our positions. We were pleased with the result and undertook the same operation twice more after further briefings about the targets. Weise had been convinced that such an exercise was possible when our own men were forewarned.

My battalion messenger, Marek, was struck on the helmet by a splinter as he was making his way back to me from the command post. His helmet was a little dented but Marek escaped injury, thank God. The sentries at the front were vigilant. Scouting parties could not be sent out because of low combat strengths.

The weather continued to be sunny and clear. The wind came up on 8 October, but on the very next day, it was again sunny and fine. The enemy was still only seen as fleeting figures, inasmuch as they could be seen during the day. They had noticed that we could also pick them off individually. As I've already said, snipers were feared on both sides.

I visited my elevated hide whenever my time allowed it.

11 October 1942

On 11 October, the sound of heavy fighting was heard to the left of us, from a northerly direction. We noticed it straight away because the din of battle was otherwise almost only

24. Panzer-Division   Einsatz: Sowjetunion 1942

Verleihungsliste Nr. 1

für D.K. 2. Klasse

Infanterie-Regiment 276

Lfd. Nr.	Zuname	Vorname (Rufn.)	Geburts- Ort	Tag	Dienst- grad	verliehen am
1	Bach	Fritz	Burkhardts- dorf	26. 4.13	O.Gefr.	12.lo.42
2	Erler	Werner	Meerane	14. 1.22	Schtz.	12.lo.42
3	Höhne	Alfr.	Reichenbrand	1. 5.o9	Gefr.	12.lo.42
4	Haase	Walter	Bautzen	22. 3.2o	Gefr.	12.lo.42
5	Weber	Kurt	Stockhausen	25.12.o9	Gefr.	12.lo.42
6	Meßner	Max	Jawellau	11. 9.13	O.Gefr.	12.lo.42
7	Huste	Gerh.	Dresden	9. 7.lo	Gefr.	12.lo.42
8	Reinerz	Herm.	Schoppen	11.lo.18	Gefr.	12.lo.42
9	Nokielski	Erich	Claßdorf	27. 6.21	O.Schtz.	12.lo.42
lo	Geitel	Walter	Großfurra	18.12.13	Feldw.	12.lo.42
11	Herold	Kurt	Buchholz	6. 7.11	Gefr.	12.lo.42
12	Fuss	Heinr.	Osterwick	21.lo.12	O.Gefr.	12.lo.42
13	Schrehak	Franz	Hopfendorf	14.lo.11	O.Gefr.	12.lo.42
14	Kohl	Willy	Martinskirchen	2o.1.18	O.Gefr.	12.lo.42
15	Leicher	Joh.	Mähr.Lotschnau	8. 1.14	Gefr.	12.lo.42
16	Richter	Karl	Seehausen	12. 9.14	Uffz.	12.lo.42
17	Faust	Paul	Würblitz	21.lo.11	O.Gefr.	12.lo.42
18	Lausch	Hans	Mühlhausen	lo. 8.14	Gefr.	12.lo.42
19	Drachwitz	Wilh.	Niemegk	lo. 5.lo	Gefr.	12.lo.42
2o	Tuchmann	Willib.	Georgenburg	3o. 9.13	O.Gefr.	12.lo.42
21	Kansy	Paul	Königshütte	11. 6.11	O.Gefr.	12.lo.42
22	Küßer	Otto	Dubranke	23. 9.11	Gefr.	12.lo.42
23	Röllig	Werner	Hinterherms- dorf	24. 2.23	Schtz.	22.lo.42
24	Peter	Heinr.	Neusattel	18. 7.22	O.Schtz.	22.lo.42
25	Knorr	Fritz	Chemnitz	23. 4.14	Gefr.	22.lo.42
26	Lohmann	Kurt	Fürstenwalde	17. 2.12	Gefr.	22.lo.42
27	Kunze	Paul	Maltsch	17.lo.12	O.Gefr.	22.lo.42
28	Döring	Herm.	Grunau	31. 5.14	O.Gefr.	22.lo.42
29	Mehner	Walter	Ottendorf	11.11.22	Gefr.	22.lo.42
3o	Mär	Fritz	Naunhof	3.11.13	O.Gefr.	22.lo.42
31	Müsing	Walter	Langelohe	13.12.16	O.Gefr.	22.lo.42
32	Schmiedl	Albert	Mostewitz	25.01.lo	O.Gefr.	22.lo.42

Generalmajor m.d.F.d.Div.beauft

Thirty-two members of Inf.-Rgt. 276 were also awarded the Iron Cross Second Class by 24. Panzer-Division.

heard coming from in front and to the right, that is, from the east and the south.

We got an 'involuntary deserter' the day before yesterday. A 40-year old Russian soldier had strayed in the darkness and ended up in our lines with his anti-tank rifle. Unfortunately, he only had five rounds of ammunition with him. I had exclusive use of the gun and ammunition. The prisoner was taken to the battalion staff.

On the same day, our left neighbour repulsed a localised Russian attack.

It rained yesterday morning. It was the first rain that I had experienced here. By the afternoon, the sun was again shining as if the weather was always like this.

I received two letters from my wife out of the homeland that had been written on 15 September. The direct mail link had now been re-established.

Right:

On 13 October 1942, Infanterie-Regiment 276 sent a request to the Heerespersonalamt (Army Personnel Office) in Berlin – via the divisional IIa (division adjutant, who was responsible for handling personnel matters of officers) – enquiring about the Rangdienstalter of Leutnant Holl. It says:

> *"The regiment requests to apply for a reassessment of the RDA[11] for Leutnant (active duty) Adelbert Holl at the appropriate higher authorities.*

Reason:

> *Lt. Holl was promoted to this rank with effect and RDA from 1 July 1940 (2363). In the course of his transfer to the active field officers the RDA was reduced by 5 months (1 December 1940 - Ord.Nr. 41). As per the regulation quoted above, however, reserve officers transferred to the active field officers are to keep, for the duration of the war, the RDA assigned to them as reserve officers in case an impairment of the RDA were to occur as a result of Section III, Figure 1 - 3 of the above-quoted regulation. Since this is the case here, the regiment requests the RDA to be readjusted.*

The relevant files of Lt. Holl are presently not in the possession of the regiment. Therefore the following personal data is hereafter given:

> *Leutnant (active duty) Adelbert Holl, Kompanieführer 7./Inf.Rgt.276*
> *Born 15.2.1919*

Date of first entry into the service:	*1.10.1937*	
Promotions:	*1.10.1938*	*Gefreiter*
	1.10.1939	*Unteroffizier (simultaneous commitment to 12 years service)*
	1.4.1940	*Feldwebel*
	1.7.1940	*Leutnant d.R. (RDA 1.7.40 -2363-)*
	1.10.1941	*Leutnant (aktiv)*
		RDA 1.12.40 -41-)
		Peacetime unit: Inf.Rgt.24

> *Kompanieführer since   1.8.1941*
> *4 wounds: 9.8.1941, 6.10.1941, 19.4.1942, 27.9.1942*
> *Decorations: Iron Cross Second Class 20.9.1939, Iron Cross First Class 24.8.1941, Infantry Assault Badge 8.6.1942, Wound Badge in Black 1.2.1942, Wound Badge in Silver 20.4.1942, two Tank Destruction Badges 5.5.1942, East Front Medal 1.9.1942.*

---

11. <u>RDA (Rangdienstalter)</u> - 'rank and seniority; date of seniority or substantiation'.

```
Infanterie Regiment 276          Rgt.Gef.Std., den 13.10.1942
IIa           Az. 21/42

Bezug: A.H.M.42 Ziffer 471, III, 4.
Betr.: RDA Lt. Holl, Fhr. 7./I.R.276
```

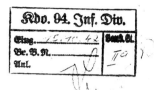

```
Der
94. Infanterie Division -IIa-
```

Das Regiment bittet, die Neufestsetzung des Rangdienstalters für
Leutnant (aktiv) Adelbert H o l l , Führer 7./I.R.276, höheren
Ortes beantragen zu wollen.

Begründung:

Lt. Holl wurde mit Wirkung undRDA vom 1.7.40 (2363) zu diesem
Dienstgrad befördert. Bei seiner späteren Überführung zu den
aktiven Truppenoffizieren wurde das RDA um 5 Monate (1.12.1940 -
Ord.Nr. 41 -) zurückverlegt. Gem. o.a. Verfügung behalten aber
die zu den aktiven Truppenoffizieren überführten Reserve-Offiziere
dann das ihnen als Reserve-Offizier zugewiesene RDA für die
Dauer des Krieges, wenn sich auf Grund obiger Verfügung Abschn.
III, Ziffer 1 - 3, eine Verschlechterung bei der Festsetzung
des RDA ergibt. Da dieser Fall hier vorliegt, bittet das Regiment, das RDA neu festsetzen zu wollen.

Die Karteimittel des Lt. Holl befinden sich z.Zt. nicht beim Rgt.
Nachstehend werden daher folgende Personalangaben gemacht:

```
        Lt. (akt.) Adelbert H o l l , Kp.-Fhr. 7./I.R.276
        geboren 15.2.1919
        1. Diensteintritt:      1.10.1937
        Beförderung:            1.10.1938  Gefreiter
                                1.10.1939  Unteroffizier (gleichzei-
                                           tig Verpflichtung auf
                                           12-jährige Dienstzeit)
                                1. 4.1940  Feldwebel
                                1. 7.1940  Leutnant d.R.(RDA 1.7.40-
                                           2363 -)
                                1.10.1941  Leutnant (aktiv)
                                           (RDA 1.12.40 - 41 -)
                                           Fr.Tr.T. I.R.24
```

```
Kompanie-Führer seit      1. 8.1941
4 Verwundungen:  9.8.1941, 6.10.1941, 19.4.1942, 27.9.1942.
Auszeichnungen:  E.K.II. 20.9.1939, E.K.I 24.8.1941, Inf.St.Abz.
                 8.6.1942, Verw.Abz.Schwarz 1.2.1942, Verw.Abz.
                 Silber 20.4.1942, 2 Pz.Nahkampf-Abz. 5.5.1942,
                 Ostmedaille 1.9.1942
                                        ,I. V.
```

```
                     Oberstleutnant
```

14 October 1942

And today, on 14 October, the sun was already high in the sky. I was up in the observation post that lay directly above my command post, as I was doing more frequently as the days passed. I preferred to look out of the right-hand window. This was the best place from which to observe the main battlefield. The Stuka strikes started going in early in the morning. The sorties were flown in continual relays[12]. The small white clouds that danced around the attacking machines indicated that the anti-aircraft guns on the opposite bank of the Volga were not asleep. I was so completely absorbed in my observations that I did not pay any attention to the salvoes the enemy was launching in our direction from the area of the Bread Factory. By the time Pawellek and Willmann called out to me: "Achtung, Herr Leutnant, the Organs!", it was already too late. I heard the roaring of the rockets, and in the same instant crashing, masonry from the chimney clattering on my helmet. Chunks from the brick oven slammed into my shoulder, arm and leg and threw me to the ground. Deathly silence. I was blinded by the smoke and dust. When I picked myself up, I quickly realised that I was not severely injured. The hatch leading down to the command post opened up. I heard my Kompanietruppführer call out in completely incredulous astonishment: "Holy mother of God, we've been lucky! Is everything alright, Herr Leitnant?" He came over to me and inspected me critically. "Herr Leitnant, if you hadn't been wearing your 'Dunstkübel'[13], you'd have been a goner."

I only nodded and checked myself. My left shoulder hurt, two fingers on my left hand were slightly crushed, and a lump had formed on the big toe of my right foot. My steel helmet − called a 'Dunstkübel' or 'Hurratüte'[14] by the soldiers − had once again proven its worth.

What had caused this chaos and confusion? I went around the oven into the larger section of the room. The smoke had cleared in the meantime. In front of me, embedded in the sand that was spread over the cellar roof − which also served as the floor of the living room − was the roughly 40-cm long remnants of a rocket. It had flown right through the front window into the room and, striking the ground, exploded. The explosive force had blown apart the front left corner; we could now look directly into the open air outside. If the oven had not been between me and the point of impact… would I have survived the pressure or the splinters from the thin-shelled projectile?

---

12. All these sorties were part of the overwhelming aerial support provided to Gruppe Jaenecke (14.Pz.-Div., 305. and 389.Inf.-Div) for its attack to capture the Dzerhezinsky Tractor Factory and the Brickworks just south of there. The ground forces moved off at 0730 hours.

13. *Dunstkübel* - literally 'fume tub', but a closer translation would be 'stink pot'.

14. *Hurratüte* - literally 'hurra bag', an obscure slang term. *Hurra!* − an old Prussian battlecry, later a taunting term for all forms of unthinking/suicidal nationalism. *Tüte* − a conical, rolled up paper wrapping; also a paper or plastic shopping bag. A paper bag as a hat is the sign of a madmen, like a dunce cap. Charging towards the enemy shouting 'hurra' while protected only by a government-issued steel helmet is probably not far from a madman's behaviour.

Pawellek and Willmann had immediately taken refuge in the cellar; the hatch had been slammed shut by the air pressure and both of them had fallen down the steps. I had to agree with my Juschko: we'd once again been enormously lucky.

"Juschko, continue observation, I'm going to get the medic to have a look at me."

Unteroffizier Paul, our medic, bandaged my fingers. The iodine stung but it had to be done as an inflammation would have been worse. My shoulder hurt but I could still move it. My big toe was swollen and had turned blue. I was glad I had not come off any worse. Unteroffizier Paul handed me his mug with a dash of Schnaps.

"Here, Herr Leutnant, have a drink, you could do with one."

Although I didn't normally appreciate this burning drink, I tipped the brew down and shook myself. "Danke, Paul, that feels better."

"Herr Leutnant, shouldn't you go to the battalion doctor?"

"Nein, Paul, that's not necessary. The few scratches will soon heal up and you know what you're doing."

To distract myself, I sat down and answered my wife's last letters and told her how I was doing. Naturally, I worded my letter so that I didn't cause needless worries for my wife and family.

My Hauptfeldwebel appeared late in the afternoon and congratulated me on the luck I'd had. Michel also took the daily report for Bataillon. Pawellek reported to me that everything was in order with the squads. In the evening, I remained at my command post and tried to go to sleep early. I had no desire to brood on events.

15 October 1942

"Herr Leitnant, wake up!" Pawellek roused me.

I was up in a flash. "What's the matter, Juschko?"

"Ivan sent out a scouting party on our right flank. Everything's already back in order. Unteroffizier Rotter took a Russian prisoner. He's outside. I've already interrogated him. Ivan said he was with a sergeant and six men. One of them was wounded. All of them made off except the prisoner. Their mission was to snatch one of us."

"Bring him in."

Pawellek fetched the Russian. He was a young man that fearlessly stared back at me. He wore a medal on his tunic. I asked him what the medal was for. He answered that he was a Komsomol (young communist). This was an odd situation for me: this soldier belonged to the youth organisation of the 'Red Tsar' and I had been in the Hitler Youth for a good five years.

"Juschko, take him to the battalion command post."

"Jawohl, Herr Leitnant, to the battalion command post."

I could no longer think about sleeping. Therefore, I shaved and had a wash. You never knew when there would be another opportunity.

My watch told me that dawn was still three hours away. Before then, something might happen over there, but I didn't think it likely because we'd been forewarned by the scouting party, and 'Ivan' knew that too.

Do I write 15 or 16 October today? It must be 15 October. Standing guard every day, you almost lose the feeling of time and have to check what the date is and whether it's a Monday or a Tuesday. For those of us in the front-line, however, it was more important that we fulfil our mission; knowing the date was not essential to do this.

17 October 1942

It seemed like something was being prepared. Yesterday and the day before that – that is, on 15 and 16 October – our Luftwaffe saw heavy action here. The weather was favourable and the sun still shone throughout the day. Our army command had to exploit that.

I'd been ordered to the battalion command post tonight and had to be there at 1700 hours.

The days were getting shorter. Morning dawned around 0900 hours and it was already dark by 1600 hours.

Shortly before 1700 hours, I reported to my commander, Major Weigert. Nemetz, my messenger, was with me. The welcome by our 'Papa Weigert' was – as always – warm, earnest and dignified. As we had not seen each other for days, he congratulated me on my soldier's luck. My friend Joachim also said as much. The commanders of the other companies of the battalion also reported punctually.

The commander came straight to the point. "Gentlemen, our holding role here is over as of tomorrow. We are going over to the attack! Here, look at the map: the pocket in the northern part of the city really bulges towards us. At both the large factories, Red October and Barrikady, the distance of our comrades fighting there from the banks of the Volga still amounts to about 1000 metres. Here, to the north-west, it's still about a good three kilometres to the Volga. 24. Panzer-Division has succeeded in pushing a wedge into the enemy from south to north. The enemy in our sector is now encircled, back to the Bread Factory. The pocket will be eradicated tomorrow. 24. Panzer-Division, who we are subordinated to for the time being, will support us with five panzers. Their commander is aware of our low combat strength, which is why we have the five panzers. To the right of us is Hauptmann Rittner's III. Bataillon, to the left is Infanterie-Regiment 544 of 389. Infanterie-Division. At dawn, the panzers will

Enemy pocket north-west of the Gun Factory, 17 October 1942.

drive out of III. Bataillon's sector along the street that is currently our front-line. They have been assigned the task of removing these resistance nests. Once the panzers are past us and over the street, they'll be in the enemy trench system. They will then clean up the pocket – from the south – in a generally northern direction. Our heavy weapons will remain in their old positions because they can reach all points of the pocket. We must reach our objective tomorrow in order to free up our troops currently occupied here for other tasks. The deployment of the battalions will stay as they are now because the men already know the ground in front of their command posts and foxholes. Any questions, gentlemen? As you haven't, let me offer you some genuine French cognac sent to me by Oberzahlmeister Knopp. And now Prost to good success for tomorrow!"

We all bid farewell with handshakes and wished each other the best. Not one of us knew whether this would be the last handshake. The lot of the soldier. Immediately after I arrived back at my command post, I had the squad commanders summoned. After the last of them appeared, I informed them about the assault scheduled for tomorrow. "Always ensure that you advance from cover to cover. Above all, make it very clear to the young 'hoppers' that they must keep their distance from the panzers. We'll have to fight for every enemy objective. We have to keep the rear of the panzers free, exactly as we did with the two Sturmgeschütze on the Tsaritsa. The mission has to be completed by the end of the day tomorrow. I'll again be in the centre with the Kompanietrupp so that we can keep in contact with one another, if possible. Does every squad have enough ammunition? One more thing: the collection point for the wounded is this command post, likewise if ammunition needs to be replenished. Are there any questions? No? Then good night, comrades, and good luck for tomorrow!"

"Gute Nacht, Herr Leutnant!"

Both Ukrainians were still with my company and they evidently felt happy to be with us. They made themselves useful by rendering numerous helpful services. It was fortunate that my Kompanietruppführer could communicate with both of them using his pidgin Polish. Over the past few nights, we were able – with their assistance – to urge our adversary to desert in their own language. The result was precisely nil. That was understandable because our battalion learned that in the past weeks, Stalin had sent in elite units, for example, students from the marine school in Astrakhan. We would meet some of them tomorrow.[15]

---

15. *On 12 October, the Soviet units opposite 24. Panzer-Division were 308th Rifle Division with Rifle Regiments 339, 347 and 351), 42nd Rifle Brigade and Guards Rifle Regiment 112 of 39th Guards Rifle Division. These had recently been supplied with reinforcements drawn from rear echelons and remnants of other destroyed units. Three days later, with the Dzerhezinsky Tractor Factory and half the Barrikady Gun Factory in German hands, the entire Soviet defence line in northern Stalingrad had been shattered, and numerous units that used to be further north were now in the area in front of 24. Panzer-Division. These included weak elements of 193rd Rifle Division and Guards Rifle Regiment 114 of 37th Guards Rifle Division.*

24. Panzer - Division   Div.Gef.Std., den .?. 10. 42

Abt.Ia/Op.   22,15 Uhr

Divisions - Befehl Nr.76

für Säubern gewonnener Stadtteile und Übernahme des Wolga-
Abschnitts nordostw. Geschützfabrik.
(Stadtplan 1 : 20 000)

1.) Masse des Feindes vor Front der 24.Pz.-Div. vernichtet bzw. ge-
fangen.
Feindteile halten sich noch vor I.R.276, vor Südhälfte Pz.Gr.Rgt.
21 und an Wolga-Ufer in 94 q, sowie anscheinend in Ziegelei um
Zahl 94.

2.) Erreichte Linie bei Nachbarn:
Rachel in 73 b West-Südwestecke Geschützfabrik — Nordrand Zahl
83 - 93 a 1 Südrand.

3.) LI.A.K. säubert am 18.10. gewonnene Stadtteile und bereitet wei-
teren Angriff vor.

4.) 24.Pz.-Div. säubert gewonnene Stadtteile vor I.R.276 und Pz.Gr.-
Rgt.21 und übernimmt Wolga-Abschnitt nordostw. Geschützfabrik mit
Pz.Gr.Rgt.26 und später ausserdem mit Pz.Gr.Rgt.21.

5.) Hierzu greifen an und säubern die restlichen Stadtteile spätestens 8,00 Uhr antretend:
a) I.R.276 in enger Zusammenarbeit mit Pz.Gr.Rgt.108 und einigen
Panzern der 14.Pz.-Div. Stadtteil zwischen Bahnlinie,Rachel
in 73 b, a und jetziger H.K.L. des I.R.276.
b) Pz.Gr.Rgt.21 in enger Zusammenarbeit mit I./Pz.Gr.Rgt.103 vor
Front des Pz.Gr.Rgt.21. Hierzu angreift I./Pz.Gr.Rgt.103 ab
6,00 Uhr.
Pz.Abt.Winterfeld zuführt und unterstellt bis 6,20 Uhr hierfür eine Pz.-Schwd. zu Rgts.Gef.Std.Pz.Gr.Rgt.21.
Zu a) u. b):
I.R.276 u. Pz.Gr.Rgt.21 nehmen vorher Verbindung mit Pz.Gr.Rgt.108
und I./Pz.Gr.Rgt.103 hierfür auf, die auch entsprechend angewiesen
sind.

                -- 2 --

Divisions-Befehl Nr. 76, as received by Infanterie-Regiment 276 for the attack on 18 October 1942. See page 111 for a full translation of this order.

6.) Pz.Gr.Rgt.26 übernimmt den in Div.-Befehl Nr.75 Ziff.11.) be-
fohlenen Wolga-Abschnitt und säubert diesen, sofern dies nicht
bereits durch das Batl. I.R.576 geschehen ist. Der Nordflügel
ist besonders zu sichern. Zur Einnahme und Säuberung des Wolga-
Ufer wird das Batl. I.R.576 dem Pz.Gr.Rgt. 26 unterstellt.

7.) Mit Morgengrauen aufklärt Pz.Gr.Rgt.21 mit Pz.-Grenadieren und
ausserdem Panzer-Abt. Winterfeld mit Panzern, ob und wie Ziegelei um Zahl 94 noch feindbesetzt ist.
Je nach Aufklärungsergebnis wird Pz.Gr.Rgt.21 spätestens ab Mit-
tag mit unterstellten Teilen der Pz.Abt.Winterfeld Ziegelei
säubern und entgegen Div.-Befehl Nr.75 Wolga-Abschnitt an Ziegelei nördl. an Pz.Gr.Rgt.26 anschliessend übernehmen und sichern.
Div.-Grenze Nordostrand der lila eingeraümten Ziegelei.
Linker Nachbar I.R.545, Rgts.Gef.Std. Mitte 85 d.

8.) Pz.A.R.89
unterstützt, soweit noch möglich, mit II.Abt. nach örtlicher
Weisung Säuberungskämpfe des I.R.276 und Pz.Gr.Rgt.21.
Mit I.Abt. und III.Abt. Angriff und Abwehr des Pz.Gr.Rgt.26 und
später den evtl. Angriff des Pz.Gr.Rgt.21 gegen Ziegelei mit
II. u. III.Abt.

9.) Pz.-Abt.Winterfeld sammelt nach Durchführung der Angriffe vor
jetziger Front des Pz.Gr.Rgt.21 u. bei Ziegelei anschliessend
im Raum um 65.

10.) Ferner zur Verfügung der Division nach Abschluß der Kämpfe:
   a) K.4 (ohne 1. u. 2.Schwd.) mit unterstellter 3./Pz.Pi.Btl.40
      und Fla-Zug 74b bzw. 64 B.
   b) Pz.Jäg.Abt.49 um 34.
   c) 2./K.4 im Leerfahrzeug-Raum K.4 zur Auffrischung.
   d) 1./K.4 u. Pz.Pi.Btl.40 (ohne 3.Kp.) wie bisher.
      2 Pz.-Spähtrupps ab 7,30 Uhr auf vorgeschobenem Div.Gef.Std.
      Sonst abkommandierte Pz.-Spähtrupps sind heranzuziehen.

11.) IV./Pz.A.R.89 wie bisher.

12.) Luftwaffenunterstützung nur auf Anforderung.

13.) Meldungen, Nachr.-Verbindungen, Gefangenen-Sammelstelle, Versor-
gungs- u. San.-Wesen wie bisher.

14.) B-Stelle des vorgeschobenen Div.Gef.Std. ab 7,45 Uhr besetzt.

                              gez. von L o n s k i
                              G e n e r a l m a j o r.
                                    F. d. R.
                              Der erste Generalstabsoffizier.

Verteiler:
Siehe Entwurf.
(Bis Rgt. u.selbst.Abt.)

Divisional-Order Nr. 76
for the mopping up of conquered districts and for taking over a sector along Volga north-east of the Gun Factory
(1 : 20000 map of the city)

1.) *The bulk of the enemy* in front of 24.Pz.-Div. has been destroyed or captured.
Enemy elements are still holding out in front of I.R.276, in front of the southern half of Pz.Gr.Rgt.21 and along the bank of the Volga in 94c, as well as apparently in the Brickworks around Number 94.

2.) *Line reached* by neighbouring units:
Gully in 73b west - south-west corner of the Gun Factory − north edge of Number 83 − 93a1 south edge.

3.) On 18.10., *LI.A.K.* will clean out conquered districts and prepare for a further attack.

4.) *24.Pz.-Div.* will mop up conquered districts in front of I.R.276 and Pz.Gr.Rgt.21 and take over the Volga sector north-east of the Gun Factory with Pz.Gr.Rgt.26 and also later with Pz.Gr.Rgt.21.

5.) *For this*, beginning at 0800 hours at the latest, the remaining districts will be *attacked* and *mopped up*:
   a) *I.R.276*, in close co-operation with Pz.Gr.Rgt.108 and a few panzers of 14.Pz.-Div., the district between the railway line, the gully in 73b, a and the present front-line of I.R.276;
   b) *Pz.Gr.Rgt.21*, in close co-operation with I./Pz.Gr.Rgt.103, the enemy in front of Pz.Gr.Rgt.21. For this, I./Pz.Gr.Rgt.108 will attack from 0605 hours.
   For this purpose, *Pz.Abt.Winterfeld* will provide and subordinate one panzer schwadron to the regimental command post of Pz.Gr.Rgt.21 before 0600 hours.
   To a) and b):
   For this purpose, *I.R.276* and Pz.Gr.Rgt.21 will beforehand establish contact with Pz.Gr.Rgt.108 and I./Pz.Gr.Rgt.103, who have also been instructed accordingly.

6.) In accordance with Fig. 1 from Divisional-Order Nr. 75, *Pz.Gr.Rgt.26* will take over the allocated sector on the Volga and clear it out, unless this has already been done by the battalion of Inf.Rgt.576. The north wing will be secured in particular. To take and clear out the Volga shore, the battalion of Inf.Rgt.576 will be subordinated to Pz.Gr.Rgt.26.

7.) At dawn, *Pz.Gr.Rgt.21* − with grenadiers −and also *Pz.Abt.Winterfeld* − with panzers − *will reconnoitre* to determine if and how the Brickworks around Number 94 is still occupied by the enemy.
Depending on the results of the reconnaissance, Pz.Gr.Rgt.21 with subordinated elements of Pz.Abt.Winterfeld will, from midday at the latest, clear out the Brickworks and, contrary to Divisional-Order Nr. 75, take over and secure the Volga sector from the Brickworks north of Pz.Gr.Rgt.26 up to the *division boundary* on the north-east edge of the lilac-outlined Brickworks.
Left neighbour is Inf.Rgt.545, Regiment command post middle of 85d.

8.) *Pz.Art.Rgt.89 will support*
with *II.Abt.*, as far as is still possible, the mopping-up operations of Inf.Rgt.276 and Pz.Gr.Rgt.21 in accordance with local instructions;
with *I.Abt.* and *III.Abt.* the assault and defence of Pz.Gr.Rgt.26 and later the possible attack of Pz.Gr.Rgt.21 against the Brickworks with II.Abt. and III.Abt.

9.) After carrying out the attacks forward of Pz.Gr.Rgt.21's front-line and near the Brickworks, *Panzer-Abteilung Winterfeld* will subsequently *assemble* in the area around 65.

10.) *Furthermore, the following are available to the Division* after the completion of the fighting:
   a) *K4* (without 1. and 2. Schwadrons) with subordinated 3./Pz.Pi.Btl.40 and Fla-Zug   74b to 64b.
   b) *Pz.Jäg.Abt.40* around 34.
   c) *2./K4* in the empty vehicle area. K4 for replenishment.
   d) *1./K4 and Pz.Pi.Btl.40* (without 3. Kompanie) as before.
   2 armoured car reconnaissance sections at the advanced Division command post from 0730 hours.
   Otherwise detached armoured car reconnaissance sections are to be drawn on.

11.) *IV./Pz.Art.Rgt.89* as before.

12.) *Air support* only upon request.

13.) *Reports, signal communications, prisoner assembly points, supply and medical services* as before.

14.) *Observation post at the advanced divisional command post* occupied from 0745 hours.

I arranged for our special weapons (concentrated charges[16], Russian anti-tank rifle[17], light mortar[18] and submachine-guns[19]) to be brought to us, ready to be used the next day by my Kompanietrupp. In this way, my Kompanietrupp formed another squad. They were to serve as a 'jack-of-all-trades'. Both Ukrainians, Peter and Paul, were assigned the task of carrying weapons and ammunition. If required, they would carry the wounded back to the collection point.

Unteroffizier Paul would remain at the command post with a medic for the time being.

I again climbed up to our observation post. It presented the same picture as it had over the last few days, and there was nothing to suggest that the enemy anticipated what was going to happen here tomorrow.

<u>Gen.Kdo. LI. A.K.</u> – 1730 hours on 17. October 1942

> 24.Pz.Div, supported by reinforced Pz.Gr.Rgt.108, reached the bend in the railway near 73c at 0930 hours and linked up with panzers of 14.Pz.–Div. near 73d1 towards 1300 hours. The enemy in districts 73a and b were mopped up in tough bunker–to–bunker fighting...

18 October 1942

<u>Gen.Kdo. LI. A.K.</u> – 0540 hours on 18. October 1942

> During the night of 17./18.10., there was harassing fire from enemy artillery along the front–line of LI. Armeekorps and attacks by the enemy air force, particular on the area west of the Gun factory and around the Tractor Factory...

I was awake early. I had slept fitfully. The responsibility and uncertainty about success or failure made me a touch nervous. I put this feeling down to the period of waiting. Over the course of hours, time appears to stand still.

I went over our preparations once again. Had anything been forgotten? Had I overlooked anything?

---

16. *Concentrated charges were constructed by binding 6 grenade heads around a central stick grenade.*
17. *Either the single-shot Degtyarev PTRD-41 (protivotankovoe ruzhe sistemy Degtyareva) or 5-shot auto-loading Simonov PTRS-41 (protivotankovoe ruzhe sistemy Simonova) anti-tank rifle, both chambered for the hard-hitting BS-41 armour-piercing incendiary bullet. The Germans thought enough of these guns to re-issue them to their own troops and give them official designations: the PTRD was known as '14.5mm PaB 783(r)' and the PTRS as '14.5mm PaB 784(r)'.*
18. *A Soviet 50mm PM40 light mortar, which had a range of about 800 metres.*
19. *PPSh-41 7.62mm submachine-gun with a 71-round drum magazine.*

To pass the time, I shaved particularly carefully, had a good breakfast – considering the circumstances – and waited for dawn to break.

It appeared to have begun. Sounds of fighting could be heard from the right. The crack of panzer cannon, machine-gun fire starting up, rifle shots resounding in between them. We watched from our observation post. The impacts of panzer shells came closer; known targets along the other side of the street were engaged with aimed fire. Individual Russian soldiers tried to get around behind them. Our men took them under fire.

The first panzer was now visible. III. Bataillon was already over the street, breaking into the enemy trench system. The enemy's defensive fire now grew heavier. Our infantry guns and heavy mortars also joined in. Two panzers drove through our sector along the street, pressing on northward. The other three wheeled around to the east and into the pocket. My right flank moved across the street. Now it was our turn. Gruppe Dittner was already over there and I followed with the Kompanietrupp. Initially, we tried to take the ground straight ahead of us, that is, in the direction of the Volga. After the first hundred metres – there was barely any trace of resistance – we abruptly ran into defensive fire. We came under fire from long-range machine-guns, falling mortars shells

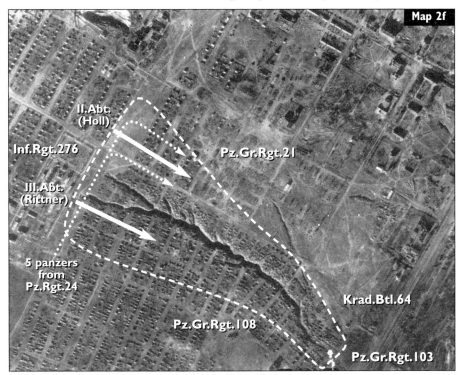

Attack on the pocket west of the Gun Factory, 18 October 1942.

and well-aimed rifles. Our panzers performed well but they couldn't manage it alone: the spadework was left to us infantrymen. To the right of us we saw the windowless rear wall of a long, rectangular building. Our forward progress was hindered by flanking machine-gun fire from this direction. We took cover in a communication trench. Juschko called to me: "Herr Leitnant, there's a hole in the wall over there. The fire is coming from there!"

The terrain faced by Holl and his men.

I looked through my binoculars in the direction indicated, saw the hole and thought I recognised some movement in the darkness.

"Nemetz, I need the anti-tank rifle!"

After a short delay, I brought it into position and waited. When a burst of fire came out of the hole, I squeezed off a shot. The machine-gun fell silent. My comrades on the right had in the meantime moved up level with us. The obstinate resistance inflicted our first casualties. We worked our way forward with mutual fire support and eliminated one nest after another. That also added to our casualties. Both Ukrainians provided splendid assistance as stretcher-bearers. The enemy defended himself to the last, none of our opponents giving themselves up.

Directly in front of us was a dug-out, apparently a command post. We worked our way up to it. Hand-grenades were thrown. Willmann was struck by a couple of splinters but was able to take himself to the first-aid post.

Juschko called: "Herr Leitnant, there's a commissar!"

"Shout to him that he should give himself up!"

When Pawellek shouted at him, he took cover and fired at us with his submachine-gun. We returned his fire. Dittner, to the left of us, sized up the situation. With one leap, he was within 10 metres of the Russian. The commissar, realising he had no way out, pulled out his Nagan pistol and shot himself. We continued on. The noise of battle could be heard to the right and left and all around. In this small pocket of approximately two square kilometres, you scarcely knew who was shooting who. The Russians in more elevated positions of course knew long ago what was happening here. Enemy artillery laid down a barrage on the sector. The Stalin Organs also launched their salvoes into the small pocket without any consideration for their own comrades still fighting there.

My Upper Silesians saw red. The higher our losses, the more doggedly they fought,

```
                    Noch Generalkommando XIV.Pz.-Korps

Verwundet: 23.10.42  Oblt.       Knappkötter,    8./Pz.A.R.16    (16.Pz.D.)
                                                 Chef

           24.10.42  Oblt.       Hilland,        2./Pz.Rgt.2     (16.Pz.D.)
                                                 Kp.Fhr.

           25.10.42  Lt.d.R.     Honert,         6./Pz.Gr.R.79   (16.Pz.D.)
                                                 Zugfhr.

Erkrankt:  29.10.42  Lt.d.R.     Vogelpohl,      9./Pz.Rgt.2     (16.Pz.D.)
                                                 Zugfhr.

Verwundet: 31.10.42  Lt.d.R.     Widmann,        II./Pz.Gr.R.54  (16.Pz.D.)
                                                 Ord.Offz.

      x)    2.11.42  Oblt.       Outschar,       4./Pz.A.R.16    (16.Pz.D.)
                                                 Chef

      x)    3.11.42  Oblt.       Schwarz,        1./Pz.Rgt.2     (16.Pz.D.)
                                                 Fhr.Stb.Kp.

            3.11.42  Lt.         Wippermann,     IV./Pz.A.R.16   (16.Pz.D.)
                                                 3.Offz.

      x)   19.10.42  Lt.         Bolten,         2./A.R.160      ( 60.I.D.)
                                                 V.B.

           23.10.42  Lt.d.R.     Ohland,         14./G.R.120     ( 60.I.D.)
                                                 Zugfhr.

      x)   24.10.42  Lt.d.R.     Hess,           9./Gr.Rgt.120   ( 60.I.D.)
                                                 Kp.Fhr.

           27.10.42  Lt.         Moritz,         6./A.R.160      ( 60.I.D.)
                                                 V.B.

           27.10.42  Oblt.d.R.   Lennartz,       4./Gr.Rgt.92    ( 60.I.D.)
                                                 Fhr.

           24.10.42  Oblt.       Mertz,          Stab A.R.160    ( 60.I.D.)
                                                 Fhr.Res.

           30.10.42  Lt.         Klose,          5./A.R.160      ( 60.I.D.)
                                                 V.B.

      x)   30.10.42  Lt.d.R.     Schönberger,    12./A.R.160     ( 60.I.D.)
                                                 Erk.Offz.

            1.11.42  Lt.         Oberwöhrmann,   3./Pz.Abt.160   ( 60.I.D.)
                                                 Kp.Fhr.

           16.10.42  Oblt.d.R.   Dr.Rosemann,    8./A.R.194      ( 94.I.D.)
                                                 Bttr.Chef

           19.10.42  Major d.R.  Wengler,        I./Gr.Rgt.274   ( 94.I.D.)
                                                 Btl.Fhr.

           19.10.42  Lt.d.R.     Röder,          Kampfgr.Wengler ( 94.I.D.)
                                                 Kp.Fhr.

      x)   19.10.42  Lt.         Holl,           7./Gr.Rgt.276   ( 94.I.D.)
                                                 Kp.Fhr.

      x)   19.10.42  Lt.d.R.     Eichhorn,       10./Gr.Rgt.276  ( 94.I.D.)
                                                 Kp.Fhr.

      x)   21.10.42  Lt.         Holl,           7./Gr.Rgt.276   ( 94.I.D.)
                                                 Kp.Fhr.

           24.10.42  Lt.d.R.     Erxleben,       7./Gr.Rgt.267   ( 94.I.D.)
                                                 Zugfhr.
```

A 6. Armee casualty list. Second and fourth from the bottom is Leutnant Holl, Kompanieführer 7./Infanterie-Regiment 276. The 'x)' on the left of his entries means that he remained with the troops and was not admitted to hospital. The date of the first wounding is incorrect: it should be 18.10.42. It is likely that this is a clerical error – the date when 94.Inf.-Div. was informed about Holl's wounding being entered, instead of the actual date.

pulling our youngsters along with them. The pocket shrunk steadily, one sensing the absolute will of the fighters to reach the set objective.

We were pushing forward when Juschko yelled out to me: "Achtung, Herr Leitnant, the 'Organs'![20]"

My comrades disappeared in a flash. Everyone threw themselves into the nearest hole or mortar crater. With one bound, I landed in a fox-hole just as they started to thunder and crash around me. A shock wave on the left side of my face stunned me for a second. The 'stove-pipes' of the salvo impacted around the edge of the hole. The shrapnel, as well as most of the pressure produced by the explosions, was directed into the air above. Some of this mighty force, however, came down into my hole. None of the rockets actually hit me – that would have been the end of me. My head buzzed and I felt as if I'd been hammered. When I looked at my comrades, I saw their lips moving but couldn't understand them. Had I been deafened? If only that roaring in my ears would stop. It felt like a steam valve constantly releasing steam. I couldn't hear a sound. I could still speak, however, and I told my Kompanietruppführer that he should substitute for me. Having lost my hearing, I was like a deaf nut here.

I would go to Bataillon – by way of my old command post – and file my report with my commander. Unteroffizier Paul and his medics had their hands full. Several of my men who could move unaided came along with me. Shells landing nearby forced us to take cover several times.

> **Gen.Kdo. LI. A.K.** – 1755 hours on 18. October 1942
>
> Today, enemy resistance has come back to life in districts captured on 16. and 17.10... Clearing up of the gully 73b3 has not yet been concluded. On 18.10., enemy artillery fire increased on the northern wing of 100.Jg.–Div and ahead of 14.Pz.–Div...

When I arrived at Bataillon, I learned from my friend Leutnant Schüler that Major Dr. Weigert had to leave the battalion on the urging of the battalion doctor. He had – like his predecessor Major Dr. Zimmermann – quite suddenly fallen ill with jaundice. Shit!

The adjutant now commanded the Bataillon. My company, or rather, the miserable remnants, were being led by my Kompanietruppführer.

We communicated with each other in rather a bizarre fashion. Jochen wrote the

---

20. *Although there was a regiment of Stalin Organs located on the west bank of the Volga – they would reverse out of large dug-outs in the riverside cliffs to fire a salvo and then quickly drive back in – most were situated on Zaitsevskii Island or on the east bank of the Volga. On 15 October, German Beobachtungsabteilungen (observation battalions) spotted a total of 18 enemy artillery batteries, including several rocket-launcher batteries, in the forests on the east bank of the Volga. Nine were suppressed by artillery fire.*

answers to my questions on a message pad. When he had questions, he wrote them down, and I then answered them.

The day would be over in an hour. Hopefully, the action to eliminate the pocket had been successfully concluded. How did our combat strength look now? The daily report would first be given to us for a close look.

I told Jochen that I would spend the night near the baggage train and that my Hauptfeldwebel should take me along when he started back from the delivery of rations. Until then, I would lie down and try to get some sleep.

A shake on the shoulder woke me up. It was Jochen. Standing next to him was my Hauptfeldwebel.

I had to first remember where I was, then everything became clear. The whistling in my ears told me that I hadn't been dreaming. I had been fast asleep for four hours and was removed from the world around me. Now I had returned to the present, hard and pitiless.

To my question as to how it looked at the front, Jochen wrote: "Pocket eliminated, 5., 6. and 7. Kompanien together have a combat strength of 23 men. Seven of those belong to 7. Kompanie. III. Bataillon has a total of 21 men in its rifle companies. Our battalion had 8 killed, 14 severely wounded, the rest medium and lightly wounded. Leutnant Weingärtner and Leutnant Fuchs were wounded."

I was dumbstruck and couldn't utter a word. What had become of our Regiment? Where were the replacements? If no experienced and battle-hardened men arrived – what use was the framework of staff and supply units, as well as units of heavy weapons? We infantrymen were the ones in close contact with the enemy. The day's high casualties proved that once again.

Jochen wrote again: "Order from Regiment Commander. You should report to him tomorrow at 1000 hours to file your report."

I nodded, offered my hand to my friend and followed my Hauptfeldwebel. After arriving at the baggage train, I had something to eat and had only one wish: sleep, sleep.

<u>Gen.Kdo. LI. A.K.</u> – 2240 hours on 18. October 1942

    LI.A.K. carried out mopping-up operations on 18.10. with elements of 24.Pz.-Div... In the gully 73b1-3, the enemy – compressed into the narrowest area – still holds out.

<u>Prisoners and materiel captured on 18.10.</u>:
    537 prisoners, including 10 deserters, 19 machine-guns, 2 anti-tank guns, 32 anti-tank rifles, 2 mortars, 10 submachine-guns

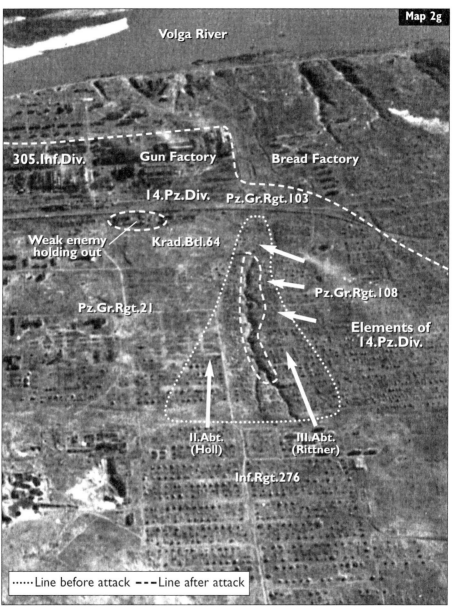

Results of the attack on the enemy pocket west of the Gun Factory, 18 October 1942. Even though the pocket was greatly reduced, stubborn Soviet defenders continued to hold out in the gully. By the end of 18 October, most of the Barrikady factory had also been captured by 305. Infanterie-Division and 14. Panzer-Division but the next few days would bring tough fighting as fresh Soviet units (Colonel Lyudnikov's 138th Rifle Division) counterattacked and recaptured many of the factory's massive workshops.

```
8.) Division-Reserven:
    a) K.4 (ohne 1., 2., 5.Schwd.) mit 3./Pi.40 und Fla-Zug,
       2./K.4,
       1./K.4,
       Pz.Pi.Btl.40 (ohne 3.Kp.),
       wie bisher.
       3./Pi.40 abstellt 2 Gruppen an Bahnübergang 94 a Mitte
       19.10.früh zur Instandsetzung.
       1./K.4 abstellt 2 Pz.-Spähtrupps ab 7,30 Uhr zu vorgeschobenem
       Div.Gef.Std.
    b) Pz.Jäg.Abt.40 Korps-Reserve südostw. Gumrik.
    c) I.R.276 erreicht zur Verfg. der Div. bis 9,00 Uhr Gegend 84 a.
       Befehlsempfänger ab 7,30 Uhr nur Gef.Std. Pz.Gr.Rgt.21.
       Rechtzeitig eintreffende schw.Waffen sind zur Angriffsunter-
       stützung einzusetzen.
       Vorbereitungen sind entsprechend zu treffen.
```

An extract from 24. Panzer-Division's Divisional-Order Nr. 77 released at 2245 hours on 18 October 1942. It was titled: "Attack in the direction of the Volga". After assisting in the reduction of the pocket, Infanterie-Regiment 276 was designated part of the Divisions-Reserve:

c)   "I.R.276 *will reach the area of 84a by 0900 hours to be at Division's disposal. Recipient of the orders will be at the command post of Pz.Gr.Rgt.21 from 0730 hours.*
     Heavy weapons that arrive punctually will be employed to support the assault.
     Preparations are to be made accordingly."

Infanterie-Regiment 276 was ordered to report its arrival in area 84a. According to 3d) of LI. Armeekorps' Korpsbefehl Nr. 90, the regiment was being sent to help 389. Infanterie-Division.

19 October 1942

I was awake around 0700 hours. It was still dark outside. The field kitchen was still in business. As always, the men at the front had already received their rations. I reached for a mug of hot coffee. Aah, that's good!

The cooks talked amongst themselves. I concluded happily that I could again hear sounds in my right ear. It sounded as though the voices were quite far away, but still, I could hear again. There was no change in my left ear but I was sure that with time, hearing would also return to this ear. In any case, I was completely confident.

The Hauptfeldwebel told me who was still at the front: Dittner, Pawellek, Nemetz and three of the old company members, as well as one of the last replacements. In addition to them, Sanitäts-Unteroffizier Paul was still there along with the Ukrainian Pavel. I asked about the second Hiwi, Pjotr. Michel said: "He was killed on his way from the first-aid station to the company troops. Pavel was so enraged that he joined the fighting, rifle in hand."

Thinking of my fallen friends, I knew how he felt.

Our company barber Grund cut my hair and gave me a shave. He was also to escort me to the Regiment command post. At 1000 hours, I reported, as ordered, to the commander, Oberstleutnant Müller. This was the first time I'd seen him: he was lean and not much taller than me. His face was lined by deep furrows. He appeared to be about 40 years-old[21]. He greeted me seriously. His adjutant, my friend Rudi Krell, was not present.

"Now, my dear Holl, tell me about yesterday. Krell has already told me a few things about you. During the last weeks, I've seen some things as deputy to Oberst Grosse. – You've repeatedly had good luck. Well, nothing runs without luck."

"Jawohl, Herr Oberstleutnant, nothing runs without good fortune."

He listened attentively to my report. I said to him quite openly that combat strength after yesterday's casualties was virtually zero and the companies needed to be urgently replenished.

"You're right, Holl. I've sent my adjutant to our Division[22]. Krell will personally describe the situation of the Regiment to General Pfeiffer[23] so that we are pulled out of 24. Panzer-Division's formation and again incorporated into our 94. Division. We require replacements and rest in order to achieve combat readiness again. – I'm also not particularly well at the moment, my rheumatism is troubling me."

A messenger entered the dug-out. "Herr Oberstleutnant, an Oberleutnant from the Division staff of 24. Panzer-Division wants to speak to you."

"Show him in."

An Oberleutnant in panzer uniform appeared, saluted and approached the commander: "Oberleutnant Jesco von Puttkamer[24], O2 of 24. Panzer-Division." My commander introduced us.

"What brings you to me, Herr von Puttkamer?"

"Herr Oberstleutnant, since the pocket near the Bread Factory was straightened out yesterday, your Regiment will occupy a new sector[25]. General von Lenski would like to know when your Regiment can be ready to march."

---

21. *He was 45 years-old.*

22. *While Inf.Rgt.276 was subordinated to 24. Panzer-Division, which was located in the Barrikady estate, the rest of 94. Infanterie-Division was a few kilometres further north as part of XIV. Panzerkorps.*

23. *Generalleutnant Dr. Georg Pfeiffer. Born 5 May 1890 in Wendessen / Wolfenbüttel; German Cross in Gold on 16 January 1942; flown out of the Stalingrad Kessel on 11 December 1942; Knight's Cross on 15 January 1943; died 28 June 1944 near Mogilev as General der Artillerie and Kommandeur VI. Armeekorps.*

24. *Oberleutnant Jesco Carl Eugen von Puttkamer. Born 20 February 1919 in Neustrelitz; captured at Stalingrad on 2 February 1943; died January 1987 in Oberaudorf*

25. *The new task set for Inf.Rgt.276 is shown in the extract from Divisions-Befehl Nr. 78 on page 121.*

```
c) I.R.276 u. K.4 erkunden ab sofort Einsatzmöglichkeiten für Gegen-
   stoß und Abriegelung im Div.-Abschnitt, besonders am rechten Flügel
   der Gruppe Below. Im Einvernehmen mit dieser ist erfolgte Erkundung
   mit etwaigem beabsichtigtem Einsatz bis 20.10., 18,00 Uhr an Di .
   mit Skizze zu melden.
        Sonstige
d) Div.-Reserve unverändert.
```

An extract from 24. Panzer-Division's Divisional-Order Nr. 78 released at 2200 hours on 19 October 1942. It was titled: "Defence of positions attained in and south of the Brickworks in Stalingrad":

5c)   *"I.R.276 and Krad.Btl.4 will immediately reconnoitre for operational possibilities to counterattack and seal off enemy intrusions in the divisional sector, particularly on the right wing of Gruppe Below. In conjunction with this, reconnaissance will be carried out for possible future operations and be reported to Division, with sketches, by 1800 hours on 20.10.*

5d)   *Divisions-Reserve remains otherwise unchanged."*

This new operational area was around the Brickworks, just north of the dreaded Barrikady Gun Factory.

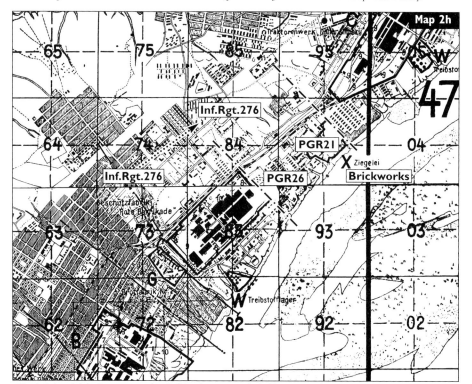

After helping shrink the enemy pocket, Inf.Rgt.276 was to be held in reserve for possible counterattacks by moving from its current location to the area of 84a, behind 24. Panzer-Division's new sector along the Volga.

I couldn't believe what I was hearing. Was this gentleman mad or didn't the Division know the whole picture?

My commander looked at me, then he said to Puttkamer:

"Leutnant Holl is one of my last company commanders. He took part in the fighting yesterday, and is half deaf at the moment. Listen to what he has to say and report it back to your commander."

He turned to me: "Go ahead."

I repeated my report and mentioned the number of men still fit for action (two battalions with 44 infantrymen all together). While doing this, my thoughts were with the dead and wounded. With tears of anger welling up, I ended with the sentence: "Should those few men also serve as cannon-fodder?!"

Von Puttkamer listened to me attentively, his face unflinching. Then he said: "Ja, I can see there's nothing you can do. I'll report that to my commander." He saluted and left.

Oberstleutnant Müller dismissed me and wished me a speedy recovery. Feeling bitter, I went with my messenger Grund back to the baggage train. That was just so typical when you were 'lent' to another unit. You were employed to the last man, then – when you'd served your purpose – you were simply discarded.

CHAPTER 3

Operations near Rynok and Spartakovka

19 October 1942

After arriving at the baggage train, my Hauptfeldwebel told me that the meagre remnants of our battalion were still in the Barrikady. As my hearing was gradually getting better in my right ear, I decided to go back to my company at the front on the following morning, 20 October. If, in the meantime, we got back several lightly wounded men that were now fit for action, it would be more expedient to form one unit out of all the remnants. I used the evening to write to my loved ones. In addition, I carried out a 'thorough body cleansing operation' with a change of underwear, as I did not know when the opportunity would present itself again.

20 October 1942

St Peter was still being kind to us as the day was again sunny and clear. After a good breakfast, I headed back to my Bataillon. It was about three kilometres away. Here, I felt relatively safe – approximately four to five kilometres behind the front. I watched with interest as our combat aircraft droned overhead en route to Stalingrad and – as they had been doing for weeks now – dropped their load of bombs on the city. For them too, the weather was also ideal. When would this cursed city finally fall! At no time had the resistance of the enemy been so obstinate and bitter as it was here. I thought of Artemovsk or Kaganovicha in the Donets area or later in Voroshilovgrad: the fighting was also hard there, yet, not so unrelenting as it was here. I was sure that the reason for this was because the city bore Stalin's name. The Red Dictator could see his prestige disappearing once Stalingrad fell. And fall it would. I was convinced of that.

I was now half way there. Three comrades from battalion staff were with me. All of a sudden – out of the clear blue sky – a high-pitched whistling could be heard and after that, the whizzing of shrapnel flying about. We threw ourselves to the ground. The same thing immediately occurred again four more times. We remained prone for some time, hugging the ground and waiting in case there was more to come. Then, as quickly as we could, we dashed to a gully that provided cover from view. Thank God this 'morning blessing' hadn't inflicted a great carnage. We looked at each other.

"Herr Leutnant, what's that on your right arm?" One of my companions pointed out two small holes on the right sleeve of my jacket. I took it off and saw that there were two small splinters in my arm above the elbow[1]. During the sudden artillery barrage, when we had thrown ourselves to the ground, I hadn't felt a thing. Our battalion doctor, Dr. Szcepanski, would see to it. I could still move my arm. My life had already been saved once before by Stabsarzt Dr. Szcepanski when I had been shot through the lung on 19 April. He was quickly on the spot and applied expert first-aid treatment. This trifling wound would be child's play for him.

None of us had been able to ascertain where the shells had come from; presumably from the other bank of the Volga.

We continued to walk to the Regiment command post and were spared any further shelling. Once there, we caught up with the latest news: our Regiment Commander, Oberst Grosse, was back from leave. Oberstleutnant Müller and his adjutant, Oberleutnant Krell, had been transferred to Grenadier-Regiment[2] 267. Major Weigert was replaced because of jaundice; his successor was Hauptmann Israel[3], who used to command 13. Kompanie. Along with Oberst Grosse, Leutnant Westernhagen and Leutnant Augst, as well as several convalescents, had returned to the Regiment. Oberleutnant Polit from Regiment staff – he commanded the communications platoon – had been buried alive by an aerial bomb. As this had happened during the night, no-one noticed the incident and help was too late in arriving. We always had to reckon with such changes and accidents.

Dr. Szcepanski, whom I'd sought out, treated my arm and confirmed that it wasn't serious.

It rained in the afternoon for the first time in weeks; hopefully it wouldn't last too long.

A 6. Armee casualty list from October 1942. Fourth from the top is Oberleutnant d.R. Ewald Polit, Nachrichtenzugführer (commander of the communications platoon) of Infanterie-Regiment 276.

---

1. This was Holl's second wound, as reported in the 6. Armee casualty list shown on page 115. Again, the date in the casualty list seems to be wrong.
2. Grenadier-Regiment - On 15 October 1942, 'Infanterie-Regiments' were redesignated 'Grenadier-Regiments'.
3. See footnote on page 37.

In the meantime, the order to shift our battalion to an area that lay approximately eight kilometres north-west of the Barrikady had arrived. Reinforcements would join up with us there.

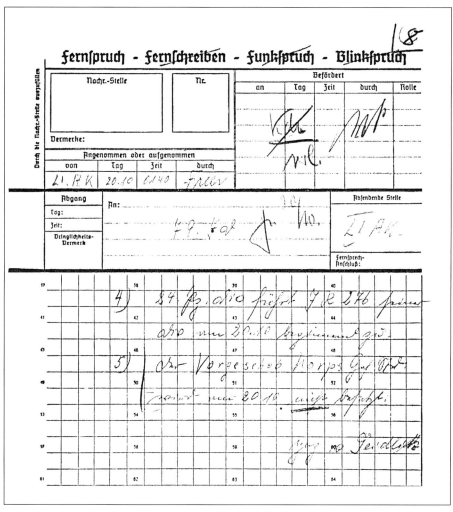

Oberstleutnant Müller's appeals to be released from subordination and returned to 94. Infanterie-Division must have had some effect because in the early morning hours of 20 October 1942, LI. Armeekorps headquarters called 24. Panzer-Division headquarters and conveyed the following message: "24. Panzer-Division will return Infanterie-Regiment 276 to its division beginning 20.10… signed von Seydlitz." As 24. Panzer-Division already had plans for the regiment on the following day, the arguments for returning it to its parent division must have been particularly convincing. It is likely that General der Artillerie Pfeiffer, Commander of 94. Infanterie-Division, spoke to General von Seydlitz personally.

24. Panzer - Division   Div.Gef.St., den 2o.1o.1942.
   Kommandeur

T a g e s b e f e h l !
- - - - - - - - - - - - -

Sold.ten des J.R. 276!

Seit 3 Wochen kämpft Ihr Seite an Seite mit den Männern
der 24. Panzer-Division in Stalingrad. Tag und Nacht habt Ihr im
schwersten Feuer eines fanatisch kämpfenden Gegners Eure Pflicht
erfüllt und zahlreiche Angriffe des Gegners abgewehrt. Tagelang
habt Ihr die Flanke der Division geschützt, die sich immer weiter
durch den Stadtkern von Stalingrad durchkämpfte.

Eurem Heldentum ist es mit zu verdanken, daß die Division
alle ihr gestellten Aufgaben restlos erfüllen konnte und seit
einigen Tagen am Wolga-Ufer steht.

Nunmehr kehrt Ihr wieder in die Reihen Eurer Division
zurück. Am Tage Eures Ausscheidens aus der Division möchte ich
Euch daher meinen und der Division tiefsten Dank sagen für Euren
Heldenmut, Eure Tapferkeit, Euere Kameradschaft und für Euren
vorbildlichen Kampfgeist, der besonders in den letzten Tagen
dazu beigetragen hat, den vor Eurer Front stehenden Gegner zu
vernichten.

Tief ergriffen gedenken wir heute gemeinsam aller
gefallenen Kameraden Eures Regiments, die in den Kämpfen um
Stalingrad in höchster Pflichterfüllung ihr Leben für Führer
und Volk hingegeben haben.

Ihr Opfer verpflichtet uns weiter zu kämpfen bis zum
endgültigen Siege für unser Volk.

Heil unserm Führer!

G e n e r a l m a j o r .

Left: Infanterie-Regiment 276 had been subordinated to 24. Panzer-Division for a total of 21 days. On the day of its departure, General von Lenski issued a Tagesbefehl that was made known to all men of the Regiment:

"Soldiers of Infanterie-Regiment 276!

"For three weeks, you have fought side by side with the men of 24. Panzer-Division. You have fulfiled your duty day and night in the heaviest fire of a fanatically defending enemy and repulsed numerous enemy attacks. Day after day, you have protected the flank of the Division as it fought its way deeper into the heart of Stalingrad.

"It is thanks to your heroic deeds that the Division has been able to completely fulfil all of its missions and has been on the bank of the Volga for the last few days.

"You now return to the ranks of your division. Before your detachment from the Division on this day, I would like to offer you – on behalf of myself and the Division – our deepest thanks for your valour, your bravery, your comradeship and for your exemplary battle spirit that, particularly in the last few days, has contributed to the destruction of the enemy along your front.

"It is with deep sorrow that we today remember all of the fallen comrades of your Regiment who, in the ultimate fulfilment of their duty, have given up their lives for Führer and Volk in the fighting around Stalingrad.

"Their sacrifice obliges us to keep fighting until the final victory for our people."

"Heil our Führer!
signed von Lenski"

21 October 1942

In the morning, we marched in battle order to the new area. It was still dark. We had to get out of sight of enemy artillery observers before it got light. Otherwise, we'd have to endure the possibility of shelling by enemy artillery.

The further away we were from the main battle area in the city centre, the easier it became for me. This city was like Moloch, the voracious giant. In a few weeks, both battalions had been worn down to a handful of men by relentless house- and street-fighting. The situation was no better with the other rifle units.

When it was light, we recognised a village to the left of us; it was Gorodishche. Our march route now led in a northerly direction. The battalion took a breather near Orlovka. Here, I received the order from Leutnant Schüler to come to the baggage train and report to the Regiment Commander, Oberst Grosse. The battalion's motorcycle messenger took me there. Apparently, it was said that we would be taking up winter positions in the northern blocking position over the next few days. Perhaps wishing for it would result in it coming about. When the soldier is on operations, he never knows what the next moment will bring in terms of new assignments.

Our Regiment Commander was still with the baggage train. There was also about forty returning convalescents who had arrived with Leutnants Augst and Westernhagen.

I reported to Oberst Grosse with the words: "Leutnant Holl reporting – as ordered!"

My commander thanked me for my salute and said with a smile: "You've taken a long time to find your way back to our Regiment."

"Jawohl, Herr Oberst, exactly six months, including a detour via 134. Infanterie-Division."

"I've already heard about that, as well as the very hard operations of our Regiment during my leave. Casualties have been extremely heavy. We must see to it that more reinforcements arrive. Until further notice, we have been designated Division reserve. And now to you, Holl. You are the last of the old experienced company commanders still available to the Regiment. In the past four weeks, you've been employed unsparingly. Oberstleutnant Müller has awarded you the Wound Badge in Gold. You were again lucky yesterday. I cannot afford to lose my last experienced company commander. You will remain here at the baggage train for a few days and be detached to the regiment staff for the next four to six weeks."

Oberst Erich Grosse, Kommandeur Inf.-Rgt. 276.

I was nonplussed because this order was not at all to my liking. The bond with my 'sevenths' was too great for me to consider a transfer. I asked: "Herr Oberst, will I have my company back after this period?"

"Of course, you retain nominal leadership of your company. Leutnant Augst will deputise for you during this time. You are my z.b.V.[4] on the Regiment staff, especially after Oberleutnant Polit lost his life in such a tragic manner."

Relieved, I said: "I'm grateful, Herr Oberst."

I spent the next half hour answering questions put to me by my commander. In the main, these were questions about the fighting we had conducted in certain parts of the city. I left nothing out since I didn't think it was the right thing to do. It made no sense to hide the truth. The high command would then receive a false picture.

When it was announced that the motorcycle/sidecar driver had arrived from

4. *z.b.V.* - *zur besonderen Verwendung*, 'on special assignment'.

Regiment, I was dismissed. I watched the motorcycle driving away. Oberst Grosse was a remarkable personality. Judging by his outer appearance, home leave had done him good. Two pale-blue eyes looked out of an unwrinkled face. His sparse head of hair was almost completely white. His body was well proportioned. I reckoned he was about 55 to 60 years-old[5]. His voice was quiet, measured and not hurtful when he had to be critical. I regarded him a good judge of men. Well, yes, at this age.

Now to my people, however. First, I met my paymaster, Unteroffizier Holm. A quiet and conscientious man, he'd been with the company since its formation. His friendly greeting was warm and sincere. Futtermeister Greguletz arrived soon after, followed by Gefreiter Fischer, driver of the horse-drawn wagon, that is, the vehicle that belonged to the assistant armourer and everyone in the baggage train. Everyone had his own assignment – like cogs in a machine – and without them, we wouldn't be able to function. And so it was with all units, whether they were horsedrawn or motorised, Heer, Luftwaffe or Kriegsmarine.

I asked a lot of questions but also had plenty to talk about. Greguletz took me out to the horses. Several of the old four-leggers were still there, including my horse Mumpitz. All of them had seen better days, and now they stood on the brink of another hard winter. Their carers did everything possible for them, I'm sure of that, but they couldn't work miracles. If the weather stayed fine, I would take Mumpitz out for a little ride tomorrow or the day after. I was already looking forward to it and was curious to see whether he would recognise that his old rider was once again sitting on him.

> <u>Gen.Kdo. LI. A.K.</u> – 2210 hours on 21. October 1942
>
> I.R.276 is being returned to 94.Inf.Div...

25 October 1942

I'd been at the baggage train for four days. It was cold, the difference being noticeable when leading a relatively peaceful life ten kilometres to the rear compared to fighting with the troops at the front and being constantly in action.

On 22 October, we watched sixty bombers flying over us in the direction of Stalingrad. A short while later, the explosions of the bombs could be heard at the baggage train.

Yesterday, I was able to say hello to our battalion paymaster, Oberzahlmeister Knopp. He had been en route for several days and had brought supplies, ammunition and mail, which also included letters dated 3 and 15 October written to me by my wife.

I went for a short ride on Mumpitz around lunchtime. After such a long time, it

---

5. *He was 57-years old.*

was a marvellous feeling to be sitting on a horse's back again, contemplating the world from on high in the sunny weather. I was lost in the moment, forgot the seriousness of the hour and thought back to happier days in Oberlausitz when I had ridden this stocky white gelding for the first time. We soon became friends, and in August 1941, when I took over the company in which I'd been a platoon commander, Mumpitz became my riding horse. He thoroughly deserved the name too. Even now, I had to keep an eye on him and show him that I was master. We returned after an hour. A happy hour was over. If the weather remained good, I would ride him again tomorrow.

28 October 1942

Thank God the days of inactivity were over. Yesterday evening, I received the order to report to the regimental command post today. I planned to ride to the commander on Mumpitz accompanied by the horse's groom. Then, however, the call came through that the commander himself would arrive by car as he had some business to attend to at the baggage train.

I was glad that I'd had the time to ride Mumpitz during the last two days. My four-legged friend also had fun. He had perked up visibly and was frisky. Who knew when I'd be able to ride him again!?

Oberst Grosse arrived at midday. Half an hour later – having received a quick helping (a full ladle) from the field-kitchen – we were on our way to the Regiment command post, which lay in a small oak forest near Spartakovka.

Spartakovka and Rynok were two small villages north of Stalingrad, separated from the city by the Orlovka Brook. The oak trees in the so-called 'forest' were still very young, only being about five metres tall. They'd already dropped most of their leaves. Nonetheless, the dug-out was well hidden from view. The entire area was about 100 x 400 metres in size and looked like a toothbrush. Sitting in the command post was a single officer, Leutnant Dr. Horst Hofmann. By profession, he was a court official in Plauen (Vogtland) and had been a platoon commander in 13. Infanteriegeschütze Kompanie until his transfer to the Regiment staff. The Regiment Adjutant, Oberleutnant Kelz, was still on home leave but was expected back any day. Until then, Leutnant Hofmann was holding the fort. I was to lend him a helping hand.

Hofmann and I would sleep in the same three square metre dug-out. I quickly stowed the few utensils that every infantryman carried. I was intending to read the mail that I picked up shortly before I left the baggage train during a quiet moment but Leutnant Hofmann entered the room and asked me to go and see the commander. The latter was already waiting for me, and after I'd reported myself 'present', he looked at me steadily and said, "My representative, Oberstleutnant Müller, has awarded you the Wound Badge in Gold for your seventh wound and injuries incurred by enemy action.

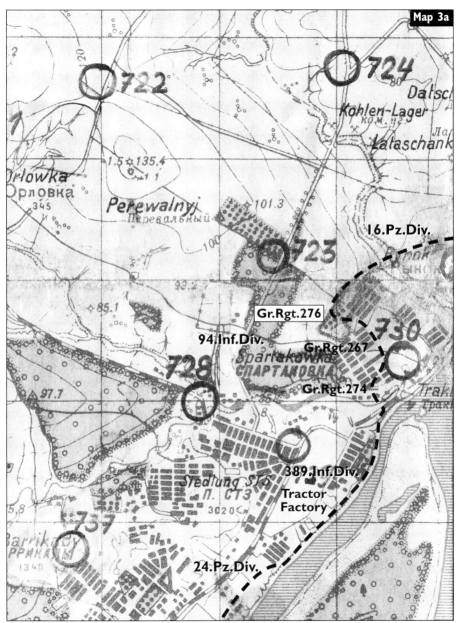

New operational area of Infanterie-Regiment 276. Oberst Grosse's regiment command post was in the rectangular forest north-west of Ref.Pt.723. 94. Infanterie-Division had been attacking Spartakovka since 19 October, and from that time until 28 October, had suffered casualties of 565 officers and men. Some of the hard-won gains would soon be lost to Soviet counterattacks.

He would have liked to personally present this award to you. The Regiment had no Wound Badges in Gold here, so it had to be requisitioned from Division. We received it yesterday, so I can now pin it on you. I wish you, dear Holl, continued soldier's luck and all the best."

I earnestly reciprocated his handshake. I was completely convinced that my destiny lay in the hands of a superior being, without which, we were all 'nothing'. It made no sense to imagine that you could cheat yourself out of responsibility by failing to do this or that. When the final moment is decided by the Lord, entreating or lamenting serves no purpose, so one must be prepared. The vow I had taken for Führer, Volk und Vaterland will always be sacred, especially since I took the oath voluntarily at 18 years of age.

That evening, I answered the mail from home. During the night, the engine noise of 'sewing machines' could again be heard.

> **Gen.Kdo. XIV. Pz.K.** – 1745 hours on 28. October 1942
>
> Assault groups of Gren.Rgt.276 still have a connection to the north wing of the assault regiments, have secured the northern flank and mopped up the shell–pocked terrain along the railway in the area of north–west corner grid square 54...

29 October 1942

29 October promised to be fine. The sun appeared in the east, and even though the nights were already cold, one could – as far as was possible – warm oneself a little in the sun's rays. My thoughts were often with my company.

On a survey near the dug-out, I discovered that there were small stray mines lying nearby and further into the forest. They were spherical in shape, about ten centimetres in diameter and had wire-like prongs protruding from them. When these wires were touched, the mine exploded and caused injuries. I reported my observation to the commander, who thereupon warned all units to look out for these dangerous 'things'.

While I viewed these 'things' with the necessary respect, an Obergefreiter from the regiment staff asked me: "Herr Leutnant, what are those?"

"They're small mines that Ivan dropped from his 'sewing-machines' last night."

"They're dangerous? They don't look it?"

"You bet they're dangerous! Give every one of these a wide berth. Everything that we don't recognise – and comes from 'Ivan' – is dangerous."

"Oh, it surely can't be as bad as that."

"I'm warning you: keep your paws off them!"

He walked away but didn't seem to be particularly convinced by my warning.

Around midday, the first Knight's Cross holder of our Regiment, Hauptmann Artur Rittner, Commander of III. Bataillon, appeared and reported to Oberst Grosse that he was departing for his 'Sonderurlaub'[6]. Rittner had performed particularly well in the fighting for southern Stalingrad. We were all happy for him. Hauptmann Rittner was a 'Zwölfender'[7] and received his training in the Reichswehr.

```
Armee-Oberkommando 6                A.H.Qu., den 4. November 1942.
        IIa
_____

                    Armee-Tagesbefehl Nr.40.
                    --------------------------

  1.) Verleihung des Ritterkreuzes des Eisernen Kreuzes:
              Der Führer und Oberste Befehlshaber der Wehrmacht ver-
              lieh das Ritterkreuz des Eisernen Kreuzes an:

                  Oberst      Barnbeck,        Kdr.G.R.211
                  Hptm        Rittner,         Fhr.III./G.R.276
                  Obfw.       Strauß,          10./G.R.267
                  Obfw.       Fleischer,       2./G.R.517
                  Obgefr.     Becker,          10./A.R.(mot) 3.
                                                            (IIa)

  2.) Verleihung des Deutschen Kreuzes in Gold:
              Das Deutsche Kreuz in Gold wurde verliehen an:

                  Major       Gießer,          Kdr. II./Pz.A.R.16
                  Major       Zinkel,          Kdr.III./Pz.A.R.16
                  Hptm.       Dobberkau,       Kdr.I./Pz.Rgt.2
                  Oblt.       Wedell,          II./Pz.A.R.16
                  Oblt.       Behrens,         Chef 1./G.R.518
                  Oblt.       Zunker,          II./G.R.120 (mot)
                  Oblt.       Friedrich,       II./Pz.Rgt.2
                  Oblt.       v.Mutius,        Chef 7./Pz.G.R.64
                  Oblt.       Behne,           Chef 4./Kr.Sch.Btl.53
                  Lt.         Seyffert,        Fhr.2./Pz.Jg.Abt.389
                  Lt.         Graf Ledebur,    Adj.I./Pz.Rgt.2
                  Obfw.       Friemelt,        2./Kr.Sch.Btl.160
                  Obfw.       Wolfshausen,     3./Kr.Sch.Btl.160
                  Obfw.       Hendess,         10./G.R.132
                  Feldw.      Wollmar,         2./G.R.518
                  Wachtm.     Winter,          2./A.R.295
                  Uffz.       Koellmann,       11./G.R.194.
                                                            (IIa)
```

6. Armee Order of the Day Nr. 40 from 4 November 1942 announcing the names of soldiers who have recently been awarded the Knight's Cross or the German Cross in Gold. Hauptmann Rittner is second in the list of Knight's Cross recipients.

6. Sonderurlaub - 'special leave', in this case awarded to recipients of the Knight's Cross.

7. Zwölfender - A career soldier who signed up for 12 years service.

My instructors, in part, had also previously served in the Reichswehr, for example, my first company commander. Without the cadre of the Reichswehr, our leaders could not have built up the Wehrmacht in such a short space of time.

When Hauptmann Rittner left on home leave, he took with him all the mail for the homeland that he would post in Breslau. We thought we could save a few days on the transport of the letters. There was more happy news. My old, revered commander, Major Dr. Zimmermann, had been awarded the German Cross in Gold. He was still in the homeland on convalescent leave.

The days were constantly getting shorter. Daylight had to be utilised for the clerical work that piled up in every staff, otherwise the Hindenburg lamps had to be endured. We were also given several captured petroleum lamps.

6. Armee Order of the Day Nr. 39 from 28 October 1942 announcing the names of soldiers who have recently been awarded the German Cross in Gold. Major Zimmermann is seventh from the top.

30 October 1942

On 30 October, we received a delegation from the neighbouring regiment of 16. Panzer-Division. It was the commander of Panzergrenadier-Regiment 79, Oberst Reinisch[8], with his adjutant, Oberleutnant Brendgen[9]. Accompanying them were several other gentlemen. Panzergrenadier-Regiment 79 had also seen heavy fighting and had – like us – suffered heavy losses. Now they were our left neighbour. With the exception of the two colonels, they were fellow landsfolk of mine from the Rhineland and Westphalia. The familiar tones from the homeland were like music to my ears. The main topic of conversation between the colonels was the situation in the front-line sectors of both regiments and how difficult it had been up to this point to gain ground in the direction of Rynok and Spartakovka to the Volga. Oberst Reinisch believed this sector could be called 'little Verdun' as there was hardly a square metre that had not been churned up by bombs and shells. In addition, he added that this fact made it impossible to deploy panzers in this area. Enemy resistance here was still unbroken.

It was interesting to meet both regiment commanders. Oberst Reinisch came from Steiermark and had an obliging manner. My commander, Oberst Grosse, was not much different. For me, these two were 'cavalrymen of the old school' from whom I could only learn. We were invited by our guests to return the visit, assuming that the general situation allowed it. Oberst Grosse said he'd be delighted. He later said to us: "It's always good to become personally acquainted with comrades from the other units. It's important for later possible operations." I could only agree with him.

31 October 1942

October was almost at an end. Still the fighting raged in the city. There were barely any advances being made. We were too weak in manpower to be employed there again. There was only enough of us to hold the positions here in this quiet sector.

Six weeks earlier, at the mouth of the Tsaritsa, when we were making almost regular headway, I wrote to my wife: "…there can only be a few more days and we will have taken Stalingrad."

Now winter was almost upon us. Fresh troops had to be brought forward if the rest of the city was to be conquered. The morale of the men was high and we all had complete confidence in our leadership.

A call from Division notified us of a visit by General Pfeiffer. He had been with our Division since the fatal accident of our first Division Commander, General der

---

8. *Oberst Johann (Hans) Reinisch. Born 12 November 1896 in Stallahofen; captured at Stalingrad on 2 February 1943; died 22 January 1948 in Soviet captivity.*

9. *Oberleutnant Dr. Franz Brendgen. Born 3 September 1916 in Rheydt; German Cross in Gold on 6 November 1942; captured at Stalingrad on 2 February 1943; died April 2000.*

Infanterie Volkmann[10]. I was ordered to report to the commander. Oberst Grosse reciprocated my greetings and said with a smile: "The Regiment must designate an officer for a company commander training course at Berlin-Döberitz[11]. The course runs from 6 December 1942 until 16 January 1943. From 22 December 1942 to 2 January 1943, the participant will receive Christmas leave. The Regiment has forwarded your name. It's in recognition of your service. I know that you've already completed such a training course within the Division framework in Oberlausitz in the autumn of 1940[12]. However, this new course is sponsored by the OKH[13] and will be of use in your personal development. Further to this, if you can deliver three lectures during the course, then an additional five days of special leave can be taken."

I could not quite take in what I was hearing, and even had a nonplussed expression on my face, which amused my commander. Leutnant Hofmann had already been informed and congratulated me on the detachment.

A messenger appeared and breathlessly reported to us: "Outside in the forest – about 100 metres from here – Obergefreiter Kornek has been torn apart by a mine!" Fearing the worst, I went out to the scene. My fears had been realised: it was the same fellow who had taken such an interest the day before yesterday in those damn mines, even though I had forcefully pointed out the danger they represented. This tragic accident must absolutely be signalled to all units! The men at the front were essentially more cautious.

The Division Commander arrived shortly before 1300 hours. He was accompanied by our regiment adjutant, who'd just returned from home leave. After our Regiment Commander reported to the General, both gentlemen – with their adjutants – went into the command post. Leutnant Hofmann and I were invited to come along. The current situation was discussed on a map. The General said to us that the strength of the companies was increasing in every regiment because convalescents were continually being discharged from the hospitals to the troops. However, he was also of the opinion that these were too few in number and that a fresh intake from the homeland was expected.

Before the General climbed into the Kübelwagen, he called me over to him.

"Holl, you'll soon be leaving for this training course at Döberitz. Before you set off,

---

10. *General der Infanterie Helmuth Volkmann. Born 28 February 1889 in Diedenhofen; commanded 94. Infanterie-Division from 13 September 1939 until he was severely injured in a motor vehicle accident on 4 August 1940; died of his wounds on 21 August 1940 in hospital in Berlin-Gatow.*

11. *Other divisions in 6. Armee were also asked to send officers to attend this training course.*

12. *This company commander's training course within Inf.Rgt.276 ran from 18 October 1940 until 30 November 1940. Holl had already participated in a training course (3. Offizier-Anwärter-Lehrgang – the 3rd Officer Candidate Training Course) at the Infanterieschule in Berlin-Döberitz from 5 February 1940 until 3 May 1940. See Appendix 1 (page 240-1) for his 'performance report' from this course.*

13. OKH - *'Oberkommando des Heeres', Army High Command.*

come and see me. My family lives in Potsdam and I'd like you to personally go there and give them a letter from me."

I blurted out only too gladly: "Jawohl, Herr General!"

I still couldn't quite believe it: in five weeks, I would be in Berlin, and in just seven weeks, with my loved ones at home. It was hard to take in!

Leutnant Hofmann informed me that following soon after Major Weigert, his adjutant – my friend Joachim Schüler – was also sick and in hospital. Hopefully it was not serious.

1 November 1942

November began with good weather. The nights were getting colder but it was sunny and clear during the day.

Through the arrivals in the past days, both battalions each now had the combat strength of a rifle company. Of course, that was still far too few but we were glad of every man who reported back. Officers that had registered their arrival with Regiment included Leutnant Pilz[14] – a Berliner – and Leutnant Baumann – a Bavarian. Many old familiar faces were among the returning convalescents. They were predominantly men from Upper and Lower Silesia, who still formed the backbone of our Regiment, even if individuals from other regions of the Fatherland were also being posted to this almost originally pure Silesian regiment. Everyone knew the seriousness of the situation. Everyone would have sooner been at home in a friendly homeland, and yet, they were all carrying out their duty in an exemplary fashion. Many of them were ill with jaundice and had to be in hospital. Dr. Szczepanski put it down to the monotony of the diet, which had been in place since crossing the Don. There was only a single track to Kalach over which our army was supplied, creating difficulties with the supply of various foodstuffs. The consequence of this was an increase in cases of jaundice, an illness which had previously occurred only rarely among the troops.

2 November 1942

Today, on 2 November, another fine day, we returned the visit of our left neighbour. With our commander, we – the adjutant Oberleutnant Kelz and I – drove to the command post of Panzergrenadier-Regiment 79. We were warmly welcomed by Herr Oberst Reinisch and the members of his staff. We stayed there for lunch and were invited to eat. Even here there was no extra wurst, but when you were hungry, the dried vegetable soup – appropriately called 'wire entanglement' by the soldiers – tasted

---

14. *Leutnant Herbert Pilz. Born 23 December 1919 in Dortmund-Mengede; died 6 December 1942 in Orlovka, Stalingrad.*

```
94. I.D.

a)  Verpflegungsstärke                                    7 469      100%

        dazu: Hilfswillige                     2581

b)  Gefechtsstärke:

            Inf.                               1209
            Art.                                998
            .i.Btl.                             525
            Pz.Jg.Bt.                           129
            Pidf.Bt.                             86
            Nachr.Bt.                           177
                                          ─────────────
            Gesamtgefechtsstärke:                          2 924      38%

c)  Nicht zur Gef.stärke zählen:                           4 545      62%

    davon Div.Stab                             214
          Ausbildungs-btl. 94/2                952
          Versorgungstruppen                  1180                    16%
      bei Kampfeinheiten                       2199                    29%

        Gesundheitszimmer-Pers.       208
        Fahrer, Pferdepfl. u.
                Beschlags-Pers.        996
        Waffen-Pers.                   105
        Gerät-Pers.                     69
        Kraftf. u. techn.Pers.         156
        Vers.- u. Verpfl.Pers., Handw. 431
        Nachr.Pers.                      9
        Tr.San.Pers.                    51
        Kranke                         174
                                    ─────────
        Summe:                        2199
```

A combat strength report of 94. Infanterie-Division submitted to 6. Armee on 13 November 1942. Ration strength (Verpflegungsstärke) was 7469 men, plus 2581 'Hilfswillige' (Soviet ex-POW volunteers in the German Army, usually in non-combat roles). Total combat strength was only 2924 men, barely 39% of the total ration strength (excluding Hilfswillige). The breakdown of the 4545 men not counted in the combat strength was as follows: Division staff = 214 men; training battalion 94/2 = 952 men; supply troops = 1180 men.
Non-combat personnel near the combat units:
Office personnel = 208 men; drivers (of horse-drawn vehicles), stablehands and farriers = 996 men; armoury personnel = 105 men; ordnance personnel = 69 men; drivers and technical personnel = 156 men; supply and rations personnel, craftsmen (tailors, shoemakers, etc.) = 431 men; communications personnel = 9 men; medical personnel = 51 men; sick men = 174; a total of 2199 men, or 29% of the total ration strength.

good. The main topics of conversation were again the broader general situation of Stalingrad and our concerns, namely that the enemy still occupied the villages of Rynok and Spartakovka. Oberst Reinisch also told us that the panzer units of 16. Panzer-Division were constantly in action as 'fire brigades'.

I used the opportunity to contact a distant cousin, who commanded a communications platoon in I. Bataillon. We had never seen each other but decided to make up for it as soon as possible.

It was already dark when we returned to our command post around 1500 hours. It had been quiet on the front-line during the day.

Nothing much happened on 3 and 4 November. I would like to say it's a small world. Shortly before dark, there appeared at our staff a PK[15] reporter with the job of taking photographs of front-line scenes and writing the corresponding reports. You can apparently take damn good photos in darkness. The reporter introduced himself as 'Gehrmann'. Later, sitting in my dug-out, I struck up a conversation with him. I could tell by his accent that he was Rhineländer.

I asked: "Herr Gehrmann, I can hear you're from the Rhineland. What city do you come from?"

"I'm from Duisburg."

"Me too! Strictly speaking, I come from Duisburg-Laar and know a Hermann Gehrmann there. When he was a boy, he had a serious bicycle accident"

"I know him, he's my brother!"

"Well, why don't I know you then?"

"Herr Holl, I'm twelve years older than my brother and had already been away from home for more than ten years. Now I'm a Wahl-Berliner."

We spoke for a long time about our home town and common acquaintances. It remained quiet in our sector, my compatriot snapping off several photographs the next morning before leaving.

6 November 1942

I had been on the move with Oberst Grosse since 0300 hours. We visited the most forward positions. My 'seventh' was also there. Leutnant Augst had made his affairs neat and tidy. I was happy when my Upper Silesians asked me: "Herr Leitnant, when are you coming back to the Kompanie?" My commander heard it and grinned. The weather was misty and it was drizzling. When we returned toward 1430 hours, my Oberst and I were tired and worn out.

15. _PK_ - _Propaganda-Kompanie._

It was cold during the night. The fine-weather period appeared to be over. It was at least better to be dry and cold than wet. If we were to see out the winter here, then heating material would become a large problem. The Regiment was urgently requesting winter clothing, as well as white camouflage, from Division. They should avoid getting them too late to supply our men. Soon, the first snowfalls would arrive; by then, at least the forward units must have camouflage clothing. Up to now, our troops had the normal equipment (2 pair of underwear; 2 pair of socks; 2 pair of foot-cloths; 1 pullover; trousers; jacket; cap; 1 pair of gloves; steel helmet; overcoat; 1 set of denims, 1 Zeltbahn; 1 bread-bag with canteen and cooking utensils; 1 pair of half-length leather boots, also known as 'Knobelbecher'[16]. Yet, for the icy Russian winter with its cruel, pitiless cold, even this kit was insufficient. The winter clothing consisted of a pair of quilted cotton trousers and a similar cotton jacket. Both pieces of clothing were reversible and could be worn over the other uniform, so in winter – with its snow – the white side was outward, and once the snow had melted, it was worn the other way with the camouflage colours on the outside. In addition to that, there was also felt boots.

Winter clothing was nothing new for the Russians. They'd so often had the advantage over us because of their warm clothing. Our camouflage clothing for the snow was

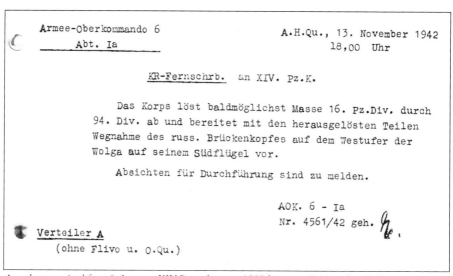

An order transmitted from 6. Armee to XIV. Panzerkorps at 1800 hours on 13 November 1942:

"Korps will replace the bulk of 16. Panzer-Division with 94. Infanterie-Division as soon as possible and with those relieved units prepare to capture on its southern flank the Russian bridgehead on the west bank of the Volga."

"Intentions for the implementation of this will be reported."

16. Knobelbecher - 'dice-cups', soldiers' slang for army boots.

makeshift. It comprised a white cloth with a hole cut for the head and two slits for the arms. They were designed to prevent the troops from being easily spotted in the snow.

The weather was changing. It was cold and very windy. It had rained the previous day and it was very slippery outside. It made life difficult for our supply vehicles bringing up the rations. It also rendered fighting in the front-line more difficult. The entire regiment staff made great efforts to procure winter clothing for the men at the front.

15 November 1942

I heard that the Americans and English had landed in North Africa but I did not have time to muse over these wider questions; other matters now pressed upon us. Hauptfeldwebel Michel appeared and reported that he was heading off for home leave. He honestly deserved it because as a single man, he had repeatedly foregone his leave in favour of family men. Now, it had been almost 18 months since he'd been home. I wished him all the best and a safe return to the troops. Feldwebel Cupal would be standing in for him. He was a Sudeten German and had already served with the Czech Army.

The mail from home brought me sad news: several friends and former childhood acquaintances had been killed or lost at sea when their U-Boat had gone down while on combat patrol.

My commander told me that I would leave on 25 November in order to arrive in time for the company commander training course. That was still ten days away.

16 November 1942

Gen.Kdo. XIV. Pz.K. – 0540 hours on 16. November 1942

> Regrouping and change of command between 16.PD and 94.ID on the Volga and north front sectors continues as scheduled...

We again drove to Panzergrenadier-Regiment 79. It was 16 November. At Oberst Reinisch's command post, an attack on the suburbs of Rynok and Spartakovka was being discussed. Both of our regiments were detailed to carry out this attack alongside each other. It was to be a surprise assault. We couldn't count on panzer support because the terrain did not permit such operations[17]. Besides, these were once again in action as a 'fire-brigade'. The beginning of the assault was fixed for the morning of 17 November. The artillery of 16. Panzer-Division would support us. As Panzergrenadier-Regiment 79 had also risen in strength in the past weeks due to returning convalescents, Korps believed we were in a position to take both suburbs.

---

17. *For their attack on Rynok, 16. Panzer-Division managed to assemble 25 repaired panzers under the command of Rittmeister Konstantin Graf Furst zu Dohna-Schlobitten.*

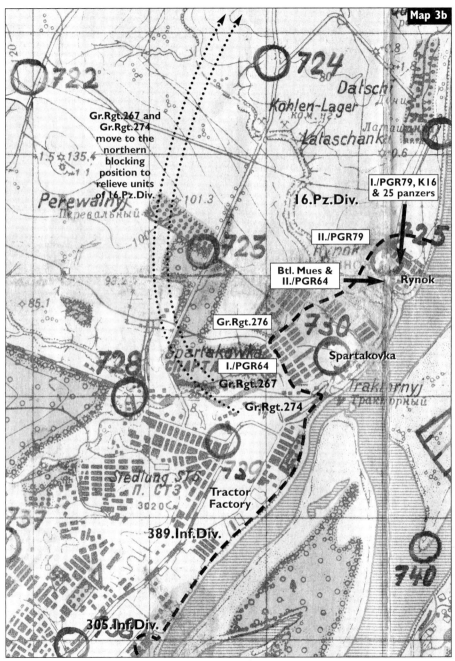

Progress of the attack on Rynok and Spartakovka, 17 November 1942.

Gen.Kdo. XIV. Pz.K. — 1600 hours on 16. November 1942

    3.ID and 94.ID relieved 16.PD along the Volga and northern front for the attack on Rynok...

17 November 1942

The hours before the beginning of the assault meant none of us could get any rest. Orders had to be transmitted. Where this was not possible by telephone, they were delivered in writing by a messenger. In vitally important matters, an officer had to be present at the battalion staffs.

Before it had been noticed, the hours had flown by. And then once again came the final hour prior to launching the assault. You thought: would it succeed this time? Could we surprise the enemy? – Questions and doubts which could only be answered later.

Several days earlier, both our sister regiments, Grenadier-Regiment 267 and Grenadier-Regiment 274, had moved into position in the northern blocking line that stretched from the Don to the Volga[18] with a front-line generally facing northward. We were also designated to spend the winter in this blocking position. Nevertheless, it still had not come to that point. First of all, we had to carry out this attack.

As I was commander of 7. Kompanie – curiously ordered to regiment staff on a six week detachment – my thoughts naturally turned to the men in my company. As so often in the past weeks, they were once again facing a difficult assignment. Silesians and Upper Silesians were about to carry out this attack together with my fellow countrymen from Rhineland-Westphal: the rest of the assault force comprised a regiment each from 24. Panzer-Division[19] and 16. Panzer-Division[20], two divisions whose men up to this point in the war – and in their own areas – had proven themselves.

I – a small cog in this large machine, who had only been trained in tactics and knew little about strategic matters – had doubts as to whether this assault would be successful[21]. When one goes from holding positions over to the offensive, a considerable numerical superiority must be available or one's own heavy weapons must be employed to keep the enemy down in his positions until the breakthrough. I didn't believe we had numerical superiority. I didn't know whether the heavy weapons assigned for the assault could keep the enemy down. The terrain was unsuitable for support by panzers; moreover, they were not currently available.

---

18. *As per the order shown on page 140.*
19. *There is no record that any units of 24. Panzer-Division participated in this attack.*
20. *Both panzergrenadier regiments (64 and 79) of 16. Panzer-Division took part, as did Kradschützen-Btl. 16, elements of Panzerpionier-Btl. 16 and the 25 panzers of Panzer-Regiment 2.*
21. *Holl wasn't the only one to have doubts about this attack. Several officers of 16. Panzer-Division also did not see any sense in the operation.*

When we heard the first sounds of battle to the north of us, we knew that the 'dance' had begun. For me, it was an unaccustomed feeling: previously, I had been directly involved in the fighting with my men. In this way, you were completely focused on the fighting and often forgot the time.

Now, for the first time, I was on a staff: a participant with entirely different duties for whom time literally crawled. I noticed that our commander, Oberst Grosse, was plagued by doubts as to whether everything was progressing well. He knew our overall situation better than we did and had also made his objections known about what the attack entailed. Ultimately, however, we were soldiers who had to obey and carry out orders. The combat effectiveness of every army stands or falls with obedience and confidence in the command.

Around midday, we received the first reports about the course of the fighting: the attack had stalled after gaining barely 200 metres of ground. Our heavy weapons hadn't succeeded in keeping the enemy down. His defensive fire had inflicted considerable casualties on both regiments, including several dead[22].

> **Gen.Kdo. XIV. Pz.K.** – 1625 hours on 17. November 1942
>
> Along the eastern front of Korps, 16.PD attacked the village of Rynok from the north and west with 2 Kampfgruppen (combat groups). Both groups initially succeeded in penetrating into the village. Poor visibility and heavy defensive fire prevented both combat groups from making contact with one another. A Russian counterattack, supported by 4 tanks, forced the combat groups to withdraw from the northern and western edge of the village. Strong anti-tank and tank fire, as well as mines, caused numerous losses amongst our own panzers... After regrouping, the Div. renewed the attack around 1300 hours. Combat is still in progress...

There was a violent exchange of artillery and mortars currently in progress which meant little progress was possible. I was ordered by my commander to go with a messenger to the staffs of II. and III. Battalion. For Hauptmann Israel, and also Oberleutnant Krause[23], substituting for Hauptmann Rittner, the situation was extremely precarious. Both battalions had no reserves and every casualty amounted to a real weakening of combat strength.

---

22. *Casualties of 16.Pz.-Div.: 4 Offz and 15 Uffz & men killed; 8 Offz and 95 Uffz & men wounded; 2 Offz missing in action; 3 Uffz & men sick*
    Casualties of 94.Inf.-Div.: 2 Uffz & men wounded
    As can be seen from these casualty figures, 94.Inf.-Div. did not suffer greatly on this day. Records seem to indicate that the Division did not take part in this attack on 17 November 1942. It is likely that Holl has confused it with an attack made by his Division against Spartakovka on 8 and 9 November 1942.
23. *Oberleutnant Krause commanded 13./Inf.Rgt.276 until he was wounded in July 1942.*

Oberleutnant Krause said in his East Prussian dialect: "If this continues, in the end, we'll have to fight with our lads from the supply train."

Secretly, I had to agree with him.

When I returned to the Regiment staff, I filed my reports with Oberst Grosse and learned that our neighbouring regiment had also suffered heavy casualties and found themselves in a similar situation to us. In the meantime, darkness was closing in and the sounds of battle were dying away. Our men had their hands full, carrying our wounded and dead and ensuring that the enemy could not carry out a counterattack. 'Ivan' laid mines in front of his line, which naturally made our men uncertain.

AOK.6. – 1840 hours on 17. November 1942

Aim: Continuation of the attack against Rynok, with the objective of taking the village and bank of the Volga into possession on 18.11...

18 November 1942

18 November also brought no change to the situation. The attack was hopelessly mired and could not be resumed without reinforcements. What the men in the forward line had to perform almost bordered on the superhuman. Most of them still lacked winter clothing. In other words, they had to make do with their normal kit. They squatted in fox-holes in front of the enemy with only their Zeltbahne as protection against the damp and cold. There, the hours were an eternity. Many of them emerged from battle with parts of their uniforms shredded and then still said laconically: "Never mind. Better the rags than my bones!"

I knew from experience and completely understood the men. And I was sure about one thing: everything we experienced would later be paid for with our health – if we were lucky enough to survive the war at all.

CHAPTER 4

18 November 1942

On the evening of 18 November, the following order came through: "Withdraw to the starting positions in the night of 19 November." An unsuccessful operation with high casualties for our side was finished.

Over the next three days, we were occupied with filling the gaps that the casualties had created amongst our combatants. Anyone who could be spared from the staffs had to go to the front.

We learned from Division that the Russians north-west of us had launched an attack against the Rumanians and broken through along a wide front. This was repeated on 20 November in the south. On 21 November, the Regiment learned that the enemy spearheads had met near Kalach-on-Don, encircling our 6. Armee. Initially, it was a shock for all of us. How could something like this happen? Had those at the top fallen asleep? Were there no German units supporting our Allied troops? We could find no answers to that.

I was convinced that this Kessel[1] wouldn't last long. Our command wasn't born yesterday and would soon break the encirclement.

Still, we had to see to it that the front was held in our sector. The northern blocking position had been solidly constructed since the thrust from the Don to the Volga. The enemy had finally halted his unsuccessful attacks. We had to improve and further strengthen our positions in our sector. As far as what they were doing west of us on the Don, we had no influence here.

23 November 1942

Towards midday on 23 November, we received the order that every serviceable lorry and motor vehicle, with the available petrol, should prepare for a break-out in a south-westerly direction. A further inquiry by Oberst Grosse to Division revealed that this order was given by General von Seydlitz, commanding LI. Armeekorps, to which we belonged. All important documents would be burnt. What could not be taken with us would be prepared for destruction. Only the necessities would be taken along, above all, ammunition.

---

1. _Kessel_ - literally 'cauldron', but in military terminology it means 'an encircled area or pocket'.

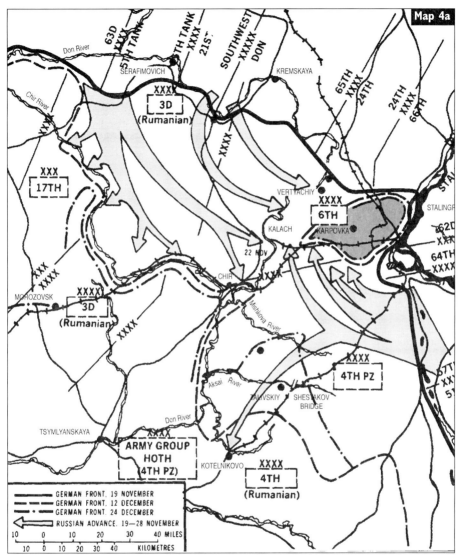

The Soviet counteroffensive that surrounded Stalingrad, 19-23 November 1942. On 19 November 1942 the Red
Army unleashed Operation Uranus. The attacking Soviet units consisted of three complete armies; the 1st Guard,
5th Tank and 21st Army: a total of 18 rifle divisions, eight tank brigades, two motorised brigades, six cavalry
divisions and one anti-tank brigade. Outnumbered and poorly equipped, the Rumanian 3. Armee, which held 6.
Armee's northern flank, was shattered after managing to hold on for most of the day.

On 20 November, a second Soviet offensive was launched to the south of Stalingrad against points held by the
Rumanian 4. Armee. The army, consisting primarily of cavalry units, collapsed almost immediately. Soviet forces raced
west, the tips of the two pincers meeting two days later near the town of Kalach-on-Don, sealing the ring around
Stalingrad. Roughly 300,000 German and allied troops found themselves trapped inside the resulting pocket.

Fortunately, a dry cold prevailed. I was not at all happy at the prospect of having to fall back. With what energy and offensive elan had we foot-soldiers fought forward to this point, and with what casualties! And now back?

My comrades – as far as I'd been able to speak to them – were of the same opinion. We didn't like the idea. And lastly, we had to cover the retreat – even though we still had unsatisfactory winter equipment. On top of all that, the bread ration for the entire Kessel was cut to 200 grams, which meant few full stomachs and hunger. Yet, in the cold, our bodies required a higher calorie intake. Nevertheless: orders were orders! We prepared everything, as ordered. We completed the preparations for the destruction of unnecessary items, as well as documents, and were now awaiting further orders. Thoughts were now totally focused on the break-out. It would be a hard and costly affair: of that, we were all sure[2].

24 November 1942

We barely found time for a short nap during the night of 23/24 November. At most, all we managed was a brief snooze. The nervous strain was great. Even Oberst Grosse joined in our conversations. We talked about everything and nothing just to pass the time spent waiting. From time to time, the commander or Oberleutnant Kelz made inquiries over the field-line in an attempt to learn whether anything had happened. Around midnight, the Oberst informed us about his inquiries: "The units in the northern blocking positions are in the process of withdrawing. Hopefully, they'll succeed unnoticed" – For us, however, it meant more waiting.

Did anyone understand what was going on! Yesterday, we were ordered to prepare to break out. And now – shortly before midday – they said to us: Break-out cancelled! Everyone to stay put![3]

---

2. *Generaloberst Friedrich Paulus, Commander-in-Chief of 6. Armee, had made repeated requests to Hitler for freedom of action. Paulus' main intention was to form a perimeter around Stalingrad, but if a front could not be constructed to the south, the only solution would be to withdraw from Stalingrad. To do this, the northern front would be given up, the army would pull together and then break out to the south-west toward 4. Panzerarmee. Paulus waited in vain throughout 23 November for a decision from Hitler. General der Artillerie Walter von Seydlitz-Kurzbach, Commanding General of LI. Armeekorps, had already concluded that a break-out was inevitable and issued an order to his divisions in the north-eastern corner of the pocket to prepare to pull back. A prerequisite for this withdrawal was the destruction of all superfluous material. Unfortunately for historians, this included all the Division's paperwork, such as war diaries, journals, orders etc.*

3. *The withdrawal of 94. Inf.-Div. turned into a minor debacle. When the Soviet soldiers noticed that a withdrawal was taking place, they immediately moved forward and attacked the retreating German soldiers. The casualties that resulted from this were very high and included many irreplaceable soldiers who had survived the previous three months of combat in Stalingrad. The exact number of casualties has not been recorded in available documents but several officers were killed and wounded while close to 200 men became casualties. These were losses the severely weakened Division simply could not afford.*

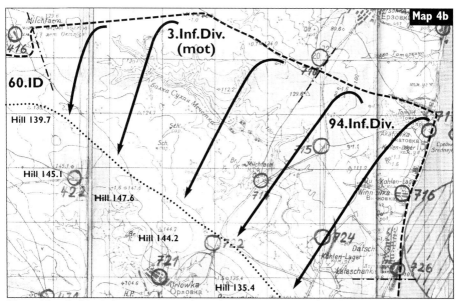

The withdrawal of 94. Infanterie-Division and 3. Infanterie-Division (mot.) from the north-eastern corner of the Stalingrad pocket. A new defensive line was set up along a railway that passed in front of a chain of dominating hills.

Were those 'up above' quite mad?[4] We were surrounded by the enemy and not on an exercise ground! There, one could 'do this' one moment and 'do that' the next, but not here, where every square metre that we'd moved forward had been paid for with our blood.

How did it look in the northern blocking position? Would our comrades be able to re-occupy it? It was fortunate that nothing had yet gone up in flames. Had 'Ivan' noticed the retreat movements? And how did he react to them? One thing was clear to all of us: without the break-out to the south-west, the coming days would be difficult if we did not succeed in winning back the northern blocking positions.[5]

The next day, I had been due to head west, having already dreamt of the homeland. Subconsciously, however, I had had doubts: it would only come about when I actually

4. *The next morning, when Hitler heard about the withdrawal, he demanded a full report and forbade any further retreats. It was explained to Hitler that the troops had been taken back to prepared positions and in this way, a division had been gained for employment elsewhere. Hitler was not convinced and, suspecting that Paulus was behind the withdrawal, gave von Seydlitz – the man who was actually responsible – command of the northern front of the Kessel!*

5. *The withdrawal placed 94. Infanterie-Division into an unfavourable tactical situation. Its former positions in the northern blocking position were well-constructed, comfortable and easily able to withstand the heaviest Soviet attack. The new positions were basically just a line drawn in the snow. In addition to the great loss of men and materiel, the new situation now forced Paulus to withdraw additional forces from other weak sectors of the Kessel to reinforce the northern front – exactly the opposite of what had been reported to Hitler.*

got there. – Now farewell, you beautiful dream. Reality looked different: everyone was to remain where they were!

In the meantime, we learned from Division that the units from the northern blocking position had been pulled back up to four kilometres in some places.

The enemy had already moved forward about three kilometres to the railway line that ran from Barrikady through Spartakovka to Gumrak and was one and a half kilometres north of our Regiment command post. The order for us: highest alarm readiness! This also applied to the rear echelons, like staffs, baggage trains, supply companies etc. These were insignificant distances for tanks provided they had broken through. Until the general situation became completely clear, we all had to be on our guard. Nevertheless, we breathed easier because we were convinced that we would be freed from outside.

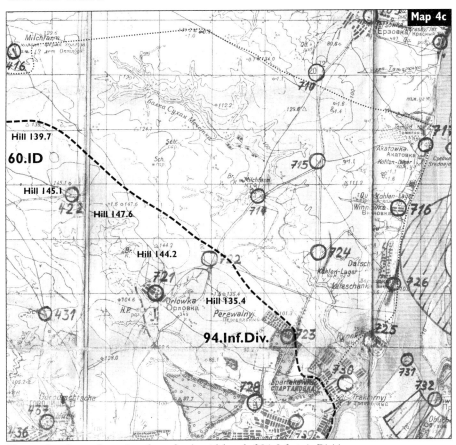

The new front-line on the northern front after the withdrawal of 94. Infanterie-Division.

25 November 1942

The situation was still unclear in our sector on 25 and 26 November. The units that had pulled out of the northern defensive line – as ordered – were endeavouring to construct a new front-line along the single-track railway line north of our command post. Amongst those units was Grenadier-Regiment 276. Fortunately, the Russians only followed up hesitantly; they had not recognised what was happening. Why should they, when we were voluntarily giving up a well-constructed position in winter which had resisted every enemy attack over the past months.

Grenadier-Regiment 274 lay in the Tractor Factory with their front facing Spartakovka and hadn't been required to take part in the withdrawals. After a short stay in hospital, my friend Joachim Schüler was transferred as regiment adjutant to Grenadier–Regiment 274, whose commander was Oberst Brendel[6].

<u>Gen.Kdo. LI. A.K.</u> – 1745 hours on 25. November 1942

At daybreak, 94.ID was attacked on a broad front by enemy infantry escorted by individual tanks. Trying to widen the breakthrough point they achieved yesterday, the enemy – moving down the Erzovka road north of Spartakovka – captured the orchard and later the forested area south of there. The enemy pushed to the north–west, behind our infantry holding out along the railway line, and captured Hill 135.4... The immediately implemented countermeasures were successful, with Hill 135.4 being recaptured... Fighting has not yet ended there.
<u>Aim for 26.11.</u>: Resolution of the situation near 94.ID. For this, the remaining elements of 24.PD with Gruppe Scheele will go into action on the right wing of 94.ID.
<u>Casualties on 25.11.</u>:
94.Inf.Div.: Killed – 1 Offz, 15 Uffz and men   (incomplete
            Wounded – 1 Offz, 28 Uffz and men   report)

- -

<u>Gen.Kdo. LI. A.K.</u> – 0700 hours on 26. November 1942

Relief of employed elements of 94.ID south–east of Hill 135.4 by Gruppe Scheele has been smoothly carried out... On the Erzovka road, two T–34s were destroyed by 94.ID.
<u>Casualties on 26.11.</u>:
94.Inf.Div.: Killed – 1 Offz, 51 Uffz and men   (incomplete
            Wounded – 3 Offz, 128 Uffz and men   report)

---

6. *Oberst Albert Alfred Oscar Brendel. Born 8 December 1893 in Sonnefeld; Knight's Cross on 20 January 1943; captured 2 February 1943 in Stalingrad; died 16 April 1943 in Frolov POW camp.*

27 November 1942

Oberleutnant Kelz informed me that my promotion to Oberleutnant had finally arrived at Regiment[7]. It was only valid once it was published in the Regiment's order of the day. On the same day – 27 November 1942 – my promotion to the rank of Oberleutnant together with a simultaneous appointment to Kompanie-Chef with effect from 1 July 1942 was announced. Everyone was happy for me, yet, it was neither the right time nor the right place for celebrations. Kelz was kind enough to give me two pips for the epaulettes of my uniform jacket.

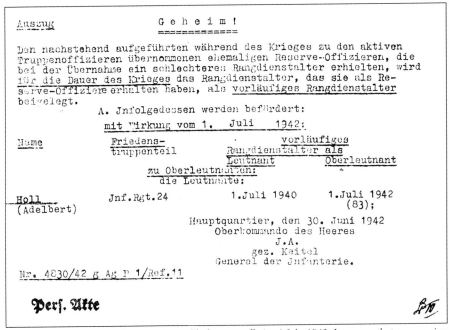

Confirmation of Adelbert Holl's promotion to Oberleutnant, effective 1 July 1942. It was exactly two years since he first became an officer.

<u>Gen.Kdo. LI. A.K.</u> – 27. November 1942

<u>Casualties on 27.11.:</u>
94.Inf.Div.: Killed – 7 Uffz and men
            Wounded – 38 Uffz and men
            Missing – 6 men

---

7. *This was due in large part to the request sent to Heerespersonalamt (Army Personnel Office) in Berlin on 13 October 1942 enquiring about the Rangdienstalter (seniority) of Leutnant Adelbert Holl. See page 103.*

28 November 1942

In the early morning hours – it was already light – an 'Alarm' was sounded! Outside the dug-outs, lively battle noises were heard coming from the north. In the meantime, the Russians had woken up to the fact that our troops had withdrawn from the north-east corner of the northern blocking position. They were attempting to break through the new front-line with tank support. In the first instance, they were attempting to take the area from Hill 135.4 to Hills 144.2 and 147.6. Following the course of the railway line in front of these prominent points was the front-line. If the enemy succeeded in taking only one of these hills, he could look into Stalingrad from the north. It would be a serious disadvantage for our troops. Our artillery and everything that could shoot was making strenuous efforts to repulse this attack. Nevertheless, there was an almighty great stink up front.

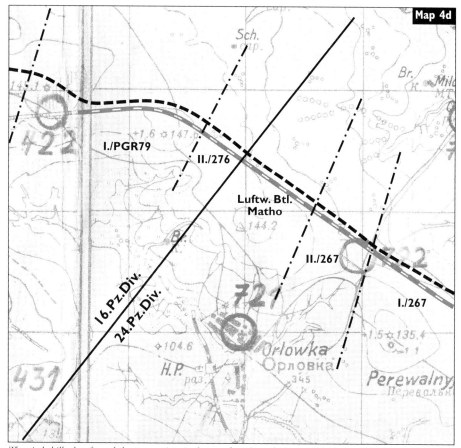

The vitals hills that formed the strongpoints in the new front-line of 16. and 24. Panzer-Divisions.

<u>Armee—Oberkommando 6.</u> — Morning report for 28. November 1942

    Renewed enemy attacks against the north—eastern front of
LI. Armeekorps. A penetration west of Rynok was straightened out by
24.PD. The enemy penetration near 147.6, which has a strength of
about two battalions and more than 6 tanks and has pushed forward to
the gully 2.5km north—west of Orlovka, has not yet been sealed off.
The elements of 16.PD that are arriving will be used to
counterattack...

Toward 1000 hours, two panzers appeared at the command post and requested instructions. Oberst Grosse gave me the order to personally direct the panzers. We sharpened up.

The main enemy objective appeared to be Hill 135.4. I ran as fast as my lungs would allow me. I had been a good long-distance runner as a boy. It now paid off. To the left of me I saw Orlovka. Now through the balka, up the opposite slope, and there it was, Hill 135.4. I stopped at the leading panzer, pointed out to the commander that he would have an overview of the battlefield behind the hill, and walked back on the return journey.

I now took my time. On the way here, every minute counted for my fighting comrades. I knew that a few panzers – even though it was only two – were in operation and they could have a breather. The first shots from the panzers were heard. Bravo boys, look after yourselves.

The ground was frozen, the weather was clear. Orlovka now lay on my right-hand side. It was still at least two kilometres away. My route headed in a southerly direction. I had already walked half way up a gently rising slope, where it levelled out for about 40 metres, then came to the last small ascent. Suddenly, hell broke loose around me! The Stalin Organs! When you'd experienced them almost once or twice a day, as I had in the past weeks in Barrikady, you knew from the roaring approach of the rockets what was happening. They came from the north, from the other side of the front-line. The first impacts struck the other side of the balka, roughly where I'd left both panzers. I looked around like a hunted animal. Not a scrap of cover was to be seen. There, a small hollow! It was about 40 centimetres wide and 10 centimetres deep. It was practically nothing! I had never tried to make myself so small before in my entire life. My legs were pressed close to the ground, face downwards, arms stretched out to the front. There was one explosion after another. I lay there unprotected, a helpless bundle of humanity submitting himself to this concentrated show of force produced by the hand of man. Rockets constantly exploded around me, one time here and the next time there. Would this never end? Shell splinters hissed through the air. I waited and didn't know whether I'd been dreaming. I lay still for several minutes – completely stunned by this 'morning blessing'. I was unable to say how many rockets there were. In such moments, you forget the numbers and just try to save your own skin. The constant exploding of shells were the seconds until eternity.

I finally composed myself and was totally amazed that I had not been injured. Were these shots meant for the two panzers or did 'Ivan' suspect we had troops here? I couldn't say.

<u>Gen.Kdo. LI. A.K.</u> — 1805 hours on 28. November 1942

Around 1100 hours, the enemy attacked along the entire north–eastern front, from the Erzovka road up to Hill 145.1 (422) with the focal point along the Erzovka–Orlovka road. The attack was repulsed by 24.PD; the enemy succeeded in breaking into the front–line south–west of 135.4 with 6 tanks that were subsequently forced to turn away. At 1500 hours, the enemy attack against Hill 145.1 was renewed with 7 tanks. The enemy took the hill and pushed over the railway to the south. Hill 147.6 is in our hands. 16.PD, which is moving into the sector, will be used to counterattack...

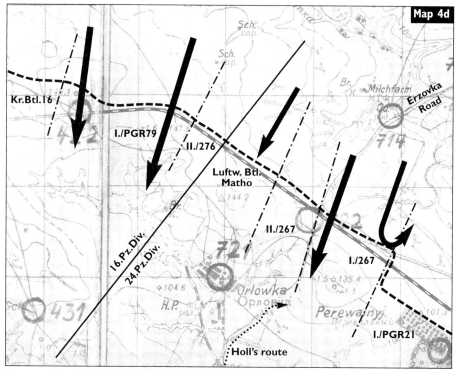

Enemy attacks on 28 November 1942.

By the time I'd arrived at the Regiment command post, I had recovered from the shock. Oberst Grosse was anxiously walking back and forth in front of his dug-out. He was awaiting my return. He had heard the rocket barrage because it came down only one kilometre from our command post.

I said: "Oberleutnant Holl reporting back. Panzers assigned as ordered."

My commander asked: "Can anything be seen here?"

I answered: "Nein, Herr Oberst, but you could get hit quite easily here. A few minutes ago I was caught without cover in a rocket barrage and am still amazed that I've come out of it in one piece. I request, Herr Oberst, that we go into the dug-out."

"You go, Holl, I'm going to stay out here for a while."

I had just gone down the six steps that led into the dug-out and closed the door when there was a booming noise outside. The door was blown off by the air pressure. One of the 'stove-pipes' from a Stalin Organ had exploded right in front of the dug-out; more impacts followed, more or less widely scattered. After it stopped, a man burst into the dug-out: "The Commander's wounded!"

Kelz, Hofmann and I looked at each other, startled. That was all we needed! Oberst Grosse was carried in by two men and placed on a plank-bed. He groaned in great pain, which he tried to suppress. A large chunk of shrapnel had penetrated his abdomen. The regimental doctor was immediately fetched. I was furious at my helplessness. There was nothing I could do and I said reproachfully to the wounded man: "Why did Herr Oberst not listen to my advice?"

Tormented by pain, my Commander replied: "You're right to scold me, Holl!"

It wasn't my intention to scold. If only he had listened to me. But I – a simple Oberleutnant – could not order my Regiment Commander to go into the dug-out.

We lost no time in immediately taking our commander – who in the meantime had received first-aid from the doctor and then slipped into a morphine-induced unconsciousness – to an army hospital in Stalingrad. I would not quickly forget this 28 November.

Armee—Oberkommando 6. — Daily report for 28. November 1942

     After artillery preparation, the enemy advanced along a broad front with infantry and tanks. He was smashed back north of Spartakovka and north—east of 135.4, while he succeeded north—east of Orlovka and later at 1300 hours near 145.1 (west of the bend in the railway) in penetrating the main defensive area with tanks and infantry mounted on those. The penetration north—east of Orlovka was straightened out after the destruction of two T34s. The enemy pushed forward with infantry and tanks up to Hill 147.6, where he was halted.

> The counterattack launched by elements of 16.PD and 60.ID (mot)
> recaptured Hill 145.1. Fighting there has not yet ended. Near 145.1,
> a KV was totally destroyed, one tank was immobilised.
>
> The process of 24.PD taking over the right sector of 94.ID up
> to the south-east side of Hill 147.6 has started...

Command carried on as usual. The adjutant, Oberleutnant Kelz, took over temporary command of the regiment until a successor for Oberst Grosse arrived.

I learned that both panzers directed by me had worked wonders. They had appeared almost literally at the last minute and shot up four or five tanks (T-34) and in so doing, forced the Russians to withdraw[8]. It consequently became possible for our men to hold the front-line on the railway track.

29 November 1942

Gen.Kdo. LI. A.K. — 1730 hours on 29. November 1942

> Enemy was quiet in the morning... At 1200 hours, 24.PD took
> over the sector of 94.ID up to a point south-east of 135.4.

We were greeted once again on 29 November with rain that immediately froze into black ice. It was an additional burden for my comrades at the front.

30 November 1942

Gen.Kdo. LI. A.K. — 0600 hours on 30. November 1942

> Busy traffic, including tanks — at times with uncovered
> headlights — was seen on the road north-east of Orlovka. Our
> positions on Hill 147.6 and south of 111.1 lay under heavy tank- and
> mortar-fire for most of the night...

At midday on the last day of November, the thermometer once more climbed above 0° Celsius. It was sunny and clear.

Heavy defensive fighting was in progress along the front-line. The enemy attacks were repulsed. The heavy Russian mortar fire made it difficult for us to cope. Hauptmann Israel[9], who had led our II. Bataillon since the departure of Major Weigert, was struck by shrapnel and killed.

---

8. *When the Soviets had been thrown back, they left behind 30 dead and 80 men who became prisoners.*

9. *Another source lists Israel's date of death as 29 November 1942. Hauptmann Walter Gustav Friedrich Israel was posthumously promoted to Major.*

The remnants of II. and III. Battalions were merged into one unit designated 'Kampfgruppe Krause'. Oberleutnant Krause was promoted to Hauptmann. He was a quiet East Prussian who knew his business. His adjutant was Leutnant Gerlach, a Saarländer, a vocational school teacher by profession. Until just a few days ago, he'd been a platoon commander in 14. (Panzerabwehr) Kompanie.

Gen.Kdo. LI. A.K. — 1115 hours on 30. November 1942

Since the early hours of the morning, the enemy has been attacking the north–east front on the sector Rynok–145.1. Tanks are on the left wing...

Gen.Kdo. LI. A.K. — 1640 hours on 30. November 1942

During the morning, there were uncoordinated enemy attacks in groups of 30 to 300 men against the entire front–line of 24.PD. The enemy has repeated his attack several times on Orlovka along the road from the north–east and towards Hill 135.4 from the north–east. With panzer support, the enemy was thrown back and the front–line was improved by local counterattacks. Combat operations have still not ended. As planned, 16.PD captured the front–line on the right wing at daybreak using assault group operations. At 0800 hours, the enemy attacked Hill 147.6 with 4 tanks and about 75 riflemen. The attack was repulsed.
The attack was renewed at 1100 hours with 4 tanks and a battalion of infantry. During this fighting, two KV1s and three T34s were destroyed, one T34 was immobilised. Continuation of these attacks must be reckoned on.

Gen.Kdo. LI. A.K. — 2055 hours on 30. November 1942

In the morning, there were several independent enemy attacks against our positions west of Rynok, on the roads to Orlovka and Spartakovka and on Hills 135.4 and 144.2. Only near 135.4 did the enemy succeed with a local penetration. Through a counterattack by panzers and armoured riflemen – who had to dismount due to strong enemy tank fire – the enemy was destroyed and as a result of this, the front–line position was improved. The very strong enemy preparatory fire, as well as the heavy fire during the enemy attacks has – as a result – caused us our own casualties. After the repulsion of the tank–supported attack on Hill 147.6, the enemy attack was renewed at 1700 hours in complete darkness. The enemy, about 100 men strong, was thrown out in hand–to–hand combat...

1 December 1942

<u>Gen.Kdo. LI. A.K.</u> – 1650 hours on 1. December 1942

The morning passed quietly. Towards 1400 hours, two enemy probes north–east of Orlovka, each of 60 men, were repulsed. Increasingly strong harassment fire on Hill 147.6...

Around midday on 1 December, as weather conditions cleared, we were able to watch a dogfight between two German and two Russian fighters, but no-one was shot down. I believe that our boys were low on gas because they suddenly veered away without being followed by the Russians.

In the evening, we received the bad news that our Regiment Commander, Oberst Grosse, had not survived his severe wounding and had been recalled to the great army. He was 57 years-old. We had all revered and respected him both as a man and a

---

Gliederung 24.Pz.Div.

Pz.Div.Kdo.	
I./Pz.Gren.Rgt.21	abgekämpft
II./Pz.Gren.Rgt.26	abgekämpft
Kradsch.Abt.4	schwac'
Pz.Rgt.24	10–15 Panzer
Pz.Artl.Rgt.89	3 l.Bttr.zu 11 Geschützen,
	1 Bttr.s.F.H. zu 2 Geschützen,
	IV.(Flak)Abt. zu einer Bttr.
	zusammengefasst.
Pi.Btl.40	
Pz.Nachr.Abt.40	
Von 94.I.D. unterstellt:	
Gren.Rgt.274	2 schwache Btl.,
Gren.Rgt.267 mit unterstelltem Btl.Matho	3 schwache Btl.,
III./Gren.Rgt.276 mit 13./276	abgekämpft,
Stab Artl.Rgt.194 mit II.A.R.194	3 l.F.H.-Bttr. und
IV./A.R.194 mit	1 l.und 1 s.Bttr.
Pi.Btl.194 (Reste) u. Rdf.Schwadr.194(Reste)	
2 schw.Pak der Pz.Jg.Abt.194	

Composition of 24. Panzer-Division on 1 December 1942. The bulk of 94. Infanterie-Division's remaining combat forces were subordinated to this division.

```
                                       ...lage 2 zu Gen.Kdo.LI...K.
                                              Ia Nr.526/42 geh.

        Gliederung der 16.Pz.Div.
        ─────────────────────────

Pz.Div.Kdo.
  Pz.Gren.Rgt.64        1 schwaches Btl.
  Pz.Gren.Rgt.79        1    "     Rtl.
  Kradsch.Btl.16        1    "     Btl.
  Pz.Rgt.2              2o Panzer (als Armeereserve dem XIV.Pz.K.
  Pz.Jäg.Abt.16         1o Pak, 2 m.Sfl., 1 s.Sfl.   unterstellt)
  Pz.Art.Rgt.16         2 le.Abt. zu je 3 Bttr.
                        1 Abt.zu 2 le.u. 1 s.Bttr.
                              1 lo cm Kan.-Bttr.
                        1 Panos-Flak-Abt.
  Pz.Pi.16              ab kämpft,dem XIV.Pz. K. unterstellt.
  Pz.Nachr.Abt.16

Von 94.I.D. unterstellt:
Gren.Rgt.276 (ohne III. 276 und 13./276)  abgekämpft.
I.Art. Abt.194 (3 l.F.H.-Bttr. zu 3 Geschützen, 1 s...-Bttr.
                      zu 2 Geschützen).
```

Composition of 16. Panzer-Division on 1 December 1942. The only units of 94. Infanterie-Division subordinated to this division were Grenadier-Regiment 276 (without III.Btl. and 13.Ko.), as well as an artillery battalion.

superior. Who could possibly be his successor?[10]

Losses were constant and there were no replacements in sight. The rear units were sifted through again and again. Everyone that was dispensable was sent to the front.

Winter had also arrived – at least superficially. Snow fell during the night of 1 to 2 December. Everything was blanketed in white as far as the eye could see. To me, it took on the appearance of an enormous shroud that compassionately covered all the misery here.

Gen.Kdo. LI. A.K. – 1640 hours on 2. December 1942

　　　Under cover of heavy artillery fire, enemy infantry supported by individual tanks pushed up to our positions on 135.4 – 144.4. The attack was smashed by our artillery. Two thrusts with 3 tanks and anti-tank guns towards 147.6 likewise came to a halt in our defensive fire...

10. *Weeks later, Oberst Erich Hugo Richard Grosse was posthumously promoted to Generalmajor, effective 1 December 1942. He was also posthumously awarded the German Cross in Gold on 25 January 1943.*

2.12.1942.

Von <u>16.Pz.Division</u> kriegsgliederungsmäßig eingesetzte Teile:

<u>Regts.Stab Gr.Regt.79</u>

      I./Gr.Regt.79,   Gefechtsstärke etwa 5 / 180

      zusammengestelltes
      Batl. K 16   "   "   4 / 160

<u>Pz.Artl.Regt.16</u>, bestehend aus

      I./Pz.A.R.16   (3 l.F.H.-Batterien)
      II./   "   (3   "   ")
      III./   "   (2 s.F.H., 1=10 cm Battr.)
      IV./   "   (3=8,8 cm, 11=2 cm Geschütze).

<u>Panzerabwehrwaffen</u>:

      10 m.Pak   (davon 2 Sfl.)
      2 s.Pak   (Sfl.)

   Im Bereich 16.Pz.Div. eingesetzte Truppen, die ihr
kriegsgliederungsmäßig nicht angehör~~i~~gen:

      II./Gr.Regt.276   Gefechtsstärke 3 / 89

      Artl.Abt.631   (3 = 10 cm Batterien)
      5./A.R.65   *(2 l. F.H.)*
      3 s.Pak   (v.100.Jg.Div.).
      1 s.Werfer.Battr. v. Regt.2
      Pz.Jg.Abt.Schönburg (1 s., 2 = 5 cm, 2 = 4,7 cm Pak)
          (angeblich von 79.I.D.) .

A report from 16. Panzer-Division on 2 December 1942 shows that II./Grenadier-Regiment 276 had a combat strength of 3 officers and 89 men.

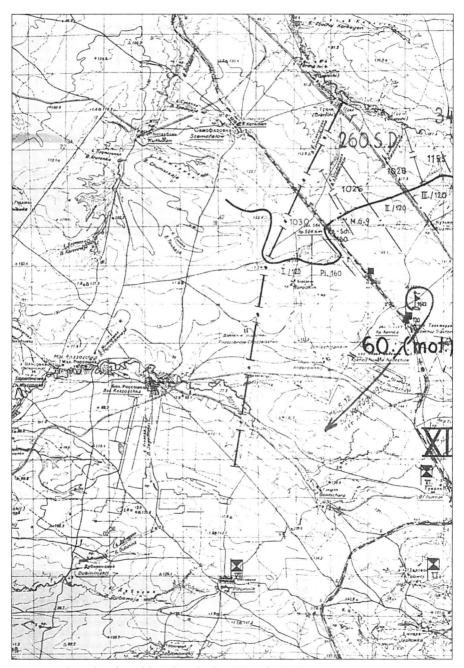

Situation on the northern front of the Stalingrad pocket, 2 December 1942.

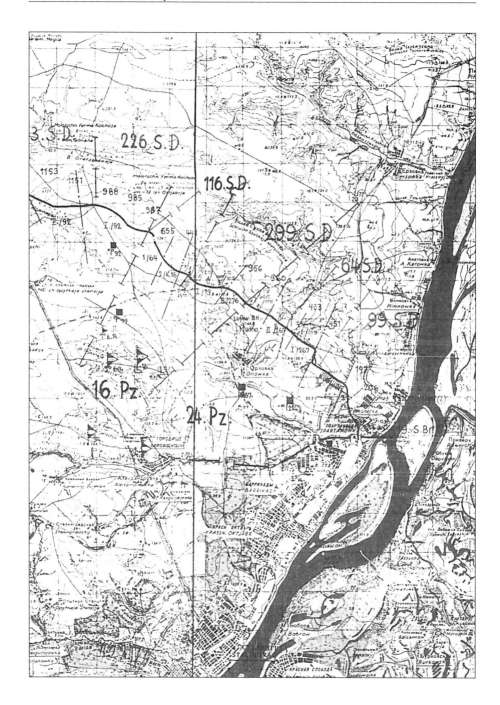

4 December 1942

On 4 December, I called my cousin Willi Nußbaum. He was very close by, on the staff of Major Wota[11], I./Panzergrenadier-Regiment 79. We would try to meet each other the next day.

Our men were firmly convinced that we would be freed from this Kessel, as I did too. A slogan made the rounds: "Hold out, the Führer will get you out". Until then, we would hold our ground with all available means.

> **Gen.Kdo. LI. A.K.** — 2034 hours on 4. December 1942
>
> North—east of Orlovka, two enemy assault groups — each of 30 men — were repulsed. Two enemy groups preparing to launch an attack towards 147.6 were smashed. Artillery and mortar harassment fire on the north—eastern and northern fronts...

5 December 1942

> **Gen.Kdo. LI. A.K.** — 1550 hours on 5. December 1942
>
> No combat activity, apart from weak enemy harassment fire.

I actually succeeded in meeting my cousin for a short while. We had never seen each other before but we immediately understood one another. Unfortunately, duty called for both of us and we hoped that we would find another passing opportunity for a conversation.

5, 6 and 7 December were very costly for 'Restbataillon 276'[12] of Kampfgruppe Krause. On 5 December, Oberleutnant Schulz[13] was killed on Hill 147.6, Leutnant Pilz[14] on 6 December on the railway embankment. Leutnant Baumann[15] was killed on the railway embankment on 7 December by a head shot. In addition to them, time was also up for some familiar old men and non-coms like my messenger, Obergefreiter Kurt Willmann[16], Obergefreiter Körner (earlier 8. Kompanie), Unteroffizier Feldmann and other proven and experienced soldiers.

---

11. *Major Kurt Wota. Born 19 May 1903; listed as missing in action 22 January 1943 but actually captured at Stalingrad 2 February 1943; died 23 March 1943 in Elabuga POW camp.*
12. *Restbataillon - literally 'battalion remnants'*
13. *Oberleutnant Wolfgang Hubertus Erwin Adolf Schulz. Born 27 July 1911 in Neisse; killed 5 December 1942 in Stalingrad. Another source lists his date of death as 6 December 1942.*
14. *Another source lists Leutnant Pilz's date of death as 9 December 1942.*
15. *No record exists of a Leutnant Baumann being killed on 7 December 1942. However, there is listed a Hauptmann Bruno Baumann; born 23 September 1909 in Ulm; died 4 December 1942 in Stalingrad.*
16. *Obergefreiter Arthur Kurt Willmann. Born 9 November 1913 in Ziegenhals; killed in December 1942 on Hill 147.6 near Orlovka, Stalingrad.*

<u>Gen.Kdo. LI. A.K.</u> — 1645 hours on 6. December 1942

 The probe towards 145.1 by a 50 man strong enemy group was repulsed by 16.PD. Two kilometres north of 147.6, the unloading of about 150 men from lorries was spotted and brought under fire from our artillery. An enemy attack in battalion strength east of 422 at 1530 hours was repulsed...

Those men suffering from jaundice had to remain with the troops. The jaundice-afflicted men were returned to their units from the field-hospitals. If it continued with this regularity, we could work out for ourselves when it would be our turn. The Russians intended to throw us out of this weak defensive line once and for all — in contrast to the northern blocking positions — and seize the crucially important hills 147.6, 144.2 and 135.4 that lay south of the railway line. The miracles my comrades were performing at the front could barely be envisaged: defensive combat in snow and cold for days on end. They were only inadequately equipped for it, yet, they obstinately defended every square metre of ground.

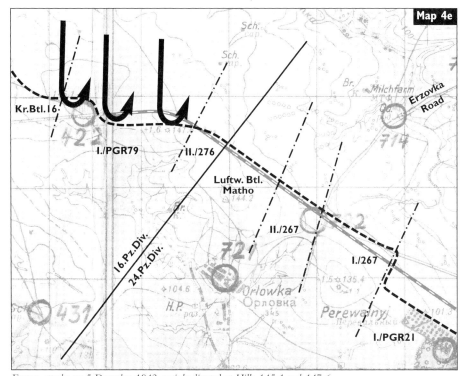

Enemy attacks on 5 December 1942, mainly directed at Hills 145.1 and 147.6.

Gen.Kdo. LI. A.K. – 2040 hours on 6. December 1942

    16.PD repelled an assault of a 50 man enemy group directed at Hill 145.1, and two attacks in battalion strength – the first at 1400 hours and the second at 1700 hours – towards our positions between 147.6 and 145.1. The disembarkation north–east of 147.6, which was caught by our artillery, movement in front of 16.PD in the direction of their right wing and the continued supply of enemy forces from the direction of Erzovka on about 70 lorries to the area of the Milchfarm (dairy) near orientation point 714 allows the further offensive intentions of the enemy against 24.PD and 16.PD to be discerned for 7.12. Tanks have so far not been observed...

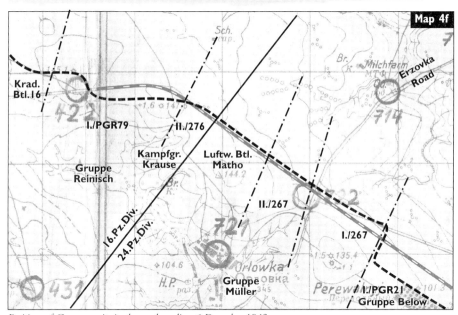

Positions of German units in the northern line, 6 December 1942.

Our neighbours to the left were in no better shape. From what I could establish, they had better winter clothing, though they faced the severity of the defensive fighting exactly like us.

In the meantime, Kampfgruppe Krause had been subordinated to 'Kampfgruppe Reinisch'. The right flank of Panzergrenadier-Regiment 79 and the left flank of the remnants of the former Grenadier-Regiment 276 – now called Kampfgruppe Krause – had time and again borne the brunt of enemy attacks. Combat raged chiefly around Hill 147.6. 'Ivan' repeatedly attacked in company strength supported by tanks. The front-line was penetrated twice, and up to now, our men had succeeded in throwing them out again. But for how long could this be kept up?

IIa Abt of 6. Armee HQ: — 6. December 1942

    Total casualties in the time from 21.11. — 5.12.1942:
    94.Inf.Div.:   981
    16.Pz.Div.:   699
    24.Pz.Div.:   584

Gen.Kdo. LI. A.K. — 2102 hours on 7. December 1942

    An assault of 60 men out of Spartakovka was repulsed. North of 145.1, two companies on skis were suppressed by our artillery...

6.12.42
08.00   Gruppe S e y d l i t z, Ia   XI.A.K., Ia.

K R

Bezug: Gruppe Seydlitz, Ia F.S. v. 2.12.42.
Betr.: Frontbreite und eingesetzte Waffen.

1.) 24.Pz.Div.:

    a) Gruppe Brendel   — 3 100 m
          "   Below   — 2 800 m
          "   Müller — 5 100 m

    b) Waffen

Gruppe Brendel	l.M.G.	42
	s.M.G.	11
	l.Gr.W.	5
	s.Gr.W.	5
	l.J.G.	8
	s.J.G.	1
	m.Pak	4
Gruppe Below	l.M.G.	63
	s.M.G.	5
	s.Gr.W.	8
	l.J.G.	4
	s.J.G.	1
	w. Pak	5

                                        wenden!

Breadth of front and weapons employed by 24. Panzer-Division and its subordinate units. Gruppe Brendel (Gr.Rgt.274) held 3100 metres of front, Gruppe Below (Pz.Gr.Rgt.21) held 2800 metres and Gruppe Müller (Gr.Rgt.267 held 5100 metres.

```
        Gruppe Müller        l.M.G.      31
                             s.M.G.      12
                             l.Gr.W.      5
                             s.Gr.W.      7
                             l.J.G.       3
                             s.J.G.       1
                             le.Pak       1
                             m.Pak        5
                             s.Pak        8


2.) 16. Pz. Div.:

     a) Kampfgruppe Reinisch       4 300 m
            "        Dörnemann      3 600 m


     b) Kampfgruppe Reinisch    l.M.G.      4 7
                                s.M.G.         2
                                l.Gr.W.      1
                                s.Gr.W.      4
                                l.J.G.       6
                                s.J.G.       2
                                lei.Pak      3
                                m. Pak       6
                                s. Pak       4


        Kampfgruppe Dörnemann   l.M.G.      30
                                s.M.G.       2
                                s.Gr.W.      1
                                l.J.G.       6
                                s.J.G.       2
                                m.Pak        8
                                s.Pak        2


3.) 60.I.D. mot.

     a) Kampfgruppe Fink (G.R.92)     7 000 m
            "        Schmidt (G.R.120) 5 000 m
            "        Bäu (G.R.         9000 m


     b) Kampfgruppe Fink        l.M.G.      81
                                s.M.G.      12
                                l.Gr.W.     14
                                s.Gr.W.      9
                                l.J.G.       2
                                s.J.G.       2
                                Pak 3,7      3
                                Pak 5,-      4
                                Pak 7,62
                                   Sfl.      2
                                              - Blatt 2 -
```

Breadth of front and weapons employed by 16 Panzer-Division and its subordinate units. Gruppe Reinisch (Pz.Gr.Rgt.79 and attached units) held 4300 metres of front while Gruppe Dörnemann (Krad.Btl.16 and attached units) held 3600 metres.

Chapter 5

8 December 1942

The situation demanded that our command post be withdrawn from the small oak forest. It was pulled back to Hill 108.8 during the night of 8 to 9 December. I didn't know which staff had been located here weeks ago. Perhaps it was only a signals position or an artillery unit?

> Gen.Kdo. XI. A.K. – Daily report from 8. December 1942
>
> 16.Pz.Div.: The counterattack against Hills 0.6 and 145.1 at 1400 hours with panzers, mounted riflemen and half-tracks – supported by our artillery – met with complete success. In daring assaults, Hill 0.6 was taken at 1430 hours and Hill 145.1 at 1700 hours. The enemy fled to the north and suffered heavy casualties. At the moment, the old front-line is still being cleared of infantry and occupied by our own riflemen, particularly between Hill 145.1 and Ref.Pt. 422...
>
> Just north of 147.6, the enemy, with a strength of about two companies, has pushed forward right up to the hill...

9 December 1942

> Gen.Kdo. XI. A.K. – Morning report from 9. December 1942
>
> 16.Pz.Div.: Mortar harassment fire on the Division's right sector. North of 147.6, engine noises and movements were observed in the enemy front-line...

We received a new commander on 9 December 1942. Why Oberst Steffler[1] – that was how he introduced himself to us – should be here, I did not know. Also, I wasn't quite clear what purpose our Regiment staff served. The few remaining troops belonged to Kampfgruppe Reinisch. We currently only had administrative duties and

---

1. *In the original German text, Holl incorrectly called him 'Scheffler' instead of Steffler. Oberst i.G. Johannes Konrad Steffler. Born 21 May 1899 in Glatz; captured at Stalingrad 2 February 1943; died 21 March 1943 in Frolov POW camp. Oberst i.G. Steffler was chief-of-staff of IV. Armeekorps from 20 June 1942 until 5 December 1942. He then took command of Infanterie-Regiment 276.*

among other things were tasked with securing rations and ammunition as well as procuring winter clothing.

I was glad when I learned that our comrades from 16. Panzer-Division were helping out our fighting men with winter clothing. Through the joint burden of defensive combat around Hill 147.6, Kampfgruppe Krause enjoyed good relations with the comrades of Panzergrenadier-Regiment 79. Instead of feeling like they were an appendage, as they had been in the past weeks when attached to other units, they now belonged to a family. The heavy defensive fighting which was still raging back and forth on 11 December particularly contributed to this. When the Russians succeeded in obtaining a local penetration, they were quickly thrown out by a counterattack. All of us were aware that if he pushed through us, the entire city could be rolled up from the north.

> <u>Gen.Kdo. XI. A.K.</u> – Daily report from 9. December 1942
>
>   <u>16.Pz.Div.</u>: At 1300 hours, 16.Pz.-Div., with panzers and half-tracks, only succeeded in penetrating to the western slope of Hill 141.0 occupied by enemy tanks and anti-tank guns. A simultaneous enemy attack carried out with superior forces and several tanks led to the loss of Hills 0.6 and 145.1...

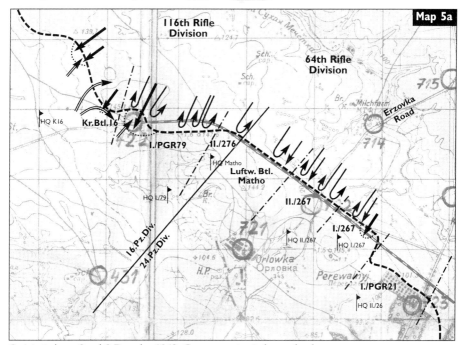

Soviet attacks on 8 and 9 December 1942. German counterattacks are also shown.

```
                    Ü b e r s i c h t

über die Aufteilung der 94.Jnf.-Division, Stand 1o.12.1942.


Reststab der Führungsabteilung (ohne
               Quartiermeisterabteilung)
          Fhr.: Ic d.94.J.D.,Oblt.d.R.Klünder    :    24.Pz.-Div.

Quartiermeisterabteilung u. Versorgungstruppen :    XI.A.K.


Gr.Rgt.274 (ohne 14.Kp.bei 376.J.D.)         )
Gr.Rgt.267                                   )
Stab Gr.Rgt.276 mit III./Gr.Rgt.276 u. 13.Kp.)
Stab A.R.194 mit II./A.R.194 (4.,5.u.6.Bttr.))
          u. IV./A.R.194 (11.,12. u. 8.Bttr.))   24.Pz.-Div.
Stab Pz.Jäg.Abt.194 mit Resten einer Kp.     )
Radf.Schwd.194                               )
Pi.Btl.194                                   )
eingesetzte Teile N.A.194                    )


II./Gr.Rgt.276                               )
14./Gr.Rgt.276                               )
III./A.R.194 mit 7., 9. u. 1o.Battr.         )   16.Pz.-Div.
Reste einer Komp.Pz.Jäg.Abt.194              )


nicht eingesetzte Teile N.A.194                  :    A.O.K.6

14./Gr.Rgt.274                                   :    376.J.D.
```

'Overview of the dividing-up of 94. Infanterie-Division as of 10.12.1942'. As can be seen, most divisional elements were allocated to 24. Panzer-Division. Other elements were parceled out to several other units, including II./Gr.Rgt.276, 14./Gr.Rgt.276, an artillery battalion and remnants of an anti-tank company being handed over to 16. Panzer-Division.

I escorted Oberst Steffler, my new commander, to various staffs so he could apprise himself of the current situation. We learned that ten gentlemen from our Division staff, including General Pfeiffer, were to be flown out of the Kessel to take over other assignments outside the Kessel[2]. I understood that our Division must give over the remnants of its regiments as reinforcements to other divisions and that they could do more for those of us in the Kessel from outside.

2. *On 10 December 1942, the following order, signed by 6. Armee Chief-of-Staff Generalmajor Artur Schmidt, arrived at 94. Infanterie-Division HQ:*
   "Generalleutnant Pfeiffer, Commander of 94.I.D., will be employed as 'Authorised representative General of the Commander-in-Chief of 6. Armee outside Fortress Stalingrad'. He will assemble a staff and with them, will be flown out of the Kessel to Morosovskaya on 11.12.1942. There, he will cooperate with Oberst i.G. Bader, Oberquartiermeister of 6. Armee, and make contact with 3. Rumanian Armee (Oberst i.G. Wenck) and XXXXVIII. Panzerkorps (Oberst i.G. Friebe)."
   Apart from Generalleutnant Pfeiffer, the following officers were also flown out on 11 December 1942: Oberstleutnant i.G. Martin Boriss (Division Ia - Chief-of-Staff); Oberstleutnant Hans-Werner von Oppell (Division IIa - Adjutant); and Oberleutnant d.R. Hans-Horst Manitz (Division O1 - Assistant to Ia).

12 December 1942

Heavy defensive combat took place on 12 and 13 December[3]. The rations were becoming leaner. It was lucky that we old 'Hot-Truppen'[4] still had horses which were distributed amongst all divisions. They formed the main rations of our troops. When prisoners were taken, our men first looked to see if the enemy still had anything edible.

Gen.Kdo. XI. A.K. – Daily report from 12. December 1942

16.Pz.Div.: ... In the early morning hours, weak enemy thrusts towards 147.6 and east of there were repelled with artillery support. During the day, weak mortar fire on our front-line, as on the previous days.
Casualties:
16.Pz.Div.:   6 dead, 36 wounded (of those, 12 stayed with
                 troops), 10 missing
Subordinated
units: 1 dead, 7 wounded (of those, 2 stayed with
                 troops)

Gen.Kdo. XI. A.K. – Daily report from 13. December 1942

16.Pz.Div.: An attack in the very early morning hours towards Hill 139.7 and west of there, with a strength of 120 men, was able to be repulsed with casualties for the enemy.
In the time from 0900 – 1100 hours, enemy movements in company strength were established in a north–west to south–east direction north–east of Hills 145.1 and 139.7.
After particularly strong preparatory fire from Stalin Organs, artillery and mortars, the enemy attacked at 1300 hours east and 1km south–east of Hill 139.7 with 3 to 5 tanks and infantry. The attack was repulsed. During the entire day, there was very heavy enemy mortar fire near Ref.Pt.422. Losses here continue to be high.
Casualties:
10 dead, 22 wounded, 1 missing

---

3. *The previous day – 11 December – had also been very difficult for 16. Panzer-Division with subordinated units of Infanterie-Regiment 276. Casualties were as follows:*
16.Panzer-Division: 1 officer and 11 NCOs & men killed,
*   51 wounded (of those, 23 remained with the troops),*
*   2 men missing and 5 men frostbitten.*
Subordinated units: 1 officer missing,
*   22 NCOs & men killed,*
*   55 wounded,*
*   5 missing and 11 frostbitten.*
4. Hot-Truppen - *A play on the term 'Mot-Truppen': Mot = motorised, Hot = horsedrawn.*

24. Panzer - Division.   Div.Gef.Std., den 13. 12. 1942.
Abt.Ia/IIa
_____

Divisions - Befehl

für Unterstellung weiterer Teile der 94.J.D.

1.) Mit sofortiger Wirkung werden der 24.Pz.-Div. unterstellt:
    a) Resttstab u. Führungsstab 94.J.D. (ohne Qu.-Abt.),
    b) Eingesetzte Teile R.A.194,
    c) Stab/Gr.Rgt.276,
    d) Stab/Pz.Jäg.Abt.194.

2.) Qu.-Abt. u. Versorgungstruppen der 94.J.D. unterstehen dem
    XI.A.K. unmittelbar und bisher nicht eingesetzte Teile R.A.194
    dem Armee-Nachr.-Führer.

3.) Kdr.Gr.Rgt.276 ist zur 389.J.D. versetzt.
    Mit der Wahrnehmung der Geschäfte des Führers Gr.Rgt.276 wird
    Kdr.Pz.Jäg.Abt.194, Major v.Northeim, beauftragt.
    An der bisherigen Verwendung des Maj. v.N. als Pz.Jäg.Abt.Kdr.
    ändert sich hierdurch nichts.

4.) ~~Kdr.~~ ~~R.A.194~~ ~~übernimmt~~ ~~Aufgaben~~ ~~bisher~~ ~~Führern~~ ~~Reserve.~~
    Ab 14.12.42 übernimmt Kdr.A.R.194, Oberst Katzke, die Auf-
    gaben des Artl.-Führers der 24.Pz.-Div.
    Über Verwendung Oberstltn. Boredorf erfolgt noch Befehl. +)
    Gleichzeitig übernimmt Oberst Katzke die Betreuung der Teile
    der 94.J.D. in enger Zusammenarbeit mit Div.-Stab 24.Pz.-Div.
    und Rest-Div.Stab 94.J.D.

5.) 24.Pz.-Div. übernimmt die truppendienstliche Betreuung aller
    Truppenteile der 94.J.D. einschl. der anderen Verbände unter-
    stellten Teile.
    Es wird das besondere Streben der Division sein, allen Teilen
    der 94.J.D. für die Zeit der Unterstellung eine neue Heimat zu
    schaffen.

6.) Führer des Restführungsstabes der 94.J.D. legt der Div. bald-
    möglichst vor:
    a) Übersicht aller Truppenteile der 94.J.D., ihr jetziger Ver-
       bleib sowie Unterstellungsverhältnisse.
    b) Verpflegungs- u. Gefechts-Stärken der neu gem.Ziff.1.)
       a) - d) der 24.Pz.-Div. unterstellten Teile.

- 2 -

24. Panzer-Division order for the subordination of units from 94. Infanterie-Division. See next page for translation.

```
c) Offz.-Stellenbesetzung:
   Takt. Offz.-Stellenbesetzung aller Truppenteile der
   94. J.D. Die Offz. der Truppenteile, die hierbei nicht
   erfasst werden ( Urlauber, ausserhalb des Kessels
   befindliche, auf Kommando befindliche ) sind unter
   Erläuterungen mit Angabe der Verwendung zu melden.
   d) Karte der Unterbringungsräume zu Ziff. 6.) a) soweit
      sie nicht der 24. Pz.-Div. unterstellt sind
7.) Befehlsempfang für Reststab 94. J.D. täglich 7,00 Uhr
    Div.-Gef.-Stand 24. Pz.-Div. Westrand Gorodischtsche -
    Alexandrowka.
```

Divisional-Order for the subordination of further elements of 94. Infanterie-Division

1.) *The following are subordinated to 24. Panzer-Division with immediate effect:*
   a) *Staff remnants and command staff of 94. Infanterie-Division (without supply group sections)*
   b) *Employed elements of Nachrichten-Abteilung 194*
   c) *Staff/Grenadier-Regiment 276*
   d) *Staff/Panzerjäger-Abteilung 194*

2.) *Supply group sections and supply troops of 94. Infanterie-Division* are under direct control of XI. Armeekorps while previously *unemployed elements of Nachrichten-Abteilung 194* are under the Armeenachrichtenführer (commander of army signals).

3.) *The commander of Grenadier-Regiment 276* is transferred to 389. Infanterie-Division. Entrusted with the responsibility of running the position of commander of Grenadier-Regiment 276 is the *commander of Panzerjäger-Abteilung 194*, Major von Nordheim. The previous assignment of Major von Nordheim as Panzerjäger-Abteilung commander is not altered by this.

4.) *From 14.12.42, the commander of Artillerie-Regiment 194, Oberst Matzke*, will take over the duties and responsibilities of artillery commander of 24. Panzer-Division.
   An order about the assignment of Oberstleutnant Borsdorf will still take place.
   At the same time, Oberst Matzke will take over supervision of the 94. Infanterie-Division elements in close cooperation with 24. Panzer-Division staff and the remnants of 94. Infanterie-Division staff.

5.) *24. Panzer-Division will take over supervision of the troop services* of all elements of 94. Infanterie-Division, including those elements subordinated to other units.
   The Division will strive to make all elements of 94. Infanterie-Division feel at home for the duration of their subordination.

6.) *The leader of the remnants of 94. Infanterie-Division's command staff will submit the following to Division as soon as possible:*
   a) *Overview of all units of 94. Infanterie-Division*, their present whereabouts as well as subordination relationship.
   b) *Ration- and combat strength of those elements newly subordinated to 24. Panzer-Division as per Fig. 1a - d).*
   c) *Officer placement list:*
      Placement list of tactical officers from all of 94. Infanterie-Division's units. The unit officers that are not registered though this (on furlough, outside the Kessel, on detached duty) are to be reported under annotations with specification of their assignment.
   d) *Map showing the billet areas of those in Fig. 6a), inasmuch as they are not subordinated to 24. Panzer-Division.*

7.) *Receipt of orders for Reststab 94. Infanterie-Division* at 0700 hours daily. Division command post is on the western edge of Gorodishche-Alexandrovka.

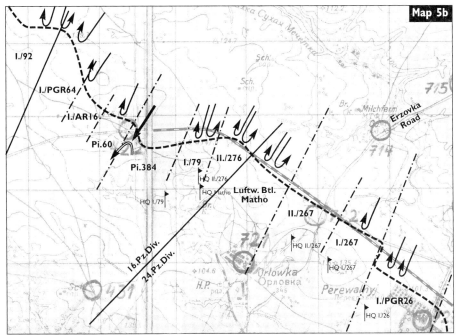

Course of the Soviet attacks on 12 and 13 December 1942.

14 December 1942

As suddenly as our new commander, Oberst Steffler, had appeared at our staff, he just as quickly disappeared. His guest appearance with us had lasted exactly five days[5]. Standing in for him was Major von Nordheim[6], last commander of Panzerjäger-Abteilung 194. He had the task of liquidating the still-functioning duties of Grenadier-Regiment 276 and dissolving the Regiment staff. Major von Nordheim was a jovial reservist of about 50 years of age. In private life, he was a director at MAN in Nürnberg. He was a passionate hunter and attempted to shorten the long hours in the evening with tales of his hunting experiences, enabling us to forget the miserable situation in which we found ourselves.

<u>Gen.Kdo. XI. A.K.</u> – Daily report from 14. December 1942

    <u>24.Pz.Div.</u>: ...On 15.12. Gruppe Brendel will hand over a platoon of light infantry guns of 13./Gr.Rgt.276 to II./Gr.Rgt.276 near 16. Panzer–Division...

---

5. *Oberst Steffler was transferred to 389. Infanterie-Division to take command of Infanterie-Regiment 545.*

6. *Major Karl von Nordheim. Born 27 September 1896 in Nürnberg; captured at Stalingrad 2 February 1943; died 9 April 1943 in Frolov POW camp.*

16 December 1942

On 16 December, the temperature once again climbed above 0° Celsius. The night to 17 December, however, already brought another hard frost and a violent, icy wind.

In the meantime, we knew that the staff had to be dissolved by 31 December 1942[7]. Major von Nordheim offered me the choice between 24. Panzer-Division or 16. Panzer-Division. There was not much to consider: I requested a transfer to 16. Panzer-Division, where I would be with my old comrades, the last men of my old 7. Kompanie. My request was granted and the corresponding papers were drawn up.

Our staff tailor used a piece of lamb-skin to make me a cap and a pair of mittens. At least now I had something warm on my head and hands.

16 and 17 December were once again difficult days for Panzergrenadier-Regiment 79, as indeed they were for the remnants of my company and, respectively, my battalion. The enemy once again tried to break into the front-line with tank and artillery support. Suffering heavy casualties, the Russian attack was repulsed.

It was incredible how my comrades at the front were coping. The icy wind with its sharp ice crystals whipped through every gap in clothing. Coming in at great speed from the east, it swept over the now naked steppe. Everyone searched for protection from it: even a wall of snow was enough to ward off the wind. Unless it was absolutely necessary, no-one left their cover or dug-outs. However, when that was required, everyone moved about in double-time, in order to quickly get to the next spot that offered some protection.

We were all happy when the wind died down four days later. It began to snow incessantly on 23 December.

> <u>Gen.Kdo. XI. A.K.</u> — Daily report from 16. December 1942
>
>   <u>16.Pz.Div.</u>: ...Light artillery and mortar harassment fire on the divisional sector focusing mostly on 145.1 and 147.6. At 1200 hours, strong mortar and anti-tank gun barrages on 147.6.
>
> ---
>
> <u>Gen.Kdo. XI. A.K.</u> — Daily report from 17. December 1942
>
>   <u>16.Pz.Div.</u>: ...Mortar harassment fire in the morning hours on 145.1 and 147.6, otherwise the course of the day was quiet. The enemy is entrenching out in front of his own forward line.

---

7. *The reason 94. Infanterie-Division was disbanded was because it was by far the weakest division on Stalingrad's northern front. Casualties had been continuous since the division first moved into the city in September. Lack of numbers, however, never alleviated the division of offensive missions. The final straw was the costly withdrawal on 23 November. It seemed to be the Division's lot during the Stalingrad battle to be subordinated to other units.*

```
            Anlage zu 24.Pz.-Div.Ia Nr.425/42 geh.
                        v.19.12.1942.


        Zur Orientierung werden Auszüge aus den Wochenmeldungen
der Truppenteile vorgelegt:

1.) Gren.Rgt.274:
    Die Btle. bzw. Abteilungen sind bedingt zur Abwehr geeignet.
    Die Zuführung einer Reserve-Einheit bleibt weiterhin unbe-
    dingt erforderlich, da irgendwelche nennenswerten Reserven
    nach wie vor nicht zur Verfügung stehen. Ebenso bleibt die
    Zuweisung eines älteren Oberleutnants als Unterabschnitts-
    führer notwendig.
    Die Stimmung der Truppe ist infolge des ununterbrochenen
    Einsatzes und der Verpflegungslage gedrückt, obwohl die
    letzte Postverteilung einen gewissen Auftrieb gegeben hat.
    Weitere Zuführung, zumindest von Briefpost, ist sehr er-
    wünscht.


2.) Gren.Rgt.276:
    Die Stimmung der Truppe ist zuversichtlich. Jeder einzelne
    ist davon überzeugt, dass von der höheren Führung alle Mass-
    nahmen getroffen werden, die eine baldige Bereinigung der
    derzeitigen Lage und damit auch unmittelbare günstige Aus-
    wirkungen, insbesondere in Bezug auf die Verpflegung für
    die Truppe, erwarten lassen.
    Der Kampfwert der Truppe, der sich mit fortschreitendem
    Stellungsbau und damit der Schaffung heizbarer Unterstände
    in den letzten Tagen gehoben hat, leidet andererseits durch
    die z.Zt. ungenügende Verpflegung.
```

Excerpts from weekly reports showing the morale and preparedness of the two regiments of 94. Infanterie-Division subordinated to 24. Panzer-Division:

1.) <u>Grenadier-Regiment 274:</u>
     The battalions, or rather, detachments, are <u>*fit for defence*</u>. The <u>*supply of a reserve-unit remains absolutely*</u> <u>*essential*</u> because there still are no noteworthy reserves at hand. In the same way, the allocation of a veteran Oberleutnant as sub-sector commander is still necessary.
     The morale of the troops is low due to permanent action and the food supply situation, even though the last delivery of mail raised their spirits. More deliveries, especially letters, is greatly desired.

2.) <u>Grenadier-Regiment 276:</u>
     The <u>morale</u> of the troops is confident. Every single soldier is certain that the high command will take every measure to resolve the present situation and with that, immediately favourable consequences can also be expected, especially in regards to the food supply for the troops.
     The <u>*fighting quality*</u> of the troops, which has risen during the last few days due to the ongoing construction of positions and therefore the provision of heated accommodation, is, on the other hand, suffering at the moment from the poor food supply.

24 December 1942

The supply by our Luftwaffe was not at all as smooth as we had hoped and as we had been promised[8]. Rations were always scanty and there was less and less ammunition. We had to conserve these precious things as never before. It was extremely lucky that we still had horses. These were also fairly distributed so that everyone received something. Our supply officer tried to procure a few supplementary provisions for Christmas Eve celebrations. Our comrades at the front received an entire loaf of bread instead of the usual 200 gram ration. An additional portion of sausage was made from horse meat. Some red wine also turned up but there wasn't enough for everyone, so the field-kitchen brewed up some punch so that everyone received a share. On top of all that, every man received ten cigarettes.

We heard the droning of our aircraft engines during the night. The Russians, having discovered that our aircraft were dropping supply canisters and ammunition at night, lit beacons just like the ones our troops were using. As a result, many of these canisters landed near 'Ivan' or in no-mans-land. It was always a heavy loss for us.

Around 2000 hours, in accordance with Major von Nordheim's order, the remnants of the Regiment staff[9] assembled in the bunker's largest room. A pine branch (where could they possibly have got hold of it?) substituted for a Christmas tree. Coarse soldiers' throats sang 'Stille Nacht, heilige Nacht'[10]. For many of them, a lump suddenly stuck in their throats. After that, Major von Nordheim addressed us. He pointed out the seriousness of the situation and that those of us here in the east – far from home and our loved ones – were fighting for our people. He concluded with the words: "And not least we owe it to our fallen comrades to continue to perform our duty as soldiers." This was followed by the song 'O, du fröhliche'[11]. After that, ten comrades sang the song 'There stands a soldier on the Volga' from 'Tsarevitch'. To finish, we all sang 'O Tannenbaum'[12].

We then returned to our dug-outs. From the faces of my comrades, I saw that their thoughts were also at home, as mine were. Not once over the past years had we experienced Christmas in such a depressing situation. I wrote to my dear little wife, not betraying the gloomy feeling and the threat of uncertainty that had befallen us.

---

8. *The aerial supply, as so pompously promised by Hermann Goering, in no way approached the levels needed to keep 6. Armee functioning as an efficient fighting force. The absolute minimum required by 6. Armee was 500 tonnes per day. As an example, the previous day – 23 December 1942 – a total of 80 planes had flown into the pocket, delivering 29 tonnes of ammunition, 86 cubic metres of fuel, 24 tonnes of rations and 5 tonnes of other items. The best day of the entire airlift was 19 December 1942, when 147 planes arrived carrying 3 tonnes of ammunition, 30 cubic metres of fuel, and 225 tonnes of rations.*

9. *For administrative purposes, the staff of Grenadier-Regiment 276 was attached to 24. Panzer-Division. Its strength on 21 December 1942 was 9 officers, 25 NCOs and 87 men*

10. *Stille Nacht, heilige Nacht* - *'Silent Night, Holy Night'*

11. *O, du fröhliche* - *'O, How Joyfully'*

12. *O Tannenbaum* - *'O Christmas Tree'*

They already had enough anxiety at home. Should I add to these while I was in this blackest of black times?

A hook-up of the German radio services enabled Christmas greetings to be broadcast to the homeland from all fronts. Comrades from northern Norway, Africa and also from the Stalingrad pocket were heard. The Reichs Propaganda Minister, Dr. Goebbels, spoke on behalf of the homeland to the soldiers fighting at the front.

Looking at these distances on a map, they appeared enormous to us Central Europeans. And what supply difficulties we've had to overcome here in Russia. We heard from some source or other that panzer units from von Manstein's army group were on their way to open the Kessel from the south-west. This report gave us new impetus, though we ourselves knew how difficult it now would be to gain ground after these heavy snowfalls. Nevertheless, we were convinced that our command would not leave us in the lurch.

It snowed the entire day of 24 December, so much so that you couldn't see more than ten metres. Where does this filthy stuff come from! Thank God our sector remained quiet. The enemy also seemed to be ill-at-ease with the weather.

Gen.Kdo. XI. A.K. — Daily report from 24. December 1942

  16.Pz.Div.: At 1100 hours, the enemy attacked Hill 139.7 with a force of 150 men in snow suits and wearing assault packs. This assault was smashed by artillery and infantry fire.
  During the course of the day, there was lively movement in front of the Division's entire forward line. The enemy was also replenishing his front—line. Division reckons on enemy assaults during the night against the left sector...

25 December 1942

We'd been mistaken about 'Ivan' because at precisely 0500 hours on 25 December, we were awoken by loud sounds of battle. The thud of artillery shells, the howling of Stalin Organs and the impact of mortars could be heard very close by – so it seemed to me – on the left flank of Kampfgruppe Reinisch. Now the crack of tank cannon could also be heard. The alarm was immediately raised at our staff. Major von Nordheim called the Reinisch command post and learned that the Russians were attacking the left flank of 16. Panzer-Division with tanks and strong infantry forces. The main objective was Hill 139.7. The fighting raged even further to the left of Sector Reinisch. The sounds of combat continued throughout the entire day. Could our men withstand the assault? We all really hoped they would, even though we knew their task was difficult.

With each passing hour, the snow piled higher and made cross-country movements more and more strenuous. In this situation, you could barely trudge, let alone run.

The Soviet attack on the morning of Christmas Day, consisting of two rifle regiment and 14 tanks, was exceedingly strong and succeeded in breaking through the front-line and seizing Hill 139.7, despite the fact that the Germans had positioned numerous anti-tank guns in this area. XI. Armeekorps submitted the daily reports of 16. Panzer-Division and 60. Infanterie-Division (mot.) to its superior office, von Seydlitz's LI. Armeekorps, as usual. A few hours later, however, XI. Armeekorps staff received a teletype that read: "The Commanding General [von Seydlitz] requests an immediate investigation and report that is to ascertain why there is a disproportion between today's extraordinarily high loss in medium and heavy anti-tank weapons and the low number of destroyed enemy tanks."

Enquiries to the divisions concerned revealed numerous causes as to why the anti-tank guns were unable to halt the Soviet tanks. The initial Soviet attack broke through the line both sides of Hill 137.8. While the accompanying Soviet riflemen were halted by German infantry weapons fire, the tanks thrust to the south-east, behind the left flank of 16. Panzer-Division. The anti-tank guns employed in the front-line there all faced north and north-east, and the icing-up caused by snowstorms meant the guns could not be swung around quickly enough. Two 88mm flak guns located on the boundary between both divisions, about 1.8km behind the front, did not have an effect because of poor visibility, and could also not be relocated because the engines of their towing-tractors would not start. Two 76.2mm Marders were knocked out at the very beginning of the attack by direct hits from artillery shells.

The following anti-tank weapons were employed in the area of the divisional boundary: 2 light, 7 medium, 2 heavy, 4 heavy self-propelled and two 88mm Flak. Of those, the following were employed in the forward line: 2 light, 5 medium and 1 heavy. An Unteroffizier from 16. Panzer-Division reported that the anti-tank guns were knocked out by well-aimed artillery and mortar fire, with the result that 6 NCOs and men were killed while 14 were wounded. He also reported that the 5cm shells had no effect on a KV tank. For the loss of most of these valuable weapons, one Soviet tank was destroyed, one was made immobile and another was set on fire.

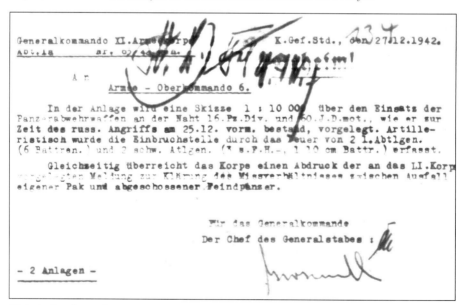

"Submitted in the attachment is a 1 : 10,000 sketch showing the deployment of the anti-tank weapons on the boundary of 16. Panzer-Division and 60. Infanterie-Division (mot.) as they were at the time of the Russian attack on the morning of 25.12. The breach was covered by the fire of two light battalions (6 batteries) and 2 heavy battalions (3 heavy howitzers, one 10cm battery).

"At the same time, Korps has handed over a copy of the submitted report to LI. Armeekorps to clarify the disparity between the losses of our anti-tank guns and knocked-out enemy tanks."

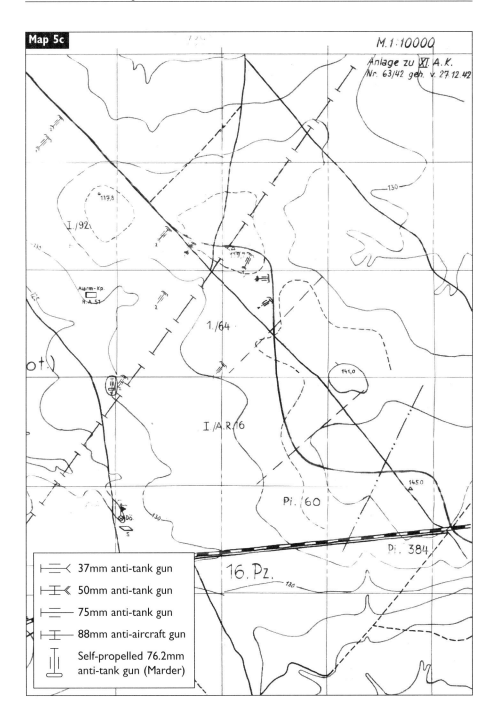

Map 5c

M. 1:10000

Anlage zu XI. A.K.
Nr. 63/42 geh. v. 27.12.42

137,8

I. /92

130

Alarm-Kp.
N.-A.51

1. /64

141,0

I. /A.R.16

145,0

Pi. /60

Pi. 384

16. Pz.

├──<   37mm anti-tank gun

├─╪«   50mm anti-tank gun

├───   75mm anti-tank gun

├─╪─   88mm anti-aircraft gun

╟╫╢   Self-propelled 76.2mm
       anti-tank gun (Marder)

In the evening, we learned that despite very heavy casualties, the enemy had succeeded in taking Hill 139.7. Our casualties were also very high.

> <u>Gen.Kdo. XI. A.K.</u> — Daily report from 25. December 1942
>
>   <u>16.Pz.Div.</u>: Around 0700 hours, after breaking in near the left neighbour[13], the enemy succeeded in taking Hill 139.7 from the west in battalion strength supported by tanks. Through heavy mortar, artillery and tank fire, the Division has suffered considerable losses. Our counterattack that began at 1130 hours with panzers and half-tracks pushed through just south of 139.7. Strong enemy forces are still on 139.7 at this time. Our losses in panzers and half-tracks are severe. Fighting is still in progress. A total of 14 enemy tanks appeared.
>
>   <u>Addition to daily report</u>: As a consequence of being strongly occupied by enemy infantry and anti-tank guns, it is no longer possible to recapture Hill 139.7 before dark.
>
>   At 1600 hours, thirty minutes of strong enemy artillery and mortar barrages fell on Hill 145.1. During the course of the day there was heavy artillery and mortar harassment fire on the Division's right sector, as well as an enemy assault in platoon strength on 147.6 and Ref.Pt.422.
>
>   <u>Aim for Division.</u>: Left wing of 16.Pz.Div., together with the right wing of 60.Inf.Div., will retake 139.7 before dawn on 26.12. and then straighten out the breakthrough position to the north-west.
>
>   <u>Casualties</u>[14]:
>   16.Pz.Div.:   7 dead, 11 wounded, 3 frostbitten, 2 missing
>   and 1 sick. Further casualties approx. 60 men.
>   <u>Enemy casualties</u>:
>   50 prisoners, 80 enemy dead counted,
>   one T-34 and one T-60 destroyed

26 December 1942

In the early morning hours of 26 December, around 0300 hours, as dawn slowly broke, renewed sounds of battle could already be heard coming from the north. An inquiry to Stab Reinisch revealed that our counterattack on Hill 139.7 had been repulsed by the Russians from their bunkers. A further Russian attack did not ensue. Our comrades, however, were ordered to dig in, construct bunkers at night – in deeply-frozen ground under artillery and mortar bombardment – and, on top of all that, be constantly ready to leap up and repulse an attack.

---

13. *The left neighbour was 60. Infanterie-Division (mot.).*
14. *Losses suffered by 60. Infanterie-Division (mot.) were particularly severe: 1 officer dead, 1 officer wounded, 1 officer frostbitten. 23 men dead, 38 men wounded. Number of men missing were to be reported later.*

Gen.Kdo. XI. A.K. — Morning report from 26. December 1942

16.Pz.Div.: Enemy assaults during the night — each with a strength of about 50 men — aimed towards 147.6 at 0100 and 0300 hours, as well as towards Ref.Pt.422, were repulsed.

At 0300 hours, the reinforced enemy on 139.7 sounded out to the south. The attack to recapture Hill 139.7 set off at 0300 hours. Our attack on 139.7 was repulsed by 0600 hours. It was carried out with 4 panzers, 8 half-tracks, 3 self-propelled light field howitzers and one company with 130 men. At this time, they are all back in the Regiment-Balka.

At the moment, the Russians are attacking in battalion strength from 139.7 to the south...

Gen.Kdo. XI. A.K. — Report to LI. Armeekorps, 26. December 1942

...Heavy snows storms have dominated since the beginning of the attack, not only reducing visibility to 40 metres but also making it impossible to hear the sound of approaching tanks...

Gen.Kdo. XI. A.K. — Daily report from 26. December 1942

16.Pz.Div.: The assault to recapture Hill 139.7 has only hard partial success. Despite strong anti-tank fire, our panzers and half-tracks pushed on to the hill. However, they did not succeed in constructing a continuous front-line with riflemen. Situation on the hill is still unclear at the moment...

Casualties:
16.Pz.Div.:   1 officer dead, 1 officer wounded. 17 men
                dead, 87 wounded, 36 missing, 7 frostbitten.

27 December 1942

During the evening of 27 December, my Futtermeister[15], Greguletz, suddenly appeared. He was concerned about the rest of the horses that were being sheltered somewhere in the city. Greguletz was very depressed. He reported: "There's barely a scrap of fodder left. In any case, the weakest animals have already been killed. Most are to be forcibly slaughtered. When something is rustled up that is suitable as fodder for the horses, then the strongest of them receive it so that they're kept alive a bit longer. Herr Oberleutnant, until now, I've been able to keep your Mumpitz alive. Now, however, even though I want to, I no longer can."

I understood him only too well, my trusted old Futtermeister, this farmer from Upper Silesia. For years, he had cared for the horses of the company and had already

---

15. _Futtermeister_ - 'NCO in charge of obtaining fodder'.

got them through the very hard winter of 1941/42. Now he stood there, helpless, unable to save his faithful four-legged friends. Without the necessary supplies, he was as powerless as all of us here.

We looked gravely at each other as I said to him: "Then you must also slaughter my Mumpitz!" With a firm handshake, we said good-bye to each other and Greguletz disappeared outside. I said a prayer for Mumpitz. I had to forcibly suppress the dark thoughts that befell me. My riding horse Mumpitz would remain in my memories: strong-willed, full of the lust for life and always causing trouble, of sorts. He was a rascal among horses.

Gen.Kdo. XI. A.K. — Daily report from 27. December 1942

    16.Pz.Div.: No occurrences except for artillery and mortar harassment fire on the Division's sector...

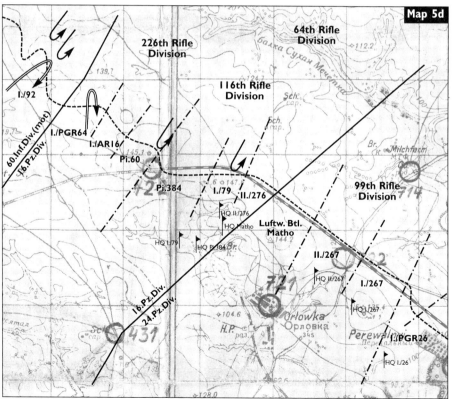

Course of the front-line and Soviet attacks on 27 December 1942. The failed German attempts to recapture Hill 139.7 at 0300 hours on 26 December 1942 are also shown.

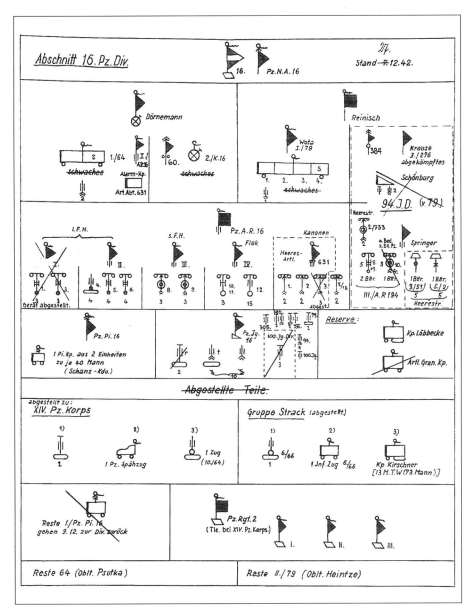

An Order of Battle submitted by 16. Panzer-Division, effective as of 27 December 1942. As the weeks in the Stalingrad pocket passed, these charts became strange patchworks of weakened companies, amalgamated battalions, units subordinated from other divisions and battle-groups: it bore almost no resemblance to charts submitted barely six months earlier, at the beginning of the 1942 summer campaign. Holl's unit ('Krause II./276') is still represented as part of Gruppe Reinisch and has been labelled 'abgekämpftes' ('worn out' or 'exhausted').

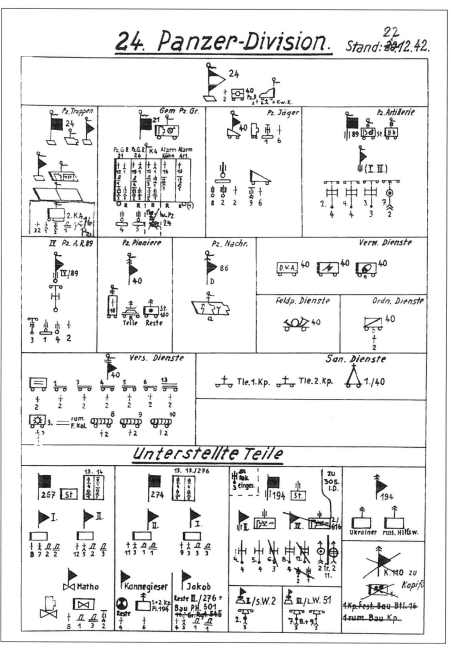

24. *Panzer-Division's Order of Battle showing the elements of 94. Infanterie-Division subordinated to it. As of 1 January 1943, these units – Gr.Rgt.267, Gr.Rgt.274, Art.Rgt.194 and others – would be integrated into it.*

28 December 1942

If nothing unforeseen happened, I would return to my company again in three days. They now bore the designation 1. Kompanie Panzergrenadier-Regiment 79 and belonged to 16. Panzer-Division, yet, these were the same men from my old II. Bataillon of Grenadier-Regiment 276. Only the Hauptfeldwebel of the old 1. Kompanie Panzergrenadier-Regiment 79 and his baggage train now belonged to us. He was responsible for supplies.

Major von Nordheim wanted us to spend the turn of the year with him because Grenadier-Regiment 276 would no longer exist on 1 January 1943. The entire staff would be divided, officers and men being split up into troop sections for 16. Panzer-Division or 24. Panzer-Division.

Gen.Kdo. XI. A.K. – Daily report from 28. December 1942

16.Pz.Div.: As a result of strong anti–tank, mortar and artillery defence, the attack to recapture Hill 139.7 in the early hours of the morning has had no success. More than 16 enemy anti–tank guns alone were counted in the narrowest possible area.
The Division holds its current occupied line and will construct a new main combat line in a series of strongpoints: Finck Balka – 800m south 139.7 – left wing I./Art.Gren.Btl.16. New dividing line to left neighbour: Hill 143.6, 119.7 (60.ID), 129.6 (16.PD)...
Losses: 2 Pz III long, 1 Pz IV long
Casualties: 1 officer killed, 4 wounded (2 stayed with troops)
13 men killed, 44 wounded (14 stayed with troops),
48 missing, 9 sick, 19 frostbitten.

Failed German counterattack on Hill 139.7, 28 December 1942.

Through a messenger from Greguletz, I learned that my riding horse had died the same night he was scheduled to be slaughtered. I did not believe it but considered it to be a merciful lie because Greguletz knew I was very attached to my Mumpitz.

31 December 1942

On 31 December, the last day for us of this momentous year, it didn't snow at all. The cook from the regimental staff had somehow been able to obtain some additional horse meat. The regimental paymaster was successful in procuring some alcohol. With tea and a shot of alcohol, we moved into the new year at midnight: Major Dr. von Nordheim, Oberleutnant Kelz, Oberzahlmeister Knopp, Leutnant Dr. Hofmann, Oberleutnant Förtsch and myself, the youngest at this gathering. We were all full of anxiety but nevertheless were calm and confident. We would have to part from one another in a few hours because each of us had a new assignment. None of us knew if and when we would see each other again. We sat together late into the night and chatted earnestly.

Before I made my way back to my company, I reported to Major von Nordheim and bid farewell to the few comrades on the staff, who were also getting ready to report themselves to their allocated units.

My winter equipment was inadequate for operations at the front: no winter boots, only the normal 'dice-cups', riding-breeches and the normal service coat, under them a shirt, pants and a pullover, a pair of woollen socks, the normal winter overcoat, the lamb-skin cap and the lamb-skin mittens. My bread-bag contained the necessary utensils for shaving and washing. That was all I had.

CHAPTER 6

Now a part of I. Bataillon Panzergrenadier-Regiment 79

1 January 1943

Trudging through the snow made me work up a sweat. I didn't feel the cold all that much as there was little or no wind. When the temperature falls below -20° Celsius, you can barely tell if it is -20° or -40° Celsius. You only know that it's bloody cold!

My destination was the command post of Kampfgruppe Krause, which should be somewhere in the Orlovka gully south of Hill 147.6. All the remaining elements of the former Grenadier-Regiment 276 had been placed under the command of Hauptmann Krause. Our commander was Oberst Reinisch of Panzergrenadier-Regiment 79.

After I reached the Orlovka gully, I still had to ask several times where I could find Hauptmann Krause. In this ravine, which had been eroded ever deeper over thousands of years by weathering and had several lateral inlets, the dug-outs clung side by side on

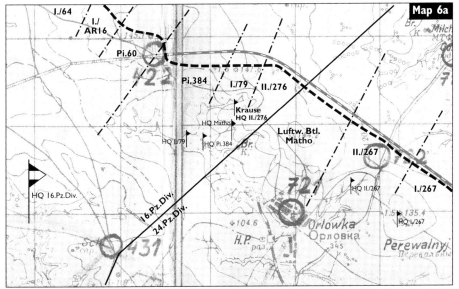

The command post of Kampfgruppe Krause (II./Grenadier-Regiment 276), as well as the headquarters of other units, were located in the north-western branch of the Orlovka Gully.

the walls like swallow's nests. Depending on the slope, these bunkers were sometimes situated higher up, sometimes lower down. Several were located directly alongside the path, while others had stairs carved from the earth. I had to pay attention to keep my footing on the slippery ground. The narrow surface had been constantly walked on over the past days, making the path as smooth as glass.

Hauptmann Krause had already been informed about my arrival. The welcome extended by him and Leutnant Gerlach was serious but very warm. Krause and I had got on well with each other since the moment we first met after the Polish campaign, when we were both posted from 21. Infanterie-Division to 94. Infanterie-Division at Königsbrück near Dresden, a unit newly formed on the exercise ground there.

"Well, you're finally here. How are you, Herr Holl?"

"Alright, Herr Hauptmann, under the circumstances. I would've preferred to say 'good'."

"Well, we're no better off. Constant casualties, extremely scarce rations, little ammunition: we must be economical with it. And then this damned cold!"

"It's also giving me cause for concern, Herr Hauptmann. Look at my uniform. In this get-up, I would make a tempting target for the enemy at the front."

"You're right about that. Fortunately, we've still got some winter equipment on hand that was allotted to us by 16. Panzer-Division. Herr Gerlach, can you please arrange for Herr Holl to receive the necessities. – Let's look at the situation map: we form the right flank of Panzergrenadier-Regiment 79. Located to the left of us is the old I. Bataillon of the Regiment under the command of Major Wota, to which we now belong. In accordance with orders, however, we are subordinated as a 'Kampfgruppe' to this Regiment until further notice. This means that our men remained with us, since we know them better. To the right of us is the left flank of 24. Panzer-Division. Our direct neighbour is the Luftwaffe battalion of Hauptmann Matho[1]. Then come our

---

1. *Hauptmann Matho, commander Luftwaffe (Luftlande) Schützenbataillon z.b.V. This battalion, formed exclusively from Luftwaffe personnel, contained five companies: 1., 2. and 3.Kompanien were rifle companies, 4.Kompanie contained heavy weapons and 5.Kompanie was – confusingly – '4./Fallschirmjäger-Flugabwehr-Maschinengewehr-Bataillon 7' (4th company from Fallschirmjäger Anti-Aircraft MG Battalion 7). On 13 November 1942, the three rifle companies each had 9 light MGs, 3 light mortars and an anti-tank rifle. The 4.Kompanie had 4 heavy mortars, 9 heavy MGs, 3 light MGs and an anti-tank rifle. The 5. Kompanie (4./Fsch.Fla.MG.Btl.7) was truly unique, being the only one of its type in existence. It was formed from young, elite paratroopers and contained four platoons, two equipped with 5cm anti-tank guns and two with 2cm anti-aircraft guns. Its initial ration strength was 5 officers and 250 NCOs and men. On 13 November 1942, it had six 5cm anti-tank guns, four 2cm anti-aircraft guns, 2 heavy MGs, 10 light MGs and 39 submachine-guns. It also had about 200 men. Since first being employed near Stalingrad in mid-September, it had sustained heavy casualties, including the loss of all 5 officers, but had performed well. Hauptmann Matho initially led 1. Kompanie but took command of the battalion on 14 September 1942 after the previous commander, Hauptmann Scherwitz, was wounded. Matho commanded the battalion until its remnants – and he himself – were captured on 2 February 1943. Matho died in Oradi POW camp in March 1943.*

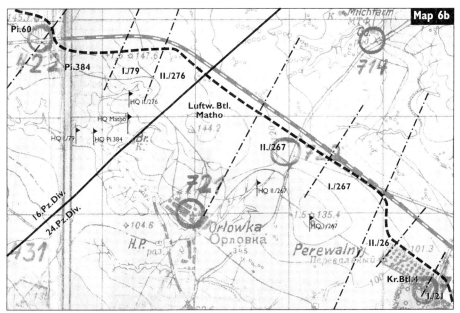

Disposition of units of 16. and 24. Panzer-Divisions, 1 January 1943.

comrades from Grenadier-Regiment 267 who have been allotted to 24. Panzer-Division. There too, there have been no personnel changes. By the way, the Luftwaffe men are dependable comrades who've been heavily involved in defending against enemy attacks in the past days[2]. – When the men are fed this evening, you can go with Leutnant Augst and take over your company again. Augst can give you a more detailed briefing in the front-line. He and his men have had another difficult day today. Early this morning, 'Ivan' once again attacked Hill 147.6., which now lies under constant artillery bombardment. However, the men of Bataillon Wota beat off the attack. We were naturally ready for action in an emergency."

"I realised something was going on at the front while on the way here. The wind carried the sound of battle to the west. It didn't seem to me to be too serious."

"You'll soon realise yourself that the deep snow muffles the detonation of explosions. The sound-waves are absorbed by the snow and don't produce the noise we usually hear."

In the meantime, Leutnant Gerlach brought me camouflaged clothing and a pair of felt boots. A few minutes later, it was slipped over my uniform. The empty space in the

2. *The soldiers of 16.Pz.-Div., 24.Pz.-Div. and 94.Inf.-Div. fought side by side with the Luftwaffe men of Kampfgruppe Matho and had nothing but the highest praise for them. The Luftwaffe men were well-trained and well-led, unlike the many Luftwaffe field divisions that would be raised during the next two years.*

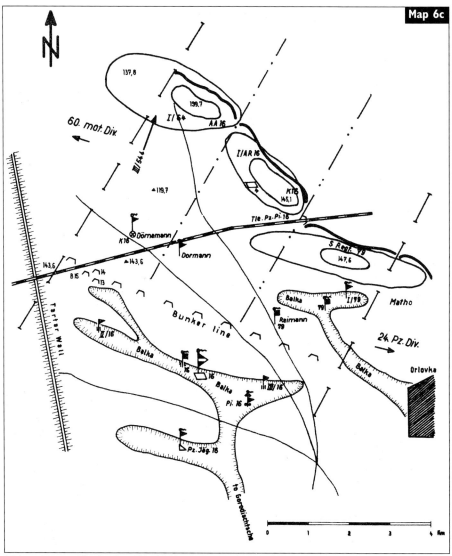

Main positions and landmarks within 16. Panzer-Division's sector, 1 December 1942 – 23 January 1943.

winter boots (I was shoe size 39) was filled with two pair of foot-cloths. I was now indistinguishable from my comrades.

"Herr Hauptmann, before I go to my men, I would like to see the Hauptfeldwebel of 1. Kompanie of Panzergrenadier-Regiment 79, Hauptfeldwebel Bigge. I don't yet know him but I need to get to know my new Spiess."

"Ja, you do that. I've already become acquainted with him, he's a methodical man."

I exchanged a few words with Leutnant Gerlach and let him show me where I could find my new Hauptfeldwebel. When I left the bunker, I could still clearly hear the impacts of shells. They came from a north-west direction.

The 'room' in which Hauptfeldwebel Bigge lived with several men did not differ very much from all the other bunkers. Most of them were 2 by 3 metres, but rarely larger. They were dug out of the clay walls of the balka. In this way, raw material was saved, given that wood was in short supply. Overhead cover, which also served as a ceiling, was primarily constructed from railway sleepers. Spread over that was soil that had been produced by the excavation. The front wall consisted of boards but the side and rear walls were carved out of the material of the balka, namely clay or dirt. Along the walls were double-plank beds for sleeping and some sort of contraption that served as an oven. No-one could exist here without heating facilities. And necessity was the mother of invention!

I greeted Bigge and introduced myself as the new company commander. Being 169cm tall, I appeared small next to my Spiess, who was a head taller. When answering my questions, I immediately recognised by his accent that he was a Sauerländer.

"How large is our trench strength at the moment", I wanted to know.

"Leutnant Augst with 48 Unteroffiziere and men."

"Have we received any replacements in the last days?"

"Herr Oberleutnant, men constantly come and go. Light casualties are handled by the battalion doctor and sent back to the Kompanie as soon as possible. – Permit me to ask if you want to escort me to our Schirrmeister[3]. I have to discuss several things with him. It'll also give you a chance to meet him."

I agreed. We made our way there together. The quarters of the Schirrmeister – his name was Schulz – were as previously described. The room measured 2 by 3 metres at the most. Counting Schulz, there were four of us and we filled the dug-out. A cylindrical iron stove roared for all it was worth. This hole was almost too hot for me.

While Bigge was discussing an official matter with his comrades and I listened with interest, there was a sudden wooff … and we stood amongst the roaring flames! I was shocked: the only exit was blocked by a wall of fire! We were our own worst enemies. The heat was unbearable. Although it was only seconds, it seemed like an eternity to us!

This was nothing new to the Schirrmeister: he ripped the blanket off his plank-bed and threw it over the full petrol can that stood near the door. Then he took his heavy overcoat and placed it over it. What a miracle: in a few seconds, the flames were smothered. However, now the smoke made breathing difficult in this small box. I

---

3. _Schirrmeister_ - '_NCO responsible for technical replacements_'.

rushed outside and deeply breathed in the fresh winter's air. The others also came out.

Bigge was furious and laid into the Schirrmeister: "Damn it all, you know that petrol canisters aren't allowed to be kept in a heated room! Put it somewhere where there's no danger of an explosion!"[4]

Bigge and Schulz apologised to me.

In the meantime, I got over the shock, since I quickly understood what had happened.

We infantry understood something about oats and nosebags but nothing about fuel. I had to adapt. I was now a company commander in a motorised unit but had no driving licence, not to mention the slightest idea of how engines worked. But that didn't matter now. We only had to hold on and see it through by whatever means possible. There was always fewer of us and always more of the enemy. We were all doggedly determined and wanted to hold out to the last.

I went forward to my company with the food-carriers. A few weeks previously, it had still been easy for my Hauptfeldwebel to drive to the front with the cook and carry the rations there in sections. Now, six men carried three canisters in which, alas, only thin 'warm rations' sloshed about. Bigge carried a few pieces of bread and lard in a sack. We followed one another along a beaten path. I brought up the rear. Every one of us was desperately trying to keep our balance. There was no talking. After about ten minutes, we reached the company command post. It was more of a hole about two square metres in size.

My second-in-command, Leutnant Augst, emerged and talked with the Hauptfeldwebel in whispered voices. Meanwhile, I went into the so-called bunker. A shoddy lamp dimly illuminated the room. A sheet metal canister, which had been converted into an oven, gave out some warmth.

Three figures got to their feet It was Pawellek, Nemetz and Grund, our company barber. I was happy to see their trusted faces again. It was very important to know the men you were with, particularly in difficult situations. Men who have been together for years and known each other in good times and bad. You know their strengths and weaknesses. Confidence in each other was greater than it otherwise would have been with new arrivals. This was not meant to belittle the others when you didn't know them. It was simply an established fact that everyone was aware of.

I shook hands with all three of them and asked Pawellek: "Juschko, what are you doing here? I thought you'd already be at home, as a lucky husband!"

The old war horse answered glumly: "It would've been beautiful but it was not to be. I got as far as Kalach; from there, I should've gone home by rail. Then the devil was

---

4. *Judging by the announcement issued by XI. Armeekorps on 9 December 1942 (shown right), this type of incident was obviously not an uncommon occurrence. Schirrmeister Schulz was lucky not to be punished.*

A b s c h r i f t :

F e r n s c h r e i b e n .

Absendende Stelle: 3.12.1942.
  XI.A.K.   An   19,oo Uhr
    Ia   24. Pz.-Div.
                          16. Pz.-Div.
                          6o. mot.-Div.

      Der Kommandierende General der Gruppe v. Seydlitz gibt bekannt: Die Zahl der Unterstandsbrände ist unverändert hoch.Es wird höchste Zeit, daß mit Strenge dagegen angegangen wird. Bei den Bränden gehen große Werte zu Grunde, die in der augenblicklichen Lage unersetzbar sind. Besonders schwer wiegt der Verlust von Munition und Lebensmitteln. Die Ursache der Brände liegt meist in grober Fahrlässigkeit oder in unsachgemässer Anlage der Öfen.

      Ich ersuche daher, eine allgemeine Kontrolle der Unterstände sofort durchführen zu lassen. Wo Öfen nach Anlage und Aufstellung nicht die nötige Sicherheit bieten, ist Abänderung sofort zu veranlassen. Es ist laufend zu überprüfen, daß brennbare Gegenstände nicht in der Nähe der Feuerstelle abgelegt werden. In Fällen festgestellter Fahrlässigkeit ist scharf einzuschreiten. Für selbstverschuldete Verluste sind die Schuldigen haftbar zu machen.

      Ich muss von dem Verantwortungsbewusstsein aller Führer und Unterführer erwarten, daß sie sich alle Mühe geben, unnötige Verluste wertvoller Güter vorsorglich zu verhindern.

                                 XI. A.K. Ia

"The Commanding General of Gruppe v. Seydlitz announces: The number of burnt-down shelters is invariably high. It's time that such accidents be stringently dealt with. Large quantities of valuable items are being destroyed in the fires, which, in the current situation, are irreplaceable. The loss of ammunition and food is especially serious. The cause of the fires is mainly due to gross negligence or the improper construction of ovens.

"I therefore ask that a general inspection of the shelters take place immediately. Where construction and installation of ovens does not offer the necessary safety, modifications must be immediately initiated. It is to be continually monitored that inflammable objects are not stored near fireplaces. Cases of proven negligence are to be severely punished. Guilty parties will be held responsible for self-inflicted losses.

"I have to expect a sense of responsibility from all officers and NCOs so that everyone exerts themselves to prevent this unnecessary loss of precious goods."

suddenly let loose: apparently, the Russians broke through near the Rumanians. They'll soon be at the Don bridge. Idiots, they acted like rear supply units: one said giddy-up, the other whoa! If there'd been regular troops like us there ... The entire thing would have turned out differently. Herr Oberleutnant, we, with our men, could have held firm there and organised a defence!"

I wanted to placate him: "Well, I doubt if we'd have made a better job of it."

"But it makes me want to puke! When the Russians did in fact appear on the far bank of the Don – only a day later – that was the end of my marriage leave. I then got a hurry on and came back to the Kompanie."

"Good grief, Juschko, and you didn't think of the airport? You know all the tricks!"

"Nope, I hadn't thought of that."

I was very moved by his bad luck: however, I was glad he was with me again.

"And our 'Figaro', how long have you been here at the front?"

"Three weeks already. As Herr Oberleutnant knows, everyone is employed at the front. Herr Leutnant Augst used me as a messenger to the Kompanietrupp after Obergefreiter Willmann was killed."

"Nemetz, who from our old crowd is still here?"

"We still have 8 men from our Kompanie, with the others from the Bataillon, about 24 men, and the rest were posted to us from different units. They're mostly men from staff units, artillerymen, radio-men, truck drivers etc. Their infantry experience is minimal but they do their duty without grumbling[5]. We even have non-coms employed as sentries."

"Well, rank no longer really matters. It comes down to every man's will to do his duty for our people and our homeland."

Leutnant Augst came in, escorted by an invisible wall of icy cold. He quickly closed the opening behind him, went to the fire and warmed up his hands.

"Damned frost, it goes straight through the gloves. Guten Abend, Herr Oberleutnant, I'm glad you're here. We can use every man here at the front. This morning, all hell broke loose again to the left of us, near Bataillon Wota. It was getting hot on Hill 147.6. We were all prepared for a counterthrust but the comrades of Bataillon Wota were able to make their presence felt. The Russian artillery, and also their heavy mortars, thoroughly plastered the hill. Unaimed mortar fire constantly fell on us throughout the entire day. It's fortunate that the nights are fairly quiet, yet, we must always be on our guard."

---

5. *Generaloberst Paulus issued an order in mid-December stating that all men who were to be sent to the front-line as replacements should receive a minimum of ten days of infantry training.*

Leutnant August was about my build, if somewhat smaller than I. He could easily have passed himself off as a southerner with his black hair and dark-brown eyes. He only needed to utter a few words, however, and his dialect revealed he was a Saxon. He had settled in well with the Silesians and was an adaptable officer on whom one could rely.

"Herr August, when you go to the positions later, I want you to accurately brief me. I want to be fully in the picture by first light tomorrow morning. Now that I'm staying here, I want to ask you where you intend to occupy positions."

"I suggest on the right flank to the Kampfgruppe of Hauptmann Matho. The new men are employed there. I'd like to take them under my wing as they've got no battle-experience. I'll stay with Feldwebel Cupal."

"That's alright with me because you know better than I what's necessary at the front."

"By the way, if you haven't yet noticed; we've got a direct line to Hauptmann Krause and Oberst Reinisch. Even the forwardmost posts have telephones to immediately raise the alarm when something happens. The 'Strippenzieher'[6] have become real night-shift workers."

"Oh, that's fine, then I can call Herr Oberst Reinisch and report to him that I've arrived."

I called the Regiment staff and reported my arrival at the company to my new commander and to Hauptmann Krause.

Then I got moving with Leutnant August to the forward posts. You couldn't lose your way. When you strayed from the beaten path by one step to the right or left, you sunk deeply into the soft snow. It was a starlit night, the snow crunched under the felt boots and there wasn't the slightest breeze. Breath was visible when exhaled because the cold made it freeze immediately. Fine crystals formed on the side of the nose when inhaling. The entire landscape lay in a diffused whiteness and was ghostly silent. Only from a distance – from the direction of that damned city which we hadn't managed to take – were faint sounds of battle discernible. Silently, I trudged behind August and took in the nocturnal scene. We arrived at the first observation post and the guards reported in a whisper. Nothing was out of the ordinary. A field-telephone stood in the corner of his observation post. A platform had been constructed for the machine-gun, which was wrapped in a tarpaulin so that it functioned when needed. On the side facing the enemy, the snow was piled so high that during the day, one was protected from sight and could quickly reach this spot from the snow holes. To call the snow holes accommodation would be an exaggeration. Only in the darkness could fires to warm up by be made, because during the day, smoke betrayed the position to the enemy. Aimed mortar fire was the result.

---

6. _Strippenzieher_ - 'Cable guys' or 'cable-layers', common nickname for the communications troops who laid and repaired cables.

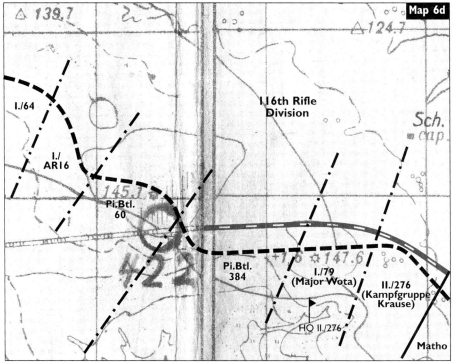

Position of Holl's unit, 1 January 1943.

We arrived at the second post. It was the most advanced post. It lay directly at the foot of Hill 147.6. At this post there was also a field-telephone. I recognised both sentries because they were from other units of our old battalion.

Augst whispered to me: "The hill up there is the critical point in this sector. Major Wota and his people are responsible for it. Whenever there's a racket up there, we go to the highest state of alert in case help is needed; likewise for Hauptmann Matho's unit to the right of us. There are two shot-up tanks up there: a T-34 and one of 16. Panzer-Division's. This morning, the men from Bataillon Wota were able to repulse the attack, but what'll tomorrow bring?"

I looked up at the hill. You could easily misjudge in the darkness but it was at least 100 to 120 metres to the top.

We still had three posts to check; we didn't go into the shelters because the men needed their rest. With the poor rations and this bloody cold, it would be irresponsible to disturb them – especially since no-one knew when the enemy would provide trouble. Only at the last post did Leutnant Augst fetch Feldwebel Cupal. As an old member of my former 7. Kompanie, I wanted to greet him. Wordlessly, we shook each others hand.

His face had become thin, his slightly bent nose was still pointed, as it always was.

"Cupal", I whispered, "Leutnant Augst will now stay with you and look after your right flank. Do you have room for him?"

"Jawohl, Herr Oberleutnant, enough for a man."

"If something happens here, call at once!"

"Jawohl, alles klar!"

I shook hands with both of my comrades and said "Take care of yourselves." – then I went back on my way.

I was now completely responsible for this 150 metre wide sector. What would the next day bring? How long could we hold on here? These were questions that I couldn't answer. Here, one could still only believe, hope and trust.

<u>Gen.Kdo. XI. A.K.</u> – Daily report from 1. January 1943

 <u>16.Pz.Div.</u>: Enemy artillery and mortar harassment fire. Otherwise no occurrences.

2 January 1943

In the first light of dawn, the spell of fire again broke upon Hill 147.6. I tried to get in touch with Post 2. The line was still working. The sentry reported artillery and mortar fire on the hill, then defensive fire from our machine-guns. I could clearly hear the sounds of battle through the earpiece. It was quiet in my sector, apart from scattered mortar fire and stray ricochets. I ordered a higher state of readiness, however, because one never knew. A situation could develop in seconds.

The battle noise died down around midday. Inquiries to my sector commanders revealed that the attack in Wota's sector had once again been repulsed. The resulting casualties were made good from disbanded supply units and staffs. We were also to receive reinforcements.

The night of 2 to 3 January again saw us at alarm readiness. A strong Russian assault group surprised the left flank of Kampfgruppe Reinisch – precisely on the border to the left neighbour – and penetrated the front-line. The enemy captured a bunker.

In this bitter cold, a bunker (which could be heated) meant life or death for a casualty. Winter combat was conducted with grim doggedness because who would like to be without shelter in temperatures that could be compared at home to those of a cool-storage room?

<u>Gen.Kdo. XI. A.K.</u> – Daily report from 2. January 1943

 <u>16.Pz.Div.</u>: Light artillery and mortar harassment fire. Otherwise no combat activity.

3 January 1943

As our comrades failed to recapture the bunker during the night, I had no doubt that this would be tried the following night. We could no longer contemplate attacks during the day because we were too weak in heavy weapons and ammunition was scarce. The deficiency of rations also had an effect on our condition. Therefore, we had to dig our heels in here, let the enemy approach and hold on with all available means. If a bunker was lost, however, none of this helped: it had to be attacked, and it had to be a surprise night-time assault.

I was not mistaken: in the night of 3 to 4 January, the bunker was the attack objective of our comrades to the left and was recaptured. A damned blasted nuisance!

<u>Gen.Kdo. XI. A.K.</u> – Daily report from 3. January 1943

    <u>16.Pz.Div.</u>: Artillery and mortar harassment fire.

4 January 1943

From 4 to 5 January, the highest state of alert was again in effect. The fighting raged further to the left of us, north-west behind Hill 147.6. 'Ivan' was now apparently trying to win back the bunker.

I went with Nemetz to a forward post. When flares climbed into the sky to the west of us, they silhouetted the entire hill for a few seconds. We had to be on our guard because the enemy could easily try to push into the front-line near us as he assumed we would be distracted by the noises of battle. At night, well-camouflaged soldiers were difficult to spot, especially when the nightly silence was interrupted by the crackle of machine-gun and rifle fire. We also rarely used flares. Sentries were ordered to use them sparingly.

After some time, I set off to inspect the right post. There, I met Leutnant Augst, who was talking with Hauptmann Matho, the commander of our right neighbours. This enabled us to get to know each other. This sector was also quiet. Nevertheless, everyone was – like us – on the alert to immediately deploy in case of an alarm.

On the way back to my command post, I could still hear furious exchanges of rifle and machine-gun fire, as well as the short bark of exploding hand-grenades. The battle was still raging. Hopefully, our men would prevail.

<u>Gen.Kdo. XI. A.K.</u> – Daily report from 4. January 1943

    <u>16.Pz.Div.</u>: Heavy artillery and mortar fire upon the entire divisional sector in the morning hours. Two new enemy batteries were spotted by the observation battery. Around 1100 hours, the enemy – for the first time – dropped a barrage in to the Balka level with the Division command post. At 1130 hours, after heavy

artillery preparation, the Russians attacked at several positions
in the eastern divisional sector, focusing mainly on 147.6. They
succeeded in breaking through in one place, just west of 147.6 .
Countermeasures are in progress at the moment. At 1330 hours,
strong artillery fire (smoke) was laid down on Hill 145.1 and 0.6.
        Addition to daily report: The counterattack to wipe out the
enemy breakthrough near 147.6 has stalled in strong artillery and
mortar defensive fire. At the moment, the breakthrough position is
sealed off. Further countermeasures are in progress.

5 January 1943

5 January brought us the bad news that the hotly contested bunker was finally lost. For us, that meant the Russians on the north-western side of Hill 147.6 were a bit closer as a result of this move forward. His repeated assaults on this prominent landmark had made it clear to us that we were to be next in line in the near future.

We received the previously announced reinforcements of comrades who had served in the supply trains, staffs and other supply units. This was literally the last levy. Feldwebels, Wachtmeister, Unteroffiziere, Obergefreite and Gefreite from all units, thus an army that now had only one purpose: defend itself to the last!

Gen.Kdo. XI. A.K. — Daily report from 4. January 1943

        Einsatz—Kompanie from 16.Pz.Div. supply services: 1
officer, 100 NCOs and men, organised in three platoons, of those,
two platoons sent to help seal off the breakthrough position at
147.6, the third platoon placed at Division's disposal in the Balka
4km north—west of 431.

All of a sudden, the headcount of my Kompanie now had a strength that had never been planned in peacetime. These reinforcements naturally brought several problems with them. The most urgent task was quickly building shelters for them. These were constructed in places behind the front-line that could not be overlooked by the enemy.

Time was pressing. The shelters had to be finished while we still occupied Hill 147.6. If the hill was lost, then even during the day, all we could expect was constant enemy fire. My comrades were aware of that and worked in uninterrupted around-the-clock shifts. New positions were also constructed in the front-line: however, these were mostly just walls of snow that only offered cover against observation. Whoever was not working went back to the dug-outs in the balka. As the ground was deeply-frozen and the physical condition of the men was increasingly deteriorating, the construction work progressed only with difficulty. Anything suitable as building material was brought forward.

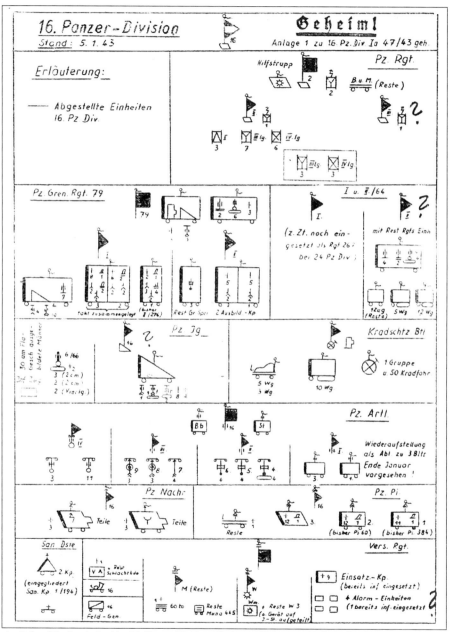

An Order of Battle submitted by 16. Panzer-Division, effective as of 5 January 1943. In this chart, II./Gr.Rgt.276 has been formally integrated into Panzergrenadier-Regiment 79 as its 1. Kompanie and is shown as being armed with 2 light machine-guns, 3 heavy machine-guns, one 50mm mortar, four 81mm mortars and 2 anti-tank rifles.

The attitude of the men was irreproachable. They knew the gravity of the situation and worked with grim faces and empty stomachs. Rank played no role; everyone pitched in as this dreadful cold was now the worst enemy.

The observation posts were strengthened and relief time for the men shortened.

<u>Gen.Kdo. XI. A.K.</u> – Daily report from 5. January 1943

    <u>16.Pz.Div.</u>: Artillery and mortar harassment fire on the left divisional sector. The counterattack on Hill 147.6 launched in the very early morning hours has been denied success, despite detailed preparations and regular attempts. The breakthrough position was sealed off. During the course of the day, the bulk of the divisional artillery has operated against the breakthrough position. More of our own assault troops will be introduced.

6 January 1943

On 6 January, the Russians tried to take Hill 147.6. They managed to break in. We were in the highest state of alert and ready to counterattack but my left neighbour, Oberleutnant Korte, straightened out this enemy penetration in his sector himself. He was killed in hand-to-hand fighting with the Russians[7]. Nevertheless, the hill remained in our possession. Once again things had worked out.

We exerted ourselves ceaselessly to construct the positions. We knew little about the general situation of the army. I was convinced that our comrades in Stalingrad and on other fronts were no better off because the cold was the same everywhere.

Hauptmann Krause told me that the Volga had frozen and the Russians now brought their troops and supplies directly over the ice. That was not welcome news for us. Nevertheless, we were soldiers who had to carry out our orders. We had to fulfil our duty and be faithful to our oath for Führer, Volk und Vaterland! No-one asked whether it was right. We believed we were protecting our people from this concept of Bolshevism that was a danger to the entire free world. Had the English and Americans not once bitterly regretted supporting these 'Reds'?

I thought back to the proclamation of Friedrich the Great: "It is not necessary that I live but that I do my duty well." And that was exactly what we soldiers of 6. Armee did, whether we came from the north, south, west or east of our homeland or from wherever we came, whether we were Prussian, Bavarian, Schwabian, Saxon, southern German or Austrian. Nobody asked when the soldiers' destiny overtook them. All of our fates lay in God's hands.

---

7. *Oberleutnant Günter Korte. Born 26 April 1914 in Essen, killed 7 January 1943 on Hill 147.6 in Stalingrad.*

Gen.Kdo. XI. A.K. – Daily report from 6. January 1943

16.Pz.Div.: Our attack to recapture Hill 147.6 in the very early morning hours had no success due to strong artillery, mortar and anti-tank fire. The old front-line around 147.6, from 150 metres east of it to 300 metres west of it, is occupied by the enemy. While firmly holding the inner edges, the breach at this moment is sealed off about 300 metres south of 147.6. A new main combat line was constructed in the dark using all available forces.

Towards 1230 hours, the enemy – with two platoons – attacked the platoon of 1./79 still holding out in the old front-line 200 metres east of Hill 147.6. The attack was repelled in the combined fire from infantry and heavy weapons, which caused casualties for the enemy.

...II./276, with elements of 13. and 14. Kompanien, were disbanded and absorbed into I./79.

9 January 1943

10 January was almost upon us. It was approaching midnight. I went with my messenger Nemetz – as I did every night – on an inspection tour of my sector from the left to right flank. The second sentry, standing directly beneath Hill 147.6, reported to me: "Herr Oberleutnant, Division called. You've been asked to immediately call Herr General from here!"

I was surprised. What would my new Division Commander want from me? Until now, I had not had an opportunity to personally meet him.

After hearing 'One moment, I'll put you through…' a few times, I heard a voice on the other end: "Angern[8] here."

"Oberleutnant Holl speaking, Commander of 1. Kompanie Panzergrenadier-Regiment 79. I was told to call Herr General."

"Ja, correct. My dear Holl, I'm happy to be able to notify you of your promotion to Hauptmann. You've been promoted by Generaloberst Paulus effective from 1 January. My congratulations and I wish you continued soldier's luck!"

The surprise lasted for a few seconds, until I said "Humbly thankful, Herr General!"

Was I dreaming or was this reality?

Nemetz asked: "What's happened, Herr Oberleutnant?"

---

8. *Generalleutnant Günter Angern, Commander 16. Panzer-Division. Born 5 March 1893 in Kolberg; Knight's Cross (145) on 5 August 1940, German Cross in Gold (83/1) on 8 March 1942; killed 2 February 1943 while attempting to break out of the Stalingrad Kessel. Other sources say he committed suicide.*

```
Auszug
                              G e h e i m !
              V o r z u g s w e i s e  B e f ö r d e r u n g e n !

          Mit Wirkung vom 1.Januar 1943 werden befördert:

Name          Friedens-       Dienst-      bisheriges       neues
              truppenteil     stellung     Rangdienstalter  Rangdienst-
                                                            alter

                   zu Hauptleuten bezw. Rittmeisteren:
                        die Oberleutnante:

Holl          Gren.Rgt.24     Kp.Chef i.   1.Juli 1942      1.Januar 1943
(Adelbert)                    e.Gren.Rgt.    (83)              (346)



                      Führerhauptquartier, den 15.Februar 1943
                              Der Führer
                          gez. Adolf Hitler
                      Oberkommando des Heeres
                              J. A.
                          gez. Schmundt
                          Generalmajor
                   und Chef des Heerespersonalamts
```

Adelbert Holl's promotion to Hauptmann, effective 1 January 1943.

"Good grief, Nemetz, I've been promoted to Hauptmann with immediate effect!"

"Fantastic, congratulations!" His sunken face showed genuine delight.

The sentry – one of my few remaining Upper Silesians – added his congratulations. We continued on our way. I thought about this surprise promotion that reached me in a forward position. This must have been arranged by my old Regiment Commander, Oberst Grosse. His adjutant, Oberleutnant Kelz[9], as well as my sector commander Krause, were both promoted to Hauptmann effective from 1 December 1942. I was the last of the old company commanders of the Regiment. A Führer Decree stated that premature promotions could be determined if a corresponding rank had been retained over an especially long period. This could be the only explanation.

Nemetz ensured that the other sentries learned of this piece of news. Wherever I went, I had to shake hands.

Despite my happiness, the hard unmerciful facts jolted me back to the present. What role would rank still play here? Everything now depended on the individual and whether he had the heart to stick it out.

In my dug-out, Pawellek suddenly asked: "Herr Hauptmann, where will you get the two pips so that everyone sees you're a Hauptmann?"

---

9. *Oberleutnant Erich Kelz had been killed two days earlier, on 7 January 1943.*

"Juschko, it's not important, we've time for that later ."

Oberst Reinisch called and congratulated me; my comrade Hauptmann Krause did likewise. He also informed me that he had two pips and that the messenger Marek would give them to me at the next opportunity. I thanked him for this nice gesture.

> <u>Gen.Kdo. XI. A.K.</u> – Daily report from 9. January 1943
>
> <u>16.Pz.Div.</u>: From dawn of the current day, conspicuous enemy movements to and from his front–line concentrated mainly near 145.1, weaker near 147.6 and 139.7. The enemy is reinforcing his front–line troops. It cannot be determined whether this is preparation or just a relief. Division reckons on an enemy attack.

10 January 1943

On 10 January, the Russians began their firestorm around 1000 hours and we feared the worst. No matter which direction you listened, sounds of fighting could be heard everywhere. The main attack appeared to be in our divisional sector. From the intensity of the bombardment, it was obvious that the Russians had been tremendously strengthened by the forces they brought across the frozen Volga.

The first enemy attack was stopped just short of the front-line. We only had machine-guns and rifles with which to defend ourselves. The few shells sent over by our artillery were well-aimed and helped us considerably.

After a short break, 'Ivan' tried a second time to reach his objective. It was once again smashed.

My comrades fought with a doggedness the likes of which they never thought possible. What other choice did we have? Captivity? By these Bolshevists? Never!

Our casualties were high; it was mostly a matter of wounded men. When it was quieter, those who weren't able to walk by themselves were taken to the rear positions. Where our field-hospital – or what served as one – was to be found, I didn't know. Our doctors would have their hands full. Did they still have enough medicine?

> <u>Gen.Kdo. XI. A.K.</u> – Daily report to Gruppe Seydlitz 10. January 1943
>
> <u>16.Pz.Div.</u>: Since 0700 hours, the enemy – after strong artillery preparation – attacked with the support of 11 tanks along a 5km wide sector (east of 422 – 139.7) focusing both sides of Hill 145.1. The enemy infantry stalled in front of our main combat line under our well–placed artillery fire and suffered heavy casualties. A smaller penetration south of 139.7 (4 strongpoints) was sealed off. In the afternoon, 3 of these were recaptured. Of the

enemy tanks that rolled over and through our front—line near 145.1, four were destroyed, the others turned northward.

At 1300 hours, the enemy relaunched his attacks on 145.1, 0.6 and the west slope of 147.6. The assaults on 145.1 and 0.6 were smashed in front of our main fighting line by concentrated fire. Enemy casualties are very high.

At 1400 hours, weaker enemy elements broke into our front—line near Ref.Pt.422. Countermeasures have been commenced.

<u>Addition to daily report.</u>: The enemy group that penetrated 500 metres south—east of Ref.Pt.422, with a strength of about 50—60 men, was thrown out by our panzers and the front—line straightened out. After nightfall, the enemy succeeded in breaking into the right wing of III./544. Sealing off of the penetration followed with the support of armoured personnel carriers and panzers...

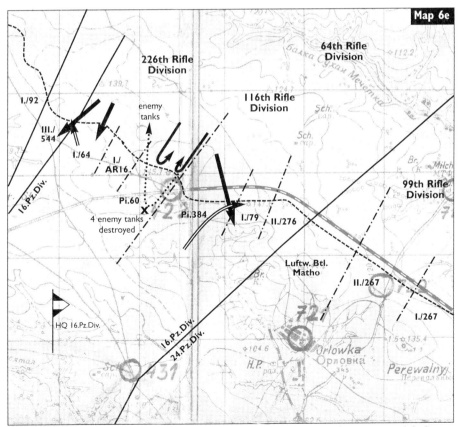

Soviet attacks on 10 January 1943. German counterattacks, carried out by armoured reserves, restored the line.

The smaller the Kessel became, the more difficult it must have become for the rear units. Those of us fighting here at the front-line knew almost nothing about that.

We were fortunate to have received men from the rear echelons. They replaced the fallen fighters. The few men with battle experience now formed the framework. They were the one constant factor and had an exemplary effect on the newcomers.

Naturally, the language of soldiers was crude and coarse, and every day, countless curses could be heard, but they were fair and by no means rebellious. Even I would swear with the soldierly coarseness of 'Landser jargon'. It was the safety valve we required to prevent us from going crazy. It was impotent rage at things that befell us and which we ourselves could not actively control.

The supply situation was deteriorating day to day. Only the combat troops still received 200 grams of bread, everyone else had to manage with 100 grams[10]. The soup consisted only of water and horse-meat that had been passed through a mincer. Flour or other additives which could thicken the soup did not seem to be used any more. I now knew what fatalism was. You had to try not to think what tomorrow or the day after would bring.

I was lucky I didn't smoke. If they managed to obtain only a few cigarettes at the front – which was becoming rarer – the heavy smokers sucked on these fags religiously. A stick was passed from mouth to mouth and smoked right down to the end, almost ending in burnt fingers. Smoke was inhaled and kept in the lungs as long as possible. Most smokers had their eyes closed while doing this. Finally, the smoke was blown out with an 'Ahhh'.

11 January 1943

Enemy fire and attacks continued on 11 January. The enemy pushed closer and closer to the front-line of our left neighbour. He took over fox-holes whose occupants were dead. This same tactic was used on 12 January. Our situation became ever more precarious.

> <u>Gen.Kdo. XI. A.K.</u> – Daily report from 11. January 1943
>
>   <u>16.Pz.Div.</u>: Despite high casualties the previous day, the Russians relaunched their attacks along the entire divisional sector beginning at 0630 hours. Near 0.6 and south–west of 139.7,

---

10. *According to 6. Armee records, the actual rations available to each man on 9 January 1943 consisted of 75 grams of bread, 24 grams of vegetables, 200 grams of horsemeat with bones, 12 grams of fat, 11 grams of sugar, 9 grams of an alcoholic beverage and 1 cigarette. However, the soldier himself usually did not receive all this: the field-kitchen of his unit combined the rations to produce a hot meal for everyone, mostly soup, whose main ingredient was melted snow.*

his attacks were supported by about 10 tanks. To begin with, the
enemy did not succeed in breaking into the main combat line. He was
thrown back everywhere with high casualties. Towards midday, enemy
pressure increased, particularly in front of the west slope of
147.6 (boundary between right and central combat groups) and in
front of Ref.Pt.422. A bunker of Strongpoint 422, temporarily in
enemy hands, was taken back in a counterattack. Under the heaviest
artillery and mortar preparation, the enemy succeeded in achieving
a break in at a point west of 147.6 on a 300 metre wide frontage and a
depth of 250 metres. Clearance of this breach is still in progress
with panzers and hastily gathered riflemen. During the course of
this counterattack, the northern branch of the Kamenaya Balka was
cleared of enemy troops. The existing holes were sealed off.

    At 1350 hours, an enemy attack in at least battalion
strength with 5 tanks broke into the right wing of Gruppe Dörnemann.
Width and depth of the penetration has still not been surveyed.
Countermeasures are under way.

12 January 1943

In the night to 13 January, the few remaining men on the left flank and in the
centre of the divisional sector were withdrawn to the Spartakovka-Gumrak railway
line. Now, only Hill 147.6 in the Reinisch sector was still in our possession. For us, it
was fortunate that the Russians didn't notice and only followed up hesitantly.

The new line of resistance, consisting of bunkers (which had been constructed by
Rumanian troops and lay about 1.5 kilometres behind the old front-line), was occupied
by our comrades to the left.

We remained in our positions and awaited further attacks on – what was for us –
the fateful Hill 147.6.

Gen.Kdo. XI. A.K. – Daily report to Gruppe Seydlitz 12. January 1943

    16.Pz.Div.: Since the morning hours, the Division has held
back the heavy undiminished attacks of the enemy against its entire
sector. Until now, they have been repelled in bitter combat with
severe losses for the enemy. Focal point of their attacks are Hills
145.1, 147.6 and south of 0.6. The enemy attacks are supported by
tanks. Of three tanks that pushed over 0.6 to the south, 2 of them
were most likely destroyed.

    The last heavy attack at 1430 hours north of 147.6, 145.1 and
south of 139.7 came to a standstill in the defensive fire of every
weapon. Our casualties are high...

14 January 1943

The enemy now understood what we were doing. He laid down concentrated fire on Hill 147.6, aiming into our positions from an almost westerly direction. This tactic put us at a disadvantage because the Division's left flank could no longer hold the old positions and had to be shifted back. It was almost flanking fire. How could we still defend ourselves?

Division quickly recognised this situation: we also received the order to pull back to the new front-line. There was much cursing from the men, which I could totally understand. All the trouble and work over the past days was now all for nothing. We knew what we had constructed for ourselves here. But what was waiting for us in the new positions? If only it wasn't for this atrocious cold.

We pulled back during the night of 14/15 January. We left practically nothing behind – if empty shellcases were ignored. We carried the two machine-guns and the pair of ammunition boxes in turns. Our overstrained and extremely weary mob painfully pushed onward through the snow. I stressed to the men that they shouldn't drop behind. The men should pair up and keep an eye on each other. The first sign of frostbite – when the nose or cheeks turned white – was something that most people would not notice by themselves. If this happened, only rubbing snow on that spot would help get the blood flowing again.[11]

I concluded with the words: "Kameraden, hold yourselves together. We don't have far to go. We have to leave stragglers behind; they'll freeze to death!"

The men understood. I composed myself. The responsibility was heavy: they all trusted me. Just don't let them down!

When such a clapped-out crowd – looked at objectively they could no longer be called an intact troop – moved forward with a supreme effort, then every metre was torture and 1500 metres an eternity. Nevertheless, we made it!

The strongest men were assigned sentry duty. Nearby, the remnants of my old men formed up and Leutnant Augst was again the nucleus of my unit.

There was nothing left of the spirit that inspired us in the past weeks and the elan with which we wanted to conquer this city of Stalin. We performed our duty like virtual machines. We felt somewhat threatened because something unknown was befalling us and we could not quite admit to it. When pressed hard, we fired and fought back like a fatally wounded animal that had been pushed into a corner and defended itself to the end with all its strength.

---

11. *Surprisingly, frostbite had been a relatively minor complaint during the preceding two months of winter fighting, but as the German troops grew weaker from lack of food and were forced out into the open after losing their dug-outs and bunkers, discipline weakened and frostbite cases rose. Frostbite was preventable if detected early but this depended largely on whether frostbite-detection was enforced by the unit commander.*

<u>Gen.Kdo. XI. A.K.</u> – Daily report from 14. January 1943

   <u>16.Pz.Div.</u>: At 0800 hours, an enemy attack with 50 to 60 men from 0.6 to the south remains stalled in the defensive fire of our infantry. Enemy reconnaissance troops and assault groups that are sounding out to the east of 147.6 were likewise repelled. During the morning, individual enemy tanks were observed driving east of 0.6. At 1230 hours, particularly strong enemy artillery fire on the entire Reinisch sector. Since 1345 hours, strong enemy attack from area of 141.0 and 0.6 in a south and south–west direction. Defence is under way.

   <u>Addition to daily report</u>: Towards 1400 hours, the Russians renewed their attack west of 147.6, around 0.6 and north of there as well as in Sector Biedermann. The attack west of 147.6 was repelled after a violent firefight, in part with counterattacks. According to earlier reports, the enemy was able to approach our front–line by having some of his men in German winter uniforms, these men then covering the others with volleys of hand–grenades. One company commander was severely wounded during this.

   The enemy attack aimed at Sector Biedermann – supported by 2 tanks – came to a standstill in our defensive fire.

   While we succeeded in halting the enemy attack, which was supported by 4 tanks, from the area south–east of 141.0 to the south before nightfall, the enemy pushed to the south from the area of 0.6 in about company strength.

   The counterattack, prepared in the moonlight with half–tracks and one panzer, as well as a company of riflemen, met considerable enemy resistance. Fighting is still in progress there.

17 January 1943

   That's what happened on 17 January: the enemy relaunched his attacks on the left flank of our neighbour. Bunkers were lost, recaptured, lost again and then won back. In the end, however, the enemy's superior numbers prevailed. Nevertheless, he took his time and acted cautiously because he knew we were as good as finished.

   My comrades and I did not want to admit it. We simply could not believe that our 6. Armee had to endure such a bitter end. We had always done our duty up to this point, performing the impossible, and yet, we now stood on the brink of disaster.

<u>Gen.Kdo. XI. A.K.</u> – Daily report from 17. January 1943

   <u>16.Pz.Div.</u>: Afternoon quiet. – Gorodishche–Position occupied in strongpoint fashion. About three companies...

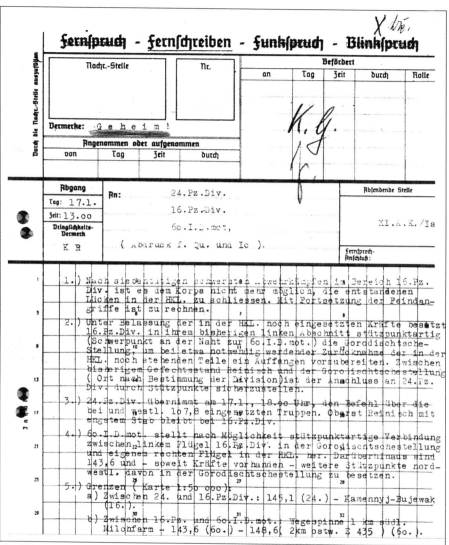

On 17 January 1943, XI. Armeekorps sent a momentous teletype message to its subordinate divisions signifying that it had lost the power to maintain a solid front-line. In part, it said:

"After seven days of the most difficult defensive combat in 16. Panzer-Division's zone, it is no longer possible for Korps to close the gaps that have formed in the front-line. Continuation of the enemy attacks must be reckoned on.

"Whilst being covered by forces still deployed in the main line of resistance, 16.Pz.-Div. will, on its present left-hand sector, occupy the Gorodishche-Position with a series of strongpoints (emphasis on the boundary to 60.Inf.-Div. mot.) in order to prepare a rear position for the increasingly inevitable withdrawal of units still holding out in the front-line. The connection to 24. Pz.-Div. between the current Reinisch command post and the Gorodishche-Position (location according to the determination of Division) is to be secured by strongpoints…"

21 January 1943

We had not received any hot food for three days. Only by moving about when we were outside and doing squats when we were stuck in the darkness of these holes that were called bunkers could we keep our blood circulating. Then, when the alarm was sounded, these human creatures shook off their exhaustion and defended themselves with their last ounce of strength. This had been going on for three days.

I sent Pawellek off with two men; he was to locate our Spiess and get us something to eat. He returned early in the morning hours with barely 100 grams of bread for each man, which we ate covetously, as if it were cake.

22 January 1943

On 22 January, my old loyal messenger Marek arrived to take me to the command post of Hauptmann Krause, my sector commander. Krause, whose staff consisted of only a handful of men, was also living in miserable conditions. Our facial expressions revealed the strain that resulted from being responsible for our comrades. Krause informed me that the whole Division would withdraw north past Gorodishche to the north-west perimeter of Stalingrad during the coming night. The resistance on the western and southern fronts of the Kessel had collapsed. Our troops had been pulled back full tilt into Stalingrad. The pocket had been split into a northern and a southern section. My company would form the rear-guard. We would only leave the front-line once darkness fell on 23 January.

With the aid of a map, Hauptmann Krause showed me the position we would occupy. It was located in the Orlovka Balka, right at the spot where the new defensive line that ran from east to west bent back to the south at almost a right angle and continued along the western edge of the city.

I learned that on 10 January, an ultimatum for the capitulation of our army had expired because our army hadn't responded to it. Capitulation and captivity were a completely new idea for us. We had never even contemplated it, let alone spoken about it.

CHAPTER 8

22 January 1943

Marek was assigned the task of immediately establishing a connection with us after our arrival in the new positions. I went back to my comrades with plenty to worry about. I hardly had any concerns about the few weapons and ammunition we still had. The only thing was how could we cope with it physically? Our stomachs were empty and the constant, bone-aching cold was bad even when there was only a light wind.

It was already dark when the platoon commanders Leutnant August and Feldwebel Cupal came to me. I told them about our current situation: "Gentlemen, the situation is shitty! Our comrades' resistance on the southern and western fronts of the Kessel has collapsed. The units have partially and hastily pulled themselves back into the city. There is now a northern and a southern pocket in the city. Tonight, our Division is going to withdraw north past Gorodishche to the western perimeter of the city. We have to form the rear-guard and then pull back early in the morning in two stages to the reception positions allocated to us. Hauptmann Krause has shown me the position on a map. Take a look here on my map: it's right here, where the Mokraya Mechetka flows into the Orlovka River. The front-line here almost makes a right-angle from west-east to north-south. We will therefore draw back in an easterly direction to the north-west edge of the city. Are there any comrades who can no longer move unaided? No! Thank God! And sharpen up the men so that we don't have any stragglers. The men will form up in pairs, as we did last time. Whoever stays behind won't be carried along by us and will freeze to death. The head of the column will move at a pace that everyone can follow. Herr August, you'll remain at the rear, I'll be at the front to ensure we make no unnecessary detours. Any questions? – Ah yes: the withdrawal begins at 0600 hours so that by daylight, we'll have covered enough ground so that the enemy can no longer see us. Auf Wiedersehen, until tomorrow!"

23 January 1943

The night eventually passed. At six o'clock, the troops set off. It was a sight that would have been laughable had the situation not been so deadly serious: the barely recognisable figures were swathed in uniform remnants which at best offered minimal protection against the cold. Only one machine-gun still remained from the men of the former heavy machine-gun Kompanie of my old Bataillon. The gun-mount had been

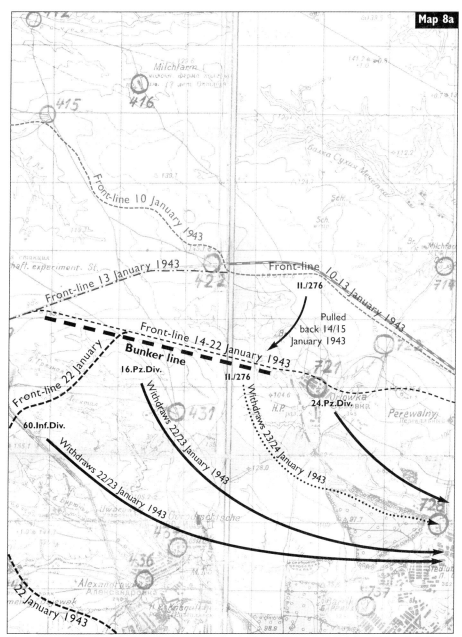

On 22 January 1943, the Soviets split the Stalingrad pocket in two. This necessitated the withdrawal of all units holding out on the north-western corner of the Kessel during 22/23 January 1943. Holl's unit pulled back on 23/24 January 1943 to its new position in the Orlovka Gully (Ref.Pt.728 on the map).

damaged and was left behind. The second machine-gun had been knocked out by shrapnel. Our 'arsenal' consisted of rifles, several 08 pistols and some ammunition; in addition to that, we still had ten to twelve egg hand-grenades.

Slowly, so that everyone could follow, I searched for the best route with my Kompanietrupp. A serious mistake could be made in this landscape covered by deep snow. We did not stop for a rest until I thought we could no longer be seen by the enemy. Thank God it had so far remained quiet. It was a while, however, until Leutnant Augst came up with the stragglers.

It was quite difficult to accurately recognise your own comrades. You had to approach them very closely and exchange words in order to ascertain who you were speaking to. Helmets and hoods were pulled so far down over the head that only eyes were visible. Few words were uttered as these brave, dutiful men lay apathetically in the snow and took a breather. I told them that we would take more numerous breaks but they would only be for a short time so that body sweat didn't freeze. In this way, we hauled ourselves further to the east, into the city – a rear-guard that deserved any other name apart from that one. Nevertheless, we carried out this order.

We reached a hill just on twilight. Of the roughly eight kilometres – as the crow flies – to the edge of the city, approximately four kilometres had been covered. We were all completely done in.

There were three old dug-outs on the slope of the hill. They might once have been occupied by supply troops, or perhaps a communications switchboard. We had no idea. The holes were covered by snow and the interiors were completely coated with a layer of ice.

I decided that this was where we would spend the night. Some comrades were practically on their last legs. Two sentries were assigned half hour shifts. They moved from bunker to bunker. Augst, Cupal and I split up amongst the night quarters. Like sardines, we huddled together and warmed one another with the little body heat we had. After a little while, a fresh snow-flurry swept in and I allowed the sentries to move into shelter.

More than anyone, I was conscious of the fact that all of our fates still lay in God's hands. I was prepared to patiently endure it.

24 January 1943

It became light outside. Someone near the entrance pushed aside the tarpaulin that had provided scant protection against the cold outside. Snow fell in. We had been well and truly snowed in over night. Today, 24 January, the sky was again clear and cloudless. We dug our way out through the drifting snow and set off again to the east. The deep snow was a considerable hindrance to our progress. Apart from us, not a soul was in sight as far as the eye could see. We had to reach the city perimeter today.

We had all survived the seemingly endless night. The thick snowfall kept the frost out of our caves. Now, however – with the clear weather – we felt it again in all its severity.

We were not able to progress in as straight a line as we would have liked. Many hollows, covered by snow, forced us to make difficult detours. If my watch was still showing the correct time, it was now past noon. On a plain, appearing through the snow almost as planned, we once again took a rest. We had somewhat split up from each other so as not to form a group.

Pawellek, who had eyes like a hawk, suddenly pointed in the direction of the city that could not yet be seen from here, and said: "Herr Hauptmann, look over there! There's a huge flock of crows, and where there's crows squabbling, there's bound to be something edible." He was right! Three to four hundred metres away from us – in a hollow – the crows were squabbling. They fluttered up and then dived down on a dark object. I saw it clearly through my binoculars but could not make out what it was.

"Go ahead Juschko, take Nemetz with you. Let us know whether your assumption is correct."

They both waded through the snow. The hope of coming across something edible drove them onwards. They were back after barely half an hour. The walk had been worth it: they were dragging a burst supply-bomb behind them that contained over thirty loaves of bread. Some of the loaves had been pecked by the crows, yet, we didn't begrudge them this because without them, Pawellek's attention wouldn't have been attracted.

I thought of the other comrades of Kampfgruppe Krause and then of the Armee Order stating that supply-canisters must be handed in. I kept ten loaves and divided them up amongst the men. Dittner and two men took the rest. He would find 'Command Post Krause' and stay there with the men until we were in the new position. Marek would then bring them along with him.

The bread was frozen, so even the unthinking couldn't devour it. We stuck the slices of bread in the pockets of our pants to thaw and put up with the cold emanating from them. The last crust of bread had just been cut into pieces with a bayonet when there was a shout: "Russians to the front!"

I looked through my binoculars and thought I was dreaming: about 1000 metres away a living black wall was marching toward us. I looked once more to make certain I wasn't going mad. No, there it was: advancing on a width of a good 100 metres – with arms linked – were several rows of Russians, one after another, heading straight toward us. They were following several figures spread out along the entire breadth of the extended line. These ones were keeping a distance of about 30 to 40 metres from one another and toted submachine-guns under their arms. Altogether, there were definitely

400 men, but there could well have been 600 or 800 of them. I could make no sense of it. Were they convicts or freed Russian prisoners? – Whoever they were, this wall of men was marching, and not only that, they were coming directly toward us.

My men took cover behind snow-walls and stared spellbound at what was an unreal image for all of us.

What should I do? Our weaponry consisted of one machine-gun, with everything else only being carbines, several submachine-guns and the remaining hand weapons, which were required for close combat. In addition, there were 08 pistols and a few egg hand-grenades.

Imagine if we had had one of those legendary MG-42s about which we had heard so many amazing things! Then everything would have been clear: allow them to come to within 200 metres and then: "Fire at will!"

However, I decided to open fire at the earliest possible moment. When we opened fire, there was still about 800 metres between us and this wall of men. The barely 150 men I had with me opened up with some desultory shooting. Most of them couldn't pull back their rifle bolts because they'd frozen. The machine-gun kept jamming, again after again. It was a stubborn mule!

Urging on my comrades, I grabbed a carbine for myself – and was also unable to work the bolt. It seemed that everything was conspiring against us. Now, at last!

Our machine-gun unleashed a burst of fire. Br, br, br, br, br; there were 15 to 20 shots, then it refused to work again. Nevertheless, that single burst of fire worked because the living wall was suddenly no longer standing, but lying down. About 600 metres still separated us.

A few rifle shots from us ensured that this state of affairs remained unchanged over the next hours. I sent Nemetz to the rear as a bloodhound. He would sniff out the next staff and inform them. He was in luck.

After quite a long while, a Nebelwerfer shell landed near the Russians. The shot was undirected and caused no damage to the enemy. As long as it was still light, however, the Russians did not move.

My comrades were totally exhausted. Time and again I went to the individual groups and exhorted the men to watch out for any signs of frostbite. I moved around unhindered because, for some reason, not a single shot had so far come from the Russian side.

Several comrades crouched together and wanted to sleep. It was too much for them. I tried with all my might to resist that overwhelming desire to sleep.

"Lads, hold out for a bit longer, until it's dark. Then we'll head out to the new positions. You can sleep there."

I shoved one that had squatted down. He fell over and didn't move.

"Take a look: this is what happens. He's frozen to death!"

My comrades looked; several no longer comprehended what I'd said. On others, white spots could be seen on faces. When this was seen, they picked up a handful of snow and rubbed it into that spot.

Darkness finally fell. I gave the order for departure. A figure was dragged up. The man could only stammer: "I'm so tired… Let me sleep…"

"For heavens sake, you'll freeze and we can't carry you with us. Pull yourself together!"

"Tired, let me sleep…"

We moved on. Two of our country's sons fell by the wayside. They had fulfiled their duty to the last. In the end, the cold had taken their lives.

When I thought about those deaths, I realised that freezing to death was merciful. You were so unspeakably tired that you only desired to sleep, to sink into an eternal sleep where everything was the same.

We struggled tortuously cross country through the snow for several hundred metres before reaching the Orlovka Brook, where we moved into the bottom of the valley of the brook. The well-trodden path was a huge relief for all of us. It allowed us to conclude that it had been used during the day by comrades from other units for their retreat. Now, however, there was not a soul to be seen.

We were utterly exhausted but we had to press on in the direction of the city until we reached our destination at Mokraya Mechetka. That was our objective. It was a good two hours before we saw this, although the thought that we would soon be crouching in accommodation with a fireplace spurred every one of us on.

We were finally there. We bumped into a sentry who indicated to me the route to the command post of his company commander. I detailed Leutnant Augst and Feldwebel Cupal to get our men warmed up in the nearby shelters before doing anything else.

One could almost call it a miracle: we had been tramping for a day, a night and then a further day until late into the night to cover a distance that would under normal circumstances have only warranted a full day's march. And all without the possibility of keeping ourselves warm and with practically no rations. In so doing, we had 'only' two deaths from freezing.

With my Kompanietrupp, I went to the command post pointed out to me by the sentry. It lay half way up a hill on the east side of the balka. Although the bunker was poorly heated, we felt that we had suddenly come from the Arctic into a tropical climate.

CHAPTER 9

24 January 1943

The company commander, Oberleutnant Jensen[1], had a 'cobbled-together mob' just like me. He belonged to 60. Infanterie-Division (mot.) and had been waiting for us so that his unit could take up another position in the city. He advised me that there had been no enemy contact in this sector: it was expected on the coming day, 25 January, however.

He further told me and pointed out that the positions had formerly been the summer quarters for supply units and couldn't endure heavy shelling. As we had been fighting in an eastern direction throughout the summer, these shelters had up to this point been correctly constructed as rear-slope positions, but because we now had to defend to the west and north, they were now forward-slope positions – as if on a platter. Every entrance opened in the direction of the enemy, so if the enemy attacked during the day, we would be sitting in a mousetrap. If fires were lit during the day, they would betray our positions to the enemy and would mean the end for these shelters.

Oberleutnant Jensen also reported that there had been no connection to the right for two days as the men there had retreated into the city. In any case, it had been a makeshift union of many different uniforms.

I asked Jensen to hold off moving out with his men until first thing in the morning because we all urgently required sleep. He agreed. Shortly after that, we all dropped into a deep – almost deathlike – sleep.

25 January 1943

0600 hours in the morning

Oberleutnant Jensen and his company left the positions. It was quiet outside. With Pawellek, Augst and Cupal, we thoroughly surveyed the sector. On our right flank we found a small hollow in which a large dug-out had been constructed. It was not suitable for defensive fighting because there was no view of the battlefield from there. Those of our comrades that were not fit for action were taken there. Sanitäts-Unteroffizier Paul and two medics cared for them.

The other positions all lay directly in the front-line, a few half way up the slope somewhat higher than the valley floor, others further down, in the vicinity of the brook.

<hr />

1. *Oberleutnant Heinrich Jensen. Born 8 November 1912 in Wittbek; killed 31 January 1943 in Stalingrad.*

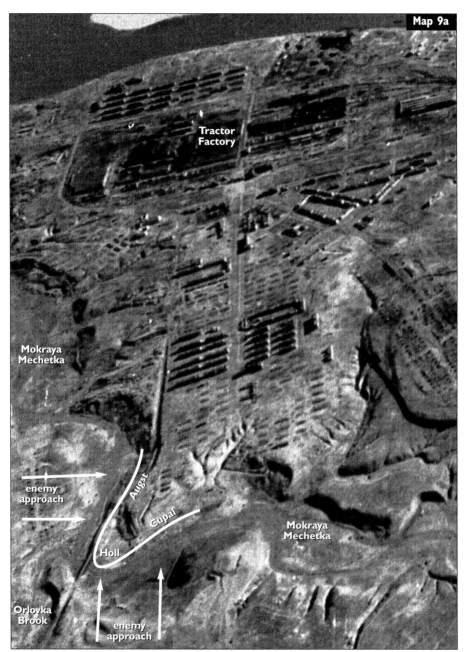

Holl's final position, at the junction of the Mokraya Mechetka and Orlovka Brook. As can be seen, Holl and his men occupied unfavourable forward-slope positions.

Augst and Cupal received their allocated sectors. Augst was located to the right of me and Cupal to the left. I decided that my command post would be positioned right on the spot where the front-line made an almost right-angled bend to the south. It was an exposed position. From there, however, I could see the entire sector, which was very important for us. Most men in my present company were not battle-proven and had only come to us a few days earlier. We were all generally in bad physical condition. The few soldiers on whom I could rely were still the twelve to fifteen comrades from our old core – the Silesians and several Sudeten Germans. I kept these men in my immediate vicinity in two shelters that lay to the right and left of my command post.

If the Russians appeared during the next few hours, we could not allow ourselves to be seen during the day but could only keep watch from our dug-outs. When it was dark, however, sentries had to be distributed along the entire sector to prevent an unnoticed enemy infiltration into our line whilst immediately sounding the alarm. Only then would I bring my 'fire-brigade' into action. These men were on a constant state of alert but were freed from all guard duty. The men to the right of me had our one and only machine-gun.

The day was frosty and clear. The men had instructions from me to construct a revetted position eighty centimetres thick and one metre high between a plank wall and their resting place, to extend from the inside to the entrance. The planks for this were taken from the rear walls of the bunkers. We dug ourselves deeper into the slope behind this position. The excavated soil – fortunately, it was sandy – was used as filling in the plank wall. The first layers of earth were still frozen but then we were able to make progress. This way, we created a traverse that would protect us from direct machine-gun and rifle fire. Small embrasures would allow the men to shoot while standing upright. We had to be economical with our ammunition; that was why I ordered shooting only in extreme cases.

The liaison to the staff of Hauptmann Krause was re-established by Marek. Nemetz and the two comrades that I'd sent with the supply-bomb appeared with him. A line was laid to me from the command post of the sector commander.

The terrain in front of us was kept under constant observation. The two brooks that converged directly in front of my dug-out – everything now was of course frozen solid – still lay some five metres below us. The furthest we could shoot from our position was a good two hundred metres directly to the west, to the balka hill. To the south-west, along the course of the Gorodishche gully, I could see about 150 metres before the projecting slope blocked my view. To the south, in the Mokraya Mechetka, I could only observe about 200 metres. The day passed with no sign of the enemy.

26 January 1943

Early in the morning, while it was still dark, my Spiess, Hauptfeldwebel Bigge, sent us rations. We received 100 grams of bread per head but only for the men that officially belonged to 1. Kompanie, which still numbered 24 men. Each of them was given two tins of Schoka-Kola[2]. Six men had to share a small circular 25 gram piece of chocolate. The five grams of fat that everyone received went into the field-kitchen so that the watery soup at least had a couple of specks of fat floating in it. It was actually a watery soup with boiled pieces of minced horsemeat

Where my other comrades – who had joined my company in the last few days – were supplied from, I could not say. The only thing I could do for them was to call Hauptmann Krause, whom I asked to look after them. I had no idea where Bigge and the field kitchen were located. I didn't know the location of the command post of my sector commander either. We were completely dependent for our supplies on our comrades holed up somewhere in the ruins of the city behind us.

The first Russians were sighted towards midday. They were wearing white camouflage clothing and stood in full view while keeping a careful lookout all around. They came down the opposite slope. It was a group of twelve soldiers. We all kept quiet. Pawellek, Nemetz and I stood behind the traverse and watched them approach. They were still about 150 metres away.

"Juschko, you take the ones in front, Nemetz, they're yours on the right; I'll take the ones on the left. Aim carefully, centre of the target. The first shot must count! After that, aim at the ones directly behind them. Then stop and wait for further instructions. Co-ordinate your fire as much as possible."

Our rifles were in good condition.

"Are you ready?"

"Ready!"

"Fire!"

Three rifle shots shattered the silence of our dug-out. The three men furthest forward of the approaching group were struck and pitched forward into the snow. The rest immediately went to ground but presented good targets on the forward slope. We immediately reloaded.

"The next ones! Ready? Open fire!"

A short bark again resounded from the rifles, and once again we hit them.

---

2. _Schoka-Kola_ - _A unique chocolate, first made in 1935, from cocoa, coffee and cola nut extract. It gave the body a boost of energy and the small (0.2%) caffeine content heightened alertness and concentration. It was packed in small, circular tins. It is still sold as a consumer product today._

The rest of the group retreated back over the hill as quickly as they could. We were once again in contact with the enemy. The enemy now knew that the 'Nyemtze' (Germans) were defending themselves here. He would be more careful because that signified to him that we were still alert. I reported the incident over the telephone.

It was important that we fired only single aimed shots so that we didn't give away our positions. I was convinced that the enemy would not keep us waiting long for his response. A few moments later, we registered the first mortar and artillery impacts. For the most part they came down several hundred metres behind us in the case of the artillery shells, and landed a bit closer if they came from mortars. 'Ivan' had not yet detected our positions. That would be bad for us. With my binoculars, I attentively surveyed the terrain lying in front of me. It was very fatiguing on the eyes to constantly search for the enemy in this glittering whiteness. I deceived myself several times because I thought I had detected something. After a short time, my eyes wandered to the positions to see if anything had changed there. And then I fixed on something that moved. It was hard to distinguish from the snow because it was also white. This thing pushed forward through the snow out to the fallen men centimetres at a time. I lowered my binoculars and tried to find it with my naked eye. I now had him again. Without taking my eyes off the target, I grabbed my carbine, supported it and aimed, hesitated and looked up again. When I fired, the shot had to count. Only the face of the enemy soldier pushing through the snow was a bit darker than the snow. He was a sitting duck! I resumed my firing position, standing behind the traverse that already proved its worth at the initial enemy sighting. It seemed like an eternity until I thought I could risk the shot. Then I slowly pulled the trigger and my bullet put a stop to the dark spot's forward movement.

Nothing more was noticed from the enemy until the onset of darkness. The outer sentries were put out and once again reminded to immediately raise the alarm if they noticed anything suspicious. Leutnant Augst reported to me that there was a gaping hole to the right of him that wasn't occupied.

The oven was now fired up so that there was at least some warmth in the bunker during the night. The squad commanders received my order to be economical with firewood and to burn it only when necessary.

Bigge again sent forward a watery soup and 100 grams of bread for each man. Now there was only one and a half cans of Schoka-Kola. The Strippenzieher were on their way because the line had been broken by the artillery fire.

It must have been just before midnight. Snow was falling outside. A sentry raised the alarm: "The Russians are here!" This shout ran through us like electricity. We grabbed our rifles and donned our helmets. We were outside in no time. There was gunfire right next to my position. Hand-grenades exploded, ricochets buzzed through the area. The enemy had worked his way over the brook and stormed up the last slope.

My comrades defended themselves desperately, even the weak ones were outside fighting with them.

"Herr Hauptmann, look out! They're also behind us!"

A quick glance behind me showed that Pawellek was not mistaken. Six Russians raced down the slope behind our position. They still thought they had not been detected.

The last machine-gun with a drum of ammunition had moved directly into position, opening fire at the onrushing enemy. In one leap, I was near the riflemen, snatched the machine-gun from them and called: "Juschko, this way!"

He immediately understood and came over to brace the machine-gun on his shoulder, holding it firmly by its bipod and the first aimed burst was quickly unleashed. Rat ta ta ta ta and again, rat ta ta ta ta. They stayed down! I saw one of them still running, the rest lay there, dead.

We now swung around 180° and banged away down the slope. Come on, let's go! 'Ivan' had not expected this. Those still capable of running disappeared as suddenly as they had appeared.

After I convinced myself that the danger was over, I allowed all of the sentries to return to the dug-outs. We had eight wounded and two dead. The wounded were taken to the medical bunker of Unteroffizier Paul. The two dead comrades were taken into a small empty dug-out that wasn't being used.

Pawellek, Nemetz and two men tried to ascertain how many attackers lay in front and behind us. They also had the task of bringing in all weapons and ammunition from the dead enemy soldiers. When they returned, Pawellek reported: "Eight Russians are lying in the brook area. We've brought back four submachine-guns with ammunition, four rifles and six hand grenades. As for food, they had several dried slices of bread in their bread-bag and some Machorka[3]."

Nemetz returned shortly after: "Five dead on the slope above us, about 20 to 30 metres from here. We've brought in three submachine-guns, two rifles, ammunition and four hand grenades, as well as a couple of pieces of dry bread and a little tobacco."

Weapons, ammunition, bread and tobacco were distributed to the squads. I made sure that everyone received his share. It was more of a symbolic gesture than anything else, since I didn't want anyone to lose out

As instructed, my men left the dead Russians as we found them. In daylight, the Russians should not be able to draw any conclusions as to where we were located.

Pawellek said that one of the enemy soldiers lying out in the front-line in the brook area was severely wounded. He had been pleading in Russian for us to help him: "Comrade, you also have a mother, help me!"

---

3. _Machorka - raw Russian tobacco._

Pawellek gnashed his teeth: "This shitty war! How can I help him? We're finished ourselves and don't know what to do with our own wounded."

I understood my Juschko only too well. These men had set out with the mission of taking us out of the battle. Whether they wanted to or not – they had no choice in the matter, just like us and every other soldier on this earth. Pitting man against man in close-quarters combat usually ends in death. When speaking to this supposed enemy, you established that man's humanity to his fellow man had not died. Human sympathy, the soul, felt for this pitiful creature. One would like to help but could not because duty to one's own comrades did not allow it. I tried to put myself in the shoes of my opposite number. It didn't take much imagination to establish that the bend in which my command post was located was an important landmark for the defence. The enemy concluded quite correctly that the focal point of resistance lay here. The seven dead that he suffered in the past days showed him that we weren't going to give up without a fight. So during the night, with two assault troops, he tried to achieve what he hadn't succeeded in doing during daylight: the first group – approaching frontally – should have distracted us while the second assault troop infiltrated through the unoccupied section to the right of us. They almost succeeded but Pawellek, that great chap, spotted them at the last moment.

When the telephone connection to staff Hauptmann Krause was re-established, I reported the night-time surprise assault and our successful defence.

27 January 1943

The rest of the night passed without further incidents. The sentries returned to their dug-outs just as dawn broke. The fireplaces cooled down. There was nothing to show that in these inadequate fox-holes German soldiers had established defensive positions: men who had a heavy feeling in their hearts about the uncertainty of their future and were ready to defend themselves to the utmost. We constantly relieved each other from observation duties. Concerns that we could be taken by surprise didn't allow me to get much sleep. I was aware that my comrades looked up to me and I could not show any sign of weakness. The sense of responsibility kept me going and gave me the strength not to despair. I spent most of the time with both observation sentries, searching the terrain lying in front of me with my binoculars. I counted the dead attackers. There were fifteen, with five more lying on the slope behind us, twenty dead in all.

Artillery and mortars had again opened up their concert. Soon after that, the field-telephone was cut again. Like yesterday, we were now completely dependent on ourselves. Shortly before midday, we received aimed anti-tank fire from the direction of the Gorodishche Balka. The shots were directed along the line of positions in the valley floor. We kept quiet so as not to reveal ourselves. A bullet meant for our command post got lodged in the traverse. Soldiers appeared from the Gorodishche Balka. They were trying to get us to fire. My men knew the order from yesterday however: only shoot in an extreme emergency. Three rounds from my rifle that did not miss their target forced the rest to turn back and left the Russians guessing as to where the shots had come from.

We were on full alert, scanning the terrain continuously. Throughout the day, the shelling by enemy artillery was heavy, but not aimed. He therefore still didn't know exactly where we were hidden. I did not believe that our bunker could withstand a direct hit. Better protection against shell impacts came from that part of the bunker that we had dug out for this purpose, with the traverse at the front.

As darkness fell, the sentries were drawn out of their positions. We were almost snow-blind in my position from lengthy observation. Fires were again quickly stoked in our makeshift ovens. With the outside temperature between 30° and 40° below zero, the dug-outs cooled down quickly during the day. As we couldn't leave them, we were all soon very cold. For us, however, they were essential because without them, we were defenceless and at the mercy of the weather. Deprived of our dug-outs, we would no longer be capable of offering the slightest resistance.

Today we had a death to mourn. During the anti-tank shelling towards midday, an Obergefreite in a bunker to the right of me was fatally wounded by shrapnel. He had previously belonged to 8. Kompanie in my old Regiment. Pawellek came over with me to bid farewell to this brave comrade. He was as stiff as a board because of the frost. We left him lying out front on the traverse.

28 January 1943

I said to the men that I'd come over to them at the start of the new day and would stay throughout the day. Then we'd go through the remaining dug-outs – or rather – bunkers. We didn't talk much; everyone knew how serious our situation was. If I could only conjure up a full stomach for my emaciated comrades. They performed their duty without grumbling.

When we arrived back at my command post, our so-called rations, which had arrived shortly before, were allocated. On this occasion, they consisted of one and a half loaves of bread for 23 men, one and a half boxes of Schoka-Kola and warm broth with a few pieces of horse meat. Where rations came from for the more than one hundred others that were under my command was still not made clear to me. Apparently, the supply organisation had up to now not managed to set up an arrangement by units. The quantity and the quality did not differ at all from ours.

In any case, we precisely distributed the miserable rations. The men from the squads who fetched the food departed. I was about to swallow the first spoonful of the 'broth' when an Obergefreite appeared in my dug-out. I immediately saw that he was from our old Regiment. He looked much worse than most of my men.

"Herr Hauptmann, I'm Obergefreiter Hübner, former orderly of Oberleutnant Böge. Do you remember me?"

"Ja, I remember you. What are you doing here?"

"Herr Hauptmann, I've had nothing to eat for five days!"

"How come?"

"I was wounded and went to a hospital in Stalingrad. Everything is hopelessly overcrowded there. I was told to look for my unit and report myself there because they had no rations for me. I then set out and asked my way here, but no other unit was able to give me anything to eat. It was the same story everywhere: 'We ourselves have nothing to eat, sorry.' Finally, today, I have found your unit here!"

"And we have nothing either", answered Pawellek for me.

"You cannot let me go hungry!" It was the cry of a man who was close to madness. I could never forget that tormented look, that tear-stained face, that hopelessness. I couldn't gulp down this soup in the presence of this comrade. "Here, take my soup, we don't actually have any more. You'll stay with us and go to Gruppe Dittner."

Hübner wanted to greedily gulp down the soup.

"Good grief, pal, not so hasty! Take your time, there'll be no more until tomorrow night." Pawellek warned our comrade to eat slowly and carefully.

In the night to 28 January, the enemy left us in peace. Our sector staff gave up trying to repair the line. It was destroyed so often by shells that it was senseless to patch it together again.

Because of that, Marek came to me and received the daily report. He now had the task of maintaining the connection from Hauptmann Krause to me. Nemetz again had to establish the liaison from us to 'Staff Krause'.

Before the outer sentries were called back, I went into the bunker to the right of my command post. Located there was Gruppe Dittner with five of our old company members as well as three men of the former 8. Maschinengewehr-Kompanie with the last MG-34, which could only be employed as a light machine-gun. All the remaining weapons were repaired as far as we were able in the past days. The captured weapons we took from the dead Russians were also made ready.

The dug-out was considerably lower than my command post. The men couldn't stand upright. The traverse out front was not as high as it was near mine. For that reason, my comrades excavated a trench about 40 to 50cm deep directly behind it and thereby received better protection from enemy fire. The machine-gun was placed in a way that it could immediately be brought into action.

As in the previous days, my main activity again consisted of observation. The allocated observation duty of the Gruppe was not affected. From time to time, Dittner relieved me.

Our new arrival Hübner had settled down. He was once again near his Silesian landsfolk and that was almost like home.

We didn't have enough proper winter boots in the Kompanie. For this reason, it had become necessary to ensure that at least the sentries standing on guard during the night were equipped with boots. That was why I'd been wearing lace-up shoes for several days, even though they were two sizes too big. While cursing the condition of my shoes, one of the squad said to me: "Herr Hauptmann, I've got a felt panel left over from a box for optical equipment. The box has already been burnt but we could make two inner-soles out of the felt."

I stood with both feet on the felt panel. It was more than adequate. It wasn't long before they were fitted into my shoes and made them warmer.

When on observation duty, I counted the dead bodies every time. I could see if anything had changed there. We could count on the enemy to use every trick in the book.

The observation post I was now in provided a somewhat wider field of view to the left. I could hear the thump of heavy enemy weapons, as on the previous day. Today, for a change, scything machine-gun fire swept our positions. As always, we kept quiet, observing, but with increased attention. On this day, I fired off two shots from my rifle. The number of dead increased continually. Our dead comrades were placed in the trench out front, in the farthest corner, adjacent to the traverse. The small amount of warmth that radiated from the fire-places during the night didn't penetrate that far. There they remained, stiff, their corpses unable to decompose. When it became dark, I moved over to my command post.

The supply of rations worsened day by day. The last airfield, Stalingradski, had already been lost on 23 January. The few supply canisters dropped over the city during the night by our Luftwaffe arrived sporadically and fell far short of what was required for sufficient nourishment. Naturally, this wretched state of affairs did nothing to raise morale. The feeling of helplessness coupled with the uncertainty as to what the future had in store for us gave rise to a defiant determination. We wanted to sell our lives as expensively as we could. Comrades collecting rations for their squads said little or nothing when they carried the meagre supplies back. That evening, we received one and a half loaves of bread, a box of Schoka-Kola and the watery soup. That was all there was to assuage the hunger of 23 full-grown men!

After I ate my small portion, I carried out an inspection, starting with the post on the left. There, Feldwebel Cupal reported that everything was in order. After that, I went to Leutnant Augst on the right flank. He told me that a few men had lice. I was not surprised because we hadn't been out of our uniforms for a long time. Livestock in the homeland had it better than us.

On my way back, I visited my wounded and severely ill comrades in the medical bunker. Unteroffizier Paul and both his medics did what they could, but it was precious little. What I saw there was a scene of sheer misery. Thirty comrades lay there, some severely wounded, some very sick. The air in the room was polluted with the sickly stench of pus, excrement and urine. I tried to find some words of comfort. I found it difficult. Outside, I drew the fresh – if somewhat icy – air deep into my lungs. If only I could help. We were much better off: we were still able to move and fight. Although we were just as malnourished, these poor men were not given better rations. In addition, they had to cope with physical pain, and with that, mental problems increased. We fighters, performing our duty, did not have much time to ponder. When one was disabled, however, there was plenty of time to think.

The entire night was dominated by lively activity on the enemy's side. We could hear it as if we had been right in the middle of it. The dry, cold air carried noises a particularly long way. 'Ivan' also didn't even take the trouble to speak softly any more. Even snatches of conversations could be heard. We were wide awake and preparing for the end.

29 January 1943

On the morning of 29 January, the entire sector lay in front of me again, as if nothing had happened during the night. Yet, I felt that the end was near. I think my comrades had the same thought but we didn't speak about it. We had our assignment and we would carry it out.

Marek notified us that during the past night, the enemy attacked north and south of us with heavy weapons and tanks. Our casualties there were very high but with a supreme effort, the last combat-ready men repulsed the attack. Nobody spoke about capitulation. That was not our business. Over there, they had to decide one way or another, since they bore the responsibility for this situation.

My eyes stung from searching too long with the binoculars. To vindicate myself, I counted the enemy dead (for the umpteenth time) around me and in front of us. There were twenty three. A single tank would have been enough to break our desperate resistance. Instead, our opponent had time and again sent men against us. They stood no chance. In the final analysis, that would barely change anything. A few soldiers still fighting meant nothing at this stage of the battle. A once proud and victorious army continued to hold out, although everyone sensed that the end had arrived.

The Russians were allowing themselves time to deal with us because nothing happened in my sector on 29 January. We didn't know either how the other fronts looked, in particular whether the southern pocket – in which our Commander-in-Chief Paulus was located – was still holding out.

Our rations were cut once again. A whole loaf of bread and three-quarters of a tin of Schoka-Kola was allocated for 23 men. Only the warm broth remained in the same quantities because there was more than enough thawed snow to make up the difference. Still, we had to search really hard to find specks of fat and pieces of horse meat.

My men didn't make it hard for me. They performed their duty without grumbling as they saw that I too exerted myself and was there for everyone. In these last days, 'comradeship' was not just a word: we actually lived it! I believe that only someone who has endured the same or similar situation can truly know the meaning of the words 'comrade' and 'comradeship'. Every man showed his true colours. Nothing else counted more, not rank, not acquired conventional empty phrases, not the slightest advantage, but only the unconditional responsibility of the individual towards his fellow man.

30 January 1943

Today, on 30 January, the Third Reich had been in existence for exactly ten years. At that time, I was not yet fourteen years old. I had participated with enthusiasm and faithful confidence. I volunteered for the infantry as an eighteen year old. I believed in the future of my people and still firmly believe in it. If our operations and sacrifice contributed to preventing this red flood, known as Bolshevism, from reaching our people and Europe, then these operations were not for nothing. Hopefully our people would survive this war!

The enemy took it upon himself to put on a special performance for us on this day of commemoration. As far as I could hear from my command post, it was 'booming'. Calibres of all sizes had only one target: the northern pocket. We weren't left out. It was indeed their intention to take the northern pocket on this day, 30 January. I would only be able to establish if my Kompanie had casualties in this 'blessing by fire' that evening – presuming that we survived it. It was clear to all of us that the enemy wanted to make short work of us because his dead lying in front of and behind our position had told him enough. Yet, we still had enough ammunition to play a small melody. As for myself, I was absolutely certain that the last bullet was for me. However, it was not quite time.

31 January 1943

It appeared that the enemy had not attained his objective yesterday. Marek reported that casualties were heavy, but wherever there were still German soldiers fighting, they defended themselves and threw back the attack. He said: "Everyone is really despondent." And we felt the same way.

Marek still had a piece of news: our commander-in-chief was promoted to Feldmarschall. In addition, Goering had broadcast to the German people yesterday evening and compared our battle in Stalingrad with Leonidas and the fighting at the Thermopylae. I found that tasteless and was disappointed with our Reichsmarschall. We fought as long as we could but had already been written off by the higher-ups.

1 February 1943

The night was comparatively quiet. As I had done over the past days, I stood at the observation post and scanned the terrain as far as it could be surveyed. It felt as if we'd already been here for an eternity. The homeland, my wife, my parents and all the other people that were near and dear to me, were so far away and yet, so close. We had endured this relentless strain for them and now our only choice was to take the final journey with dignity. If only we didn't have to wait so damn long. In a hopeless situation, there is nothing more gruelling than waiting. Where would the enemy come from? From the rear? From all sides? Would he starve us out? All of these thoughts went through my head, again and again. Of course they were foolish thoughts. Soldier, switch off your brain, dig in your heels! I managed to banish all foolish thoughts. In this way, it was easier to endure.

Once again, darkness fell without anything special happening in our sector. I didn't know how long my comrades could continue to hold out. How should I cut up half a loaf of bread into 23 portions? And what about the slice of Schoka-Kola? The broth was still no more than a warm drink. God, let there be an end to this!

As I sat there, brooding, Marek appeared.

"Herr Hauptmann, I have to immediately take you to Hauptmann Krause. The position here is to be given up."

"Nemetz, get yourself ready and come with me. Juschko, Leutnant Augst will take command of the Kompanie while I'm away. Come on, Marek, let's go!"

Marek went directly past my command post up the slope. I followed him, Nemetz brought up the rear. The route led across the terrain over several hills and valleys to ruins on the edge of the city. I remembered several conspicuous landmarks for the return journey. After about fifteen minutes, we reached the command post of Hauptmann Krause. His adjutant, Leutnant Gerlach, was still with him. We greeted each other with a handshake.

Krause began: "Herr Holl, we must pull back to a new defence line. Our neighbouring divisions, 60. Motorised-Division and 24. Panzer-Division, no longer exist. We have to deal with the fact that no connection exists to either the right or left of 16. Panzer-Division. You'll command the remaining combat-capable men and will brief them."

"Herr Krause, what'll happen with the wounded and sick?"

Krause looked at me with serious eyes and shrugged his shoulders. I was shocked:

"You mean that my comrades who can no longer move should be left in the lurch! That's out of the question! Herr Krause, please send Marek out at once. Leutnant Augst can withdraw from the position with all of the men. I'll return to the front and remain with the wounded men. They've trusted me and performed their duty to the last. And now, in the final hours of their lives, we would leave them with the thought: 'We've been abandoned to our fate.' That's simply impossible for me!"

"Herr Holl, I understand. Good-bye and God be with you!"

We shook hands and I left the bunker.

Leutnant Gerlach followed me: "Bert, can I speak to you for a moment?"

"Sure, Walter."

"You don't think we should try to get through to the south-west?"

"Not at all, Walter. You heard my conversation with Krause. I would be a miserable Schwein if I abandoned my wounded men. Good-bye, Walter!"

I had to hurry because it would soon be light and I wanted to be at the front. Nemetz followed me.

"Stay here, Nemetz, and wait for Leutnant Augst. You can spare yourself the trip."

"Herr Hauptmann, I'll come with you!"

"As you wish."

Half way back, Leutnant Augst came toward us with the Kompanie. I quickly filled him in. Then he set off on his way, led by Marek. The men moved silently, one after the other. Following at the rear was my Kompanietrupp and the rest of my old faithfuls. Pawellek noticed that I continued on in the direction of the old positions.

"Herr Hauptmann, where are you going?"

"To the front, to be with our wounded."

"May I go along?"

"Me too?"

"Me as well?"

"Whoever wants to go with me can come along."

When we reached the bunker full of wounded men, I established that there were now twelve men still able to defend themselves, including the three medics. A red cross flag was positioned outside the bunker entrance so that the enemy knew there were wounded and sick men inside.

My old position lay barely 100 metres away. I posted a sentry to alert us when the Russians arrived.

In the hospital bunker, it looked even more disconsolate than when I arrived for my last visit. The number of sick and wounded men hadn't changed. There were 39 people. They were all without hope and had resigned themselves. There were no lamentations, only the sound of pain when one of them changed positions on the hard wooden boards. With my appearance, their eyes looked at me questioningly.

"Comrades, the Kompanie has evacuated its positions and withdrawn to the edge of the city. We have come back to you because we cannot leave you in the lurch. Nothing will happen to you as long as we can still fight. We can only hope for the best. The homeland is looking with anxious sorrow to Stalingrad; the hearts of our relatives are now with us. I thank you in the name of our people. We have fulfiled our duty!"

Everyone was silent, and a few of them were quietly weeping to themselves. I sat in a corner and waited for what was to come.

Pawellek gave me two bread-bags with my mess-kit. Then he fetched a piece of meat out of his pocket.

"What's that?"

"A boiled cats leg. I caught the cat in our bunker. I don't know where it came from. It was damned skinny, but it's better than nothing."

It was only a mouthful. I bit some off, passed the piece on so that my comrades also had some.

In my camouflage uniform, I was indistinguishable from my comrades. I still had two egg hand-grenades and my 08 pistol; for that, I had two full clips plus a bullet in the chamber. That was still seventeen shots. Should the Russians not fairly treat my wounded comrades, then they would still be given a final battle.

In the meantime, an Oberzahlmeister and Hauptmann Michaelis turned up at the bunker. Michaelis commanded an artillery battery in our old Division.

Thus we awaited our last day in Stalingrad!

Adelbert Holl was born in Duisburg-Laar, Rheinland on 15 February 1919. His parents were Theodor and Emma (née Nußbaum) Holl. Educated in his parents' house from Easter 1925 until Easter 1933, then Volksschule (elementary school) in Duisburg-Laar from Easter 1933 until Easter 1936. Attended a commercial college in Duisburg, obtaining a school-leaving certificate in April 1937. Commenced a commercial apprenticeship but decided on a military career.

Military career

3 November 1937	Entered military service as a Schütze (Private) in 5./Inf.-Rgt. 24
12 November 1937	Sworn in
1 October 1939	Transferred to 6./Inf.-Rgt.276
5 February 1940	Detached to Infanterieschule Döberitz
5 May 1940	Transferred to 3./Inf.-Ers.-Btl.173
1 July 1940	Commissioned as an officer Transferred to Inf.-Ers.-Btl.173
29 August 1940	Transferred to II./Inf.-Rgt.276 as Ordonanzoffizier
5 September 1940	Takes temporary command of 7./Inf.-Rgt.276
18 October 1940 – 30 November 1940	Kompanieführer training course within Inf.Rgt.276
1 August 1941	Kompanieführer 7./Inf.-Rgt.276
14 April 1942	Received permission to marry Ilsa Moug
20 June 1942	Marriage
20 August 1942	Transferred to 134. Infanterie-Division
24 September 1942	Returned to Inf.-Rgt.276 as Führer 7. Kompanie
21 October 1942	'On special assignment', staff Grenadier-Regiment 276
1 January 1943	Commander 1./Pz.Gren.Rgt.79 (16. Panzer-Division)
23 January 1943	Declared missing in action at Stalingrad (V.L.83/49)

Wounds

9 August 1941	Kanev[1] - lightly wounded, stayed with the troops
6 October 1941	Somovka, Orel River - lightly wounded, stayed with the troops
19 April 1942	Nyrkovo - severe lung wound; required hospitalisation
27 September 1942	Stalingrad - light head wound
18 October 1942	Stalingrad - lightly wounded; concussion, temporary hearing loss
20 October 1942	Stalingrad - shrapnel wound to upper right arm

Decorations

20 September 1939	Iron Cross Second Class
24 August 1941	Iron Cross First Class
1 February 1942	Wound Badge in Black
20 April 1942	Wound Badge in Silver
5 May 1942	2 Tank Destruction Badges (knocked out two tanks with an anti-tank rifle near Kanev on 9 August 1941)
8 June 1942	Infantry Assault Badge
1 September 1942	East Front Medal
21 October 1942	Wound Badge in Gold

Promotions

1 October 1938	Gefreiter (announced in a Kompaniebefehl 29.10.1938)
1 October 1939	Unteroffizier (simultaneous commitment to 12 years service)
1 April 1940	Feldwebel
3 May 1940	Designated Offiziersanwärter (officer candidate)
1 July 1940	Leutnant d.R. (with RDA from 1.7.40 -2363-)
1 October 1941	Leutnant (aktiv) (with RDA from 1.12.40 -41-)
1 July 1942	Oberleutnant (with RDA from 1.7.42 -83-)
1 January 1943	Hauptmann (with RDA from 1.1.43 -346-)

---

1. *See also footnote 15 on page 11. In addition to Holl, many other officers were killed or wounded at this time. On this day, 9 August 1941, Holl single-handedly knocked out two enemy tanks with an anti-tank rifle.*

Feldzüge, mobile Verwendung, Teilnahme an sonstigen kriegerischen Unternehmungen und Kampfhandlungen, Verwundungen und ihnen gleichzuachtende Kriegsdienstbeschädigungen.	Auszeichnungen	Anerkannt	
		Datum	Unterschrift
1.9.-5.9.39 Gefechte um die Befestigung bei Graudenz und Kulm als 1.Gr.W.-Trupp-führer	Eis.Kreuz II. Klasse 1939 am 2o.9.1939 Eis.Kreuz I. Klasse 1939		
8.9.-11.9.39 Gefechte um die Narewbefestigungen Lomga,Nowogrod als 1.Gr.W.-Trupp-führer	am 24.8.1941		
12.9.-14.9.39 Gefechte um die Einschließung bei und südlich Zambrov als 1.Gr.W.-Trupp-führer		2o.1.42 Adelbert Holl.	
16.-18.9.39 Gefechte um Bialys-tok als 1.Gr.W.-Trupp-führer			
7.11.39 - 5. 2.4o Vorfeldkämpfe zwischen Mosel u. Rhein als Gruppenführer			

Holl's military service during the Polish Campaign as leader of a light mortar section in Infanterie-Regiment 24:

1.9.-5.9.39   *Combat around fortifications near Graudenz and Kulm*
9.9.-11.9.39   *Combat around Narev fortifications, Lomga, Novgorod*
12.9.-14.9.39   *Combat during the encirclement near and south of Zambrov*
16.9.-18.9.39   *Combat around Bialystok*
7.11.39-   *Outpost fighting between Mosel and Rhein as squad leader*
5.2.40

Holl was awarded the Iron Cross Second Class for his actions in Poland. The Iron Cross First Class was awarded for his bravery near Kanev on 9 August 1941.

<u>A b s c h r i f t</u>.

Lehrabteilung II
der Infanterieschule

Elsgrund über Döberitz,den 3.5.1940.
Neue Kaserne

Lehrgang I , 3.(Schtz) Inspektion,

B e u r t e i l u n g
über den

Dienstgrad,Vor= u.Zuname: Uffz. Adelbert H o l l

Feldtruppenteil: 1.R. 276

Werdegang: Kriegsauswahl

Stammtruppenteil
  bezw.
Wehrersatzdienststelle,
stellv. A.K.:   W.M.A.Duisburg, stellv. IV. A.K.

Teilnahme am Lehrgang: vom 5.2.1940 bis 3.5.1940 am 3.Offizier-Anwarter-
                       Lehrgang der Infanterieschule.

Allgemeines Urteil über Charakter und Persönlichkeit:

Offener, ehrlicher Charakter, frisches, temperamentvolles
Wesen, energisch und zielbewußt, zuverlässig und pflichttreu.

Dienstliche Befähigung:

a) Auftreten vor der Front
   und Kommandosprache: Sicher und bestimmt.
                                 Kommandosprache gut.

b) Leistungen und Verhalten
   als Führer: Hat Schwung, klare Befehlsgebung,
                                 reißt seine Mannschaft mit. Setzt
                                 sich rücksichtslos ein.

c) Dienstliche Kenntnisse:
   (auch Waffenkenntnisse)   Auf allen Gebieten sehr gute Leistungen.

d) Geistige Veranlagung und
   körperliche Leistungsfähigkeit:
                                 Gute Allgemeinbildung,
                                 schnelle Auffassungsgabe,scharfsinnig,
                                 denkt selbständig.
                                 Körperlich gut durchtrainiert und allen
                                 Anstrengungen gewachsen.

e) Führung: Sehr gut.

                                                    - Blatt 2 -

```
Außerdienstliches Verhalten:

                        Einwandfrei.
                        Sehr beliebter Kamerad.


Schlußurteil:
a) Eignung:
    (1) zum Offizier:       besonders geeignet

    (2) zu welcher Verwendung: Zugführer einer Schtz.Komp.

b) Ernennung zum Offizier-
   anwärter:                3. 5. 1940.


            (Siegel)                    gez. Unterschrift.

                                  Hauptmann u. Inspektions-Chef.


                                  Die Richtigkeit der Abschrift wird
                                  bescheinigt:

                                  U.U., den 27. Juni 1941.
                                            I.   V.
```

An '_Evaluation_' prepared on 3 May 1940 by Hauptmann Siegel at Infanterieschule Döberitz:

General opinion about character and personality:
Forthright, straightforward character, fresh, temperamental nature, energetic and focused, reliable and dutiful.

Official competence:
a) Appearance in front of his men and command language:

   Assured and determined.
   Good command language.

b) Performance and conduct as commander:

   Has energy, clear issuance of orders that sweep his subordinates along. Employs himself ruthlessly.

c) Official knowledge (also knowledge of weaponry):

   Very good performance in all areas.

d) Mental capacity and physical capabilities:

   Good general education, quick-witted, astute, thinks for himself.
   Physically well-conditioned and equal to any exertion.

e) Command

   Very good.

Social conduct:

   Faultless.
   Very popular comrade.

Concluding judgement:
a) Suitability:
   (1) as an officer

   Particularly suitable

   (2) in what role

   Platoon commander in a rifle company.

b) Nomination as an officer candidate:

   3.5.1940

Beurteilung

Von sicherem und bestimmtem Auftreten vor der Front und
guter Kommandosprache. Seine Befehlsgebung ist klar und
bestimmt und reißt mit ihrem Schwung die Untergebenen mit.
Sein frisches, temperamentvolles Wesen setzt sich bei den
Mannschaften rücksichtslos durch. Seine Leistungen und
Kenntnisse sind auf allen Gebieten gut. Er ist von ehrli-
chem, offenem Charakter und schneller Auffassungsgabe, Sein
Denken ist zielbewußt und sein Wesen zuverlässig und pflichttreu.

Zum Offizier geeignet.

Die Richtigkeit der Geburtsangabe und der Schreibweise des
Namens sind mit den vorhandenen Unterlagen verglichen.

2. 6. 1940

Major und Btl.-Kommandeur

Einverstanden.

17.6.1940

Unterschrift

Oberst d. Rgt.-Kommandeur.
Dienstgrad und Dienststellung

An 'Evaluation' written on 2 June 1940 by the commander of Infanterie-Ersatz-Bataillon 173 – and seconded by an Oberst – after Holl completed the officer's candidate course at Döberitz. Such assessments were critical to the future career of an officer. This evaluation about Holl says:

"Has an assured and determined appearance in front of his men and a good command language. His issuance of orders is clear and determined and sweeps his subordinates along with its energy. His fresh, temperamental nature is fearlessly asserted to the other ranks. His achievements and knowledge are good in all areas. He is of an honest, open character and quick-witted. His thinking is focused and his nature is reliable and dutiful.

"Suitable to be an officer.

"The accuracy of the birth data and the spelling of the name have been compared to the documents at hand."

Einreichender Truppenteil: Jnf.Ers.Btl.173

Feldtruppenteil: **Inf.-Rgt. 276**   Weißenfels   2. 6. 1940
                                              Ort   Datum

Stammtruppenteil: **Inf.Rgt. 53**   Feldpostnummer: **31 491**

Vorschlag zur Beförderung zum Offizier.

Name: **H o l l**   Vorname: **Adelbert**
Dienstgrad: **Feldwebel**   Laufbahnbezeichnung: **Offz.-Anw. d.B.**
Waffengattung: **Infanterie**   Mil. Fachausbildung: **Schtz.-Kp.**
Wehrbezirkskommando: **Duisburg**
geb. am: **15.2. 1919** in **Duisburg - Laar** Glaubensbekenntnis: **ev.**
Heimatanschrift: **Duisburg - Laar, Apostelstr. 1**
Familienstand: **ledig**   Beruf: **kaufm. Volontär**
Bildungsgang: **Volksschule, Handelsschule, kaufm. Beruf**

Dienstlaufbahn	von — bis (am)	bei (Truppenteil)
Diensteintritt	3.11.1937	5./I.R. 24
aktive Dienstzeit	3.11.37-30.9.39	5./I.R. 24
aktive Dienstzeit	1. 9.39- 3.2.40	6./I.R. 276
aktive Dienstzeit	4.2.40.	Inf.Ers.Btl. 173
aktive Dienstzeit	5. 2.40- 3.5.40	Inf.-Schule Döberitz
aktive Dienstzeit	4. 5.40	Inf.Ers.Btl. 173

Beförderungen und Ernennungen	am	zum
	bef. 1.10. 1938	**Gefr.**
	bef. 1.10. 1939	**Uffz.**
	bef. 1. 4. 1940	**Feldw.**
	ern. 3. 5. 1940	**Offz.-Anw.von Waffen- schule Döberitz**

Teilnahme am jetzigen Krieg	vom — bis	als (Dienststellung)
Einsatz im Westen	1.10.39 - 3.2.40	**Gruppen- u.Zugführer**

Offizieranwärterlehrgang im neuen Heer: **5.2. - 3.5.1940**
Offizierwahl am **23.5.1940** durch Offizierkorps **Inf.Ers.Btl. 173**
Ist Nachweis der außerdienstlichen Eignung erbracht? **ja**

Vordruck genau ausfüllen! Arbeitsanleitung zu Anlage 2 der Offz. Erg. Best. beachten! Ungenaue Bearbeitung führt zu Rückfragen und Verzögerung.

This '<u>Recommendation for promotion to officer</u>', also issued on 2 June 1940, accompanied the previous evaluation. This document lists his military career, promotions and participation in the current war, as of June 1940. Curiously, Holl's weeks of combat during the Polish campaign (shown on page 239) are not listed.